CHALLENGED HEGEMONY

CHALLENGED HEGEMONY

*The United States, China,
and Russia in the Persian Gulf*

Steve A. Yetiv
Katerina Oskarsson

Stanford University Press
Stanford, California

Stanford University Press
Stanford, California

Printed in the United States of America on acid-free, archival-quality paper

Library of Congress Cataloging-in-Publication Data

Names: Yetiv, Steven A., author. I Oskarsson, Katerina, 1983- author.
Title: Challenged hegemony : the United States, China, and Russia in the
    Persian Gulf / Steve A. Yetiv.
Description: Stanford, California : Stanford University Press, 2018. I
    Includes bibliographical references and index.
Identifiers: LCCN 2017015746 (print) I LCCN 2017017047 (ebook) I
    ISBN 9781503604261 (ebook) I ISBN 9781503602878 (cloth : alk. paper) I
    ISBN 9781503604179 (pbk. : alk. paper)
Subjects: LCSH: Persian Gulf Region—Foreign relations—United States. I
    United States—Foreign relations—Persian Gulf Region. I Persian Gulf
    Region—Foreign relations—China. I China—Foreign relations—Persian Gulf
    Region. I Persian Gulf Region—Foreign relations—Russia (Federation) I
    Russia (Federation)—Foreign relations—Persian Gulf Region. I
    Hegemony—United States. I Petroleum industry and trade—Persian Gulf
    Region.
Classification: LCC DS326 (ebook) I LCC DS326 .Y485 2018 (print) I
    DDC 327.536—dc23
LC record available at https://lccn.loc.gov/2017015746

Typeset by Bruce Lundquist in 10/14 Minion

Contents

List of Figures and Tables

Acknowledgments

We thank the dozens of people who provided input for this book over the past decade. If there are any errors in the book, we would like to blame them for it. Kidding aside, their contributions were invaluable, as were those of the external reviewers. We also thank Stanford University Press and its staff for managing this project deftly.

Abbreviations

ARAMCO	Arabian American Oil Company
bpd	barrels per day
CDI	Cooperative Defense Initiative
CENTCOM	U.S. Central Command
CIA	Central Intelligence Agency
CNOOC	China National Offshore Oil Corporation
CNPC	China National Petroleum Corporation
DCA	Defense Cooperation Agreement
EIA	Energy Information Administration
EU	European Union
FMS	foreign military sales
GCC	Gulf Cooperation Council
GSD	Gulf Security Dialogue
IEA	International Energy Agency
IAEA	International Atomic Energy Agency
IOC	international oil companies
LNG	liquefied natural gas
mbd	million barrels per day
NGOs	nongovernmental organizations
NOC	national oil company
OECD	Organization of Economic Cooperation and Development

OPEC	Organization of Petroleum Exporting Countries
OPM-MOI	Office of the Program Manager–Ministry of Interior
OSC-I	Office of Security Cooperation–Iraq
RDF	rapid deployment force
SPR	strategic petroleum reserve
SWF	sovereign wealth funds
UAE	United Arab Emirates
WMD	weapons of mass destruction

CHALLENGED HEGEMONY

1 Introduction

N O ISSUE IN WORLD AFFAIRS garners greater attention than the global role and position of the United States, and few regions dominate global headlines more than the Middle East. We address both subjects, America and the Middle East, within the context of a broader exploration into what it means to be a great power in world affairs.

From foreign capitals to local coffeehouses, opinions abound about the current and future state of the United States, especially compared to now-and-then rivals such as China[1] or Russia.[2] It has been hard to escape the pessimism about America's trajectory in world affairs. Summing up the views of a large number of scholars, Amitav Acharya, former president of the International Studies Association, asserted that the "age of global dominance by any single power as the world has previously experienced under Britain, then America, is over."[3] While some scholars challenge the notion that America is in eclipse,[4] even some optimists wonder about the durability of its position.[5]

Yet while many observers think U.S. capability is in decline at the global level, that is not what our data and analysis reveal regarding the Persian Gulf. We find that American capability, which should not be conflated with influence, has increased significantly in the past few decades at the military, economic, and political levels, with some important qualifications. Despite many challenges, America is a hegemon inasmuch as it has predominant capabilities toward and in the Gulf that are unavailable to other states in their entirety.

U.S. still a hegemon

However, we move beyond the question of U.S. capability in the oil-rich Persian Gulf in this book. We also seek to understand what American hegemony really means. What does being the strongest actor yield in the complex and unpredictable circumstances of world affairs? We do not make broad claims here but focus instead on the question of what American hegemony means for global oil security.

To be sure, the Middle East often appears to be highly unstable, and in many cases it is, such as in Syria and Libya, but we argue that the rise of American hegemony in the Persian Gulf in particular over the past several decades has, contrary to conventional views, increased oil security. The story is far more complex, as we will show, but the rise of American capabilities in the region, including its strategic cooperation with regional countries, has helped protect oil security.

Oil security can be defined in various ways.[6] We define it in terms of provisioning oil to the global economy so as to ensure reasonable oil prices, which are shaped by numerous economic, political, and security factors.[7] We can all debate what the term "*reasonable oil prices*" really means, but large spikes in oil prices or oil shocks that cause major economic dislocation are problematic and in fact have been linked to most of America's economic recessions since the 1973 Arab oil embargo.

Washington's capabilities have helped check real and perceived threats to oil security ranging from economic coercion to military actions, even though a number of thorny and costly issues have emerged that are endogenous to the American role. We explore them in detail here, especially in Chapter 11.

While the United States is central to our thesis, we chose to focus secondarily on China and also on Russia because they are America's primary historic and contemporary challengers at the global level. In fact, some scholars argue that China, Russia, and Iran have exploited the decline of the United States and assumed a much bolder foreign policy.[8] We also explore China and Russia because their position in the Persian Gulf, unlike that of other global powers outside the United States, has changed dramatically and altered oil security, a key issue area for us. Exploring their standing and role over time tells us something about change in global and regional politics and puts America's evolution in the region and in the arena of oil security into clearer perspective through comparison.

China's rise in the Persian Gulf has been meteoric over the past several decades. Although China remains far behind the United States in all areas of involvement, Beijing has expanded—in some cases dramatically—its diplomatic, trade, and energy ties to regional states. We cannot understand modern

China and its foreign policy, much less the international relations of the Persian Gulf, without understanding these developments. China's rise in the Gulf has challenged America economically and, in some measure, politically, but it has largely benefited oil security. This is because Beijing depends on economic growth to maintain its global position and boost its burgeoning middle class. Thus, it needs oil at reasonable prices. Since much of that oil is protected under a U.S.-led security system, Beijing also has had a vested interest in not undermining that system, even if it also rivals Washington. China has also become increasingly interdependent with the Arab states and therefore prefers greater regional security even if that also benefits Washington.

For its part, Russia entertains a grossly exaggerated view of its own standing and power in the world, as many would argue,[9] but it still remains an important global actor. To a far lesser degree than China, Russia has also expanded in the political and economic arenas in the Gulf. But Russia is less important strategically in and around the Gulf region than it was during the Cold War, and that has further benefited oil security.

While the rise in American capability and changes in the international relations of the region have boosted global oil security, U.S. hegemony has faced serious challenges. Indeed, it would be misleading to paint a picture of the rise of hegemony as translating easily into positive outcomes. The picture is much more complex. We stress that the real story is about both U.S. hegemony and the challenges Washington faces, which we capture in the concept of challenged hegemony. But that raises two questions: What are the challenges, and how have they manifested themselves? We are not referring to all of the problems of the Middle East that challenge Washington, such as potential domestic instabilities in the Persian Gulf[10] or possible spillover effects of conflicts outside the Persian Gulf. We address problems that are tied to hegemony and help us weigh what it really means, especially for global oil security.

Although we argue that hegemony boosts oil security, we also underscore the downside of hegemony. Several problems endogenous to hegemony cannot be ignored. Hegemony contributes to anti-Americanism and to terrorism in part because maintaining hegemony requires positive relations with autocratic regimes, places America into contested political space, and conjures up images among many of a powerful Western state seeking to dominate and exploit regional actors. Such hegemony is also very costly financially for the United States. America, in essence, protects global oil security and reasonable oil prices for the entire global economy, bearing highly disproportionate costs.

Moreover, hegemony hardly translates into direct influence. That, in fact, may be a classic conundrum in world history for any great power that has sought to translate predominant capability into desirable outcomes. Understanding these challenges yields a more balanced picture of America's standing and role in the region and how that connects to its global standing as well.

Hegemony also generates some level of soft balancing. Soft balancing has the same goal as hard balancing—to check the strongest actor—but relies on international institutions and economic and diplomatic approaches to balance rather than the hard balancing approaches of alliances and military spending. The United States has faced both types of balancing chiefly from Russia, China, and Iran.[11] That raises the interesting point that the same factors that can benefit oil security can also chip away at American hegemony. Thus, China's need for oil benefits oil security in the Gulf, but its dependence on oil also pushes it to compete with the United States economically in the Gulf and sometimes to try to check it strategically, even if Beijing does not want to undermine Washington's security role that helps protect that oil.

Furthermore, our argument does not ignore real threats to oil security. They certainly do exist, even though they are often exaggerated or misunderstood.[12] The real question is what these threats mean for our two key arguments: the rise of American hegemony and, in turn, its positive effect on global oil security. That is the scope that we have set here.

For example, some scholars have predicted the demise of the House of Saud since the 1960s. The regime has escaped that fate, but U.S.-Saudi relations are complicated and sometimes opaque, and instability in the kingdom is a real issue. What does that mean for our two key arguments?

At the broadest level, it is important to question the entire paradigm of global oil security and the U.S. role in the Persian Gulf. Indeed, protecting the free flow of oil, while vital to the global economy, is not the best path to security in the long run. The best path is to get off our reliance on oil in the first place. However, the world has not done nearly enough to move toward a new paradigm. In fact, global oil consumption has increased significantly over the years to nearly 90 million barrels a day (mbd) in 2016, and that trend is not likely to change any time soon. The U.S. Department of Energy estimates that the global use of oil will increase from 87 mbd in 2010 to 97 mbd in 2020 and 115 mbd in 2040. Until our dependence on oil decreases substantially, the Persian Gulf will remain crucial.

Why This Topic Matters

We offer a window on the vital issue of global oil security that affects politics and economics all the way down to the local gas pump; no country can escape that issue. Much excellent work exists on oil security and covers subjects ranging from the fundamentals of oil supply, to pipeline politics, to Russia's strategic use of energy for political power.[13] However, far less attention is given to how the international relations of the Gulf affect oil security. This is in part because most scholars of the Middle East are not focused on oil security,[14] and most oil security analysts do not focus on the international relations of the Middle East. We address this gap and bridge these areas by examining oil security with special attention to the role of great powers.

That few other goals are more important for the global economy than ensuring oil security is clear. Failure to do so could stunt global economic growth and cause much human suffering. As we earlier noted, past American and global recessions have been preceded or accelerated by an increase in oil prices, often the result of Persian Gulf instability, including the 1973 oil embargo, the 1979 Iranian Revolution, and the 1980 outbreak of the Iran-Iraq War. In light of most estimates, oil will only become more central in the race to find approaches for meeting increasing energy demand at reasonable prices,[15] and the Persian Gulf, as we discuss in Chapter 2, will be increasingly critical for meeting this demand.

Oil is by far the most important energy source[16] and is fundamentally tied to international politics and security. Oil is far more likely to contribute to military conflicts and to other security and political issues than other energy sources,[17] and it is central in driving climate change.[18]

Global oil trade accounts for a major part of global consumption.[19] Oil has a virtual monopoly on the transportation sector, which drives the world economy, and it is used in numerous products, including fertilizing, cultivating, processing, and, especially, transporting food. What happens in the Persian Gulf trickles down across all areas of human endeavor, making this region a fulcrum of global dynamics.

In addition, we tie into the broader debate about U.S. capability. While the questions of the United States and its challengers are ubiquitous, they focus on the global rather than the regional level. Thus, we commonly see questions of the following kind in the popular press and academic outlets: Is the United States still a global hegemon?[20] Will China or other actors overtake it as the strongest state in the world?[21] Has the world become post-American or multipolar?[22] These are great and important questions, but they are focused on capability at the global level. What is starkly missing is an understanding of how the relative capabilities of great powers have changed in regions of the world.

The question of the rise or fall of America in the world is not about one global-level story but rather many stories, each of which may tell a different tale. Thus, hypothetically, the United States could weaken in one or more regions but gain strength in others, or it may weaken or strengthen across the board. Paying attention to both the global and regional levels, and the links between them, offers additional explanatory leverage and fidelity. For example, as international relations scholars Robert Keohane and Joseph Nye have demonstrated, the relative capabilities of major powers in an issue area—in this case, regions—may well differ from the distribution of such capabilities at the global level and depending on the issue area in question.[23] Great Britain, for instance, remained the preeminent power in the ocean issue area well after its power began to flag at the global level. Global analysis may mask such differences across different issue areas and regions.

Much good qualitative analysis exists on the region, but we seek to offer the most comprehensive, data-driven portrait to date of the changing capabilities and role of America and, to a lesser extent, China and Russia, in the Persian Gulf. We compare their political, economic, and military capabilities in the region within the context of a broader narrative on hegemony, great power involvement, and oil security.

We focus on the 1970s through 2015, with an emphasis on the post–Cold War period. In covering such a relatively long period, we hope to offer insight into broader trends that are likely to remain germane for some time, even if some of the particulars that we identify change significantly.

No study of which we are aware has explored the evolution of China and Russia in the region systematically, much less in comparison to the United States.[24] In fact, there is a remarkable dearth of work on the international relations of the Persian Gulf in general. There are some excellent exceptions,[25] but the goal of these works usually is to focus on one great power in the region,[26] and they differ markedly from our work in their goals, scope, and approaches.

We also offer systematic attention to change, which is in relatively short supply in the study of international relations yet important. As international relations scholars Yale Ferguson and Richard Mansbach put it, to "know if and how change has taken place, it is necessary to have a baseline—the past—against which to compare and contrast the present."[27] Joseph Nye has cautioned that "One should be wary of extrapolating long-run trends from short-term cycles."[28] Other thinkers as well have observed that many studies are too static because they present only one-period snapshots of American and Chinese capabilities, which can be deceptive.[29]

Beyond our aim of illuminating Washington's role and position, we seek to do the same with Russia and China. Energy-thirsty China has become increasingly interested and engaged in the Persian Gulf region over the past several decades. The region is now critical to China—perhaps even more so than Europe. For its part, Russia has been a major player in the Persian Gulf over the past several decades. Thus, it is important to understand in what ways it has declined there and in what manner it continues to be involved in the Persian Gulf and in issues that affect regional security.

The International Relations of the Persian Gulf

We explore a few key questions: How have the capability and role of the United States changed in the Gulf in the past several decades? What does that mean for oil security? How have the capability and role of America's main rivals in the world, China and Russia, changed in the region, and what does that mean for America's regional role and for oil security?

To answer these questions, we had to develop an appropriate approach and method. Part of the challenge was to study capability over time. In international relations, power is traditionally defined as the ability to get others to do something they otherwise would not do or, relatedly, to achieve a desired outcome. This definition subsumes concepts such as soft power which is the "ability to attract others."[30] The second way to define power is in terms of capabilities. This is chiefly done by examining key indicators such as military and economic capabilities.

Here, we define *power* in terms of capabilities, which is one prominent way by which hegemony is usually conceived. We do not adopt a definition of *hegemony* in which the hegemon is necessarily viewed as being able to bring about the outcomes it desires.[31] We define *hegemony* as a preponderance of material resources,[32] which includes military capabilities, as many realists would emphasize,[33] and broader economic capabilities, as liberals and political economists would stress.[34] In fact, we also pay attention to political relations and security arrangements that might be missed in data analysis but are germane to exploring the capabilities, role, and interactions of great powers in regions.

Examining the capabilities of external actors in a region is a different matter from examining them at the global level. Conventionally, scholars compare the capabilities of states at the global level based largely on military and economic issues such as gross domestic product (GDP), national deficit, defense spending, population demographics, education levels, and number of allies, to mention just a few. However, these indicators are not suitable for regional-level analysis. Thus, even changes in defense spending may affect capabilities differently across regions, while fluctuations in GDP may or may not have meaning for regional dynamics. Studying change at the international level can provide insight into regions but does not substitute for a regional-level analysis.

The capabilities of outside actors in regions are shaped most importantly by the state of their diplomatic relations with area states, military presence in or near the region, arms sales and security relations, and economic ties such as mutual trade and investment. Such indicators provide a useful portrait of the capability and role of those who must act at long distances, but examining data can also yield a dotted sketch of reality. Thus, we ensconce such analysis in a broader story while acknowledging the challenges of trying to transform history with all its messiness into a coherent narrative.

To systematically examine the capabilities of the outside states in the region, their evolving roles, and critical features of regional security, we study the period of the 1970s to 2015 primarily, with a focus on the post–Cold War period from 1991 to 2015. Using original data, we explore and compare the following qualitative and quantitative indicators within a broader story that puts these indicators in perspective.

- The state of diplomatic relations between the United States, China, and Russia and regional states. In this domain, we explore diplomatic treaties and accords, high-level visits, and official and unofficial statements to capture the broader picture of ongoing relations.

- Military presence, security agreements, and arms sales of the United States, China, and Russia. In this security area, we examine changes in the level and composition of arms trade, broader defense relations, and the external powers' military presence in or near the region.

- Great power economic and energy ties. Here, we analyze changes in the level of hydrocarbon and nonhydrocarbon trade, mutual foreign direct investment, and energy agreements, cooperation, and relations.

Using multiple indicators yields a fuller picture. For example, we might assume that if diplomatic relations are poor, then strategic and economic interaction will also suffer seriously. That is a fair assumption, but sometimes it does not hold. For instance, America's relations with Saudi Arabia were very tense in the years after September 11, but their economic and strategic interaction, which fed into America's overall standing, did not suffer in the same time period.

To be sure, indicators of global capabilities are easier to collect and compare. For example, it's quick work to compare GDP, even if the data may not be fully accurate. By contrast, our indicators pose a greater challenge in this regard, but what we lose in ease and comparability, we hope to gain in explanatory potential.

The Organization of the Book

Chapter 2 sketches key signposts in the American journey into the Persian Gulf and the rise of oil as the most critical source of energy in the world. Chapters 3 to 8 deal with the United States, China, and Russia and explore the key aspects of great power capability and standing laid out in this chapter.

Chapter 9 then brings together, develops, and compares all of the empirical evidence we have presented regarding the United States, China, and Russia. Using quantitative and qualitative analysis, we provide a detailed as well as panoramic overview of change to sum up and put our more detailed analyses in context.

Part III examines the larger issues we have raised. Chapter 10 shows how the rise of American hegemony has actually boosted global oil security, as has China's growing need for oil. Chapter 11 examines the difficulties of hegemony and the challenges that America faces, which need to be considered carefully. Some of these challenges are related to the rise of China in the region and the continuing role of Russia. But the challenges run much deeper and include the high costs of maintaining hegemony, terrorism and the resentments that it generates in the region, and the fact that hegemony does not equal influence in world politics—perhaps a classic phenomenon as we look back at the fate of hegemons in history.

The conclusion in Chapter 12 expands on our key arguments. It explains what our findings mean more broadly for security studies, hegemony, international political economy, and Middle East politics.

I THE UNITED STATES IN THE PERSIAN GULF

2 The United States and the Global Oil Era

T HE MIDDLE EAST has been an arena for great power rivalry for millennia, from the time of the vast empires that followed the first civilizations, through the great game of Euro-Russian rivalry in the nineteenth century, and into the Cold War of the twentieth century and the post–Cold War period. The most ancient rivalries began at least as early as 2500 B.C. in Mesopotamia, the purported cradle of civilization between the Tigris and Euphrates Rivers in modern-day Iraq. Thereafter, a broad array of empires rivaled each other for influence, including the Babylonians, Assyrians, the Hittites of Anatolia, and the Persians, whose vast empire under Cyrus the Great stretched across the Near East from Greece to the frontier of India, only to be eclipsed later by Alexander the Great and subsequently the Romans.[1]

The goals of great powers have changed, as have the great powers themselves across eras from these ancient times to the fifteenth and sixteenth centuries, when the Europeans established themselves in the region, to the modern period of rivalry and cooperation among actors in a globalized world. But the Middle East has always enticed them for its coveted land, strategic position astride three continents, importance as a trade route, religious intrigue and centrality, and, in more recent times, its oil resources and concerns about transnational problems such as terrorism and weapons of mass destruction.

Modern actors at times have learned the high costs of seeking to secure energy. When one American official asserted in 1944, referring to the Persian Gulf, that the "oil in this region is the greatest single prize in all history,"[2] he could not have known what wars and travails awaited America, especially after it assumed responsibility from Britain in 1971 for the security of the Persian Gulf, a region that includes Iran, Iraq, Saudi Arabia, Kuwait, Oman, Kuwait, Bahrain, and the United Arab Emirates.

America has certainly benefited from the free flow of oil from the Middle East, but it would also be drawn slowly into the region by revolution, war, and regional rivalries, all set against the inherent instabilities of the region and the struggles for influence and standing among the global powers. The evolution of its position relative to the other great powers would prove critical to regional and global politics and to all countries that depend on the flow of oil at reasonable prices.

It is worthwhile sketching some key signposts in the American journey into the Persian Gulf all the way from the rise of the age of oil in the early twentieth century to the Iran nuclear accord of 2015, a journey that has been affected by, and has cross-cut, that of China and Russia. This evolution has been shaped in important ways by the concomitant rise in the importance of oil to the global economy. As the most politicized commodity in history, oil has been intricately interwoven into the domestic, regional, and international relations of the region.

The Age of Oil, Centered in the Middle East

By the advent of the twentieth century, the industrial revolution and the development of large standing armies had created enormous energy needs. To fill this potentially lucrative market, the United States and Russia started producing oil and by 1900 accounted for 90 percent of the world supply. American oil proved to be critical in World War I. Shortly before that war, the United States started to transform its coal-burning battle fleet into one that used oil for fuel, which created important military advantages, and during the war, it also supplied its allies with oil.[3]

From 1918 to 1999, America produced more oil, cumulatively, than any other country.[4] That position would be overtaken by Saudi Arabia, but the United States would try to regain its position with its oil boom that took off in 2007–2008. The opening salvo of the oil era for the Gulf was in 1907 when a large petroleum field was discovered in Iran. By May 1933, the United States and Saudi Arabia made an agreement that would fashion their oil relations, and oil in general would help contribute to American power in the twentieth century.[5]

Founded in 1870 at the outset of the Gilded Age of great capitalist enterprises and excesses, Standard Oil Company of California struck a sixty-year contract allowing it exclusive rights to explore and produce oil from Saudi Arabia's Eastern Hasa oil province.[6] By 1938, ARAMCO—the Arabian American Oil Company—discovered oil in commercial quantities.[7]

Forged on common interests in oil, America and Saudi Arabia developed relations that privileged strategy and money over democracy, while painting their interaction in a brighter light than deserved.[8] In subsequent decades, the Saudis slowly took control of the company from the Americans[9] as a forerunner of one of the biggest changes in global oil in the past seventy-five years—and one that has had an enormous impact on oil security and the American role in the Middle East.

Prior to the oil crisis of 1973, the Seven Sisters—the biggest private oil companies such as Chevron—controlled around 85 percent of the world's oil reserves.[10] By contrast, data show that national oil companies control around 89 percent of the world's reserves; national oil companies are more privatized hold around 7 percent; and private international oil companies (IOCs) control about 4 percent.[11] As one expert points out, in "virtually every oil-exporting country, NOCs, which had in the 1990s ceded ground to IOCs in the wake of globalization, have reclaimed lost ground."[12]

NOCs expanded most rapidly during the period of decolonization in the 1950s, 1960s, and 1970s but also in more recent decades. For instance, Iran initially nationalized its oil assets in 1953, though Western powers reversed that move in Operation Ajax, launched by America and Britain, but by the 1970s, Iran and the other Persian Gulf countries had nationalized energy more effectively.

Saudi Arabia and Kuwait nationalized their oil assets in the 1970s, keeping upstream production mostly closed to foreign investment thereafter while opening downstream production (refining mainly) to outside parties. Chevron, then the Standard Oil Company of California, had discovered oil in Saudi Arabia in 1938 and created the basis for ARAMCO, a predecessor of today's Saudi Aramco. The Saudis took full control of ARAMCO's assets in 1976, which launched a period in which the private companies would be contractors with production-sharing contracts rather than concessionaries and actual owners.[13]

The early 1970s saw further nationalization of oil assets by Middle Eastern producers, and by the mid-1970s, resource nationalism had spread throughout the developing world. Producers in the Persian Gulf assumed complete control over their oil industries, revoking any remaining concessions they had with the Western private oil companies.

Today, of the twenty major oil-producing companies worldwide, fourteen are NOCs, and their states also control the majority of global oil fields large enough to warrant investment from a supermajor or one of the world's biggest private oil companies. Moreover, it is well recognized that the global oil sector will need massive investment to meet rising demand. Most of this oil will come from members of the Organization of Petroleum Exporting Countries (OPEC), and they most likely will be critical in determining the path of the oil market. NOCs will be key drivers, despite the North American energy boom, which will probably reach peak production between 2020 and 2025.[14] In brief, then, the trend in control over oil resources has completely reversed since 1972, with Saudi and Iran dominant and the major private companies by and large sharing small percentages of control. This shift is vital to an understanding of global oil and security dynamics and the many issues that they affect. Such dynamics will make the international relations of the Persian Gulf even more important in the future.

Unlike the European powers, America was not directly involved in the great power rivalries of the nineteenth century that crisscrossed the Middle East and instead was caught in nation building, civil war, and reconstruction. While continental America was forged on the anvil of aggressive expansion, that policy did not extend over to the Middle East. America scarcely even intervened near the region with the exception of the Barbary wars from 1801 to 1804, which in any case were aimed at checking piracy against American shipping in the Mediterranean.

By contrast, imperial Britain was interested in the Middle East because of its rivalry with France, Russia, and Germany, especially after the rise of the ambitious but mercurial Wilhelm II in 1890. European interest in the region became increasingly more strategy oriented as the nineteenth century wore on. Under the nineteenth-century classic European balance-of-power system established at the Congress of Vienna in 1815, major European states endeavored consciously and purposefully to maintain a balance of power in Europe, but did not proscribe intense competition for domination of other regions.[15]

For its part, Britain and Russia transformed the Gulf into a playground for their so-called great game. In order to protect its crucial lifeline to India, Britain also needed unchallenged supremacy in the Gulf. This explains its dogged efforts to thwart Napoleon, undermine Russia's southward advance in search of warm water ports and improved strategic position, and sabotage Germany's provocative Berlin-Baghdad railroad plan.[16] While Britain and Russia were frittering away their energies in the great game, the United States, many thousands of miles away, was continuing the process of becoming one of the strongest countries in the world, a development that leading American thinkers and politicians understood and appreciated.

The Gulf became an important strategic foothold against Wilhemine Germany. The allies viewed Iran in particular as a vital conduit for sending arms to Russia during World War I, and both the Suez Canal and the petroleum fields of Persia were perceived as critical to allied interests. Defeating the Ottoman Empire, which had allied with Germany, meant penetrating the Middle East, which was under the influence of the far-flung Ottoman Empire, despite the advent of its demise in the nineteenth century.

During World War II, the Persian Gulf became more important to the United States as a result of the increasing military demand for oil and the region's strategic location.[17] Middle East oil was vital to the entire Allied war effort. Unlike World War I, armies required far greater mobility, and that resulted in one hundred times the use of gasoline.[18] Oil proved crucial to mechanized warfare on a global scale. Had the Nazis successfully invaded the Gulf area, their control of the oil fields could have shifted the course of the war.[19]

As an oil glut lasting almost two decades approached its end in fall 1941, Secretary of the Interior Harold Ickes advised President Franklin Roosevelt that America must secure additional oil resources to ensure near-term supply.[20] Although this was largely a false alarm of a peak oil problem, it illustrated how important oil had become to American national security. In roughly the same period, the Soviets had occupied Iranian Azerbaijan in 1941 in the effort against Nazi Germany, only to withdraw belatedly in 1946. Later, during the Cold War, perceptions of ongoing Soviet interest in the warm waters of the Gulf triggered Western states to secure the Gulf from their erstwhile wartime ally while also jockeying among themselves for primary political and economic influence.

While the United States was in a presidential year that would bring John F. Kennedy to power, the rise of OPEC was in the wings and would become one of the most significant developments of the twentieth century in global energy. OPEC was founded in 1960 by Saudi Arabia, Kuwait, Iran, Iraq, and Venezuela, with subsequent expansion that added Algeria, Ecuador, Gabon, Indonesia, Libya, Nigeria, Qatar, and the United Arab Emirates. OPEC market power slowly developed in the 1960s, but it was not until the 1970s that the Arab states in OPEC, rather than OPEC itself as an organization, demonstrated their power in the global oil arena,[21] including quite overtly against the United States. After the unsuccessful Arab oil embargo during the 1967 Six Day War, OPEC launched the oil embargo during the 1973 Arab-Israeli War. It quadrupled oil prices, causing a major American recession. The rest of the world felt the pain as well, as most of the industrialized world was targeted by the embargo. About 90 percent of the production cuts were made by Saudi Arabia, Kuwait, and Libya.[22]

The rise of oil futures trading markets in 1983 at the New York Mercantile Exchange would erode OPEC influence over oil pricing. In any case, Riyadh started to moderate its oil policy of its own volition in the mid-1970s and for many years to follow. As the de facto leader of OPEC, Saudi Arabia generally tried to work to keep oil prices from rising too high. While importing states worried about the security of supply, energy-exporting countries thought of the security of demand.[23] Fearing that high oil prices could hurt global growth, reduce demand for Saudi oil by encouraging conservation and renewable energy development, and anger its U.S. protector, the Saudis generally were able (and willing) to act as an oil price "dove." Although it sometimes deviated from this approach, Saudi Arabia tended to oppose any serious cuts in oil production within OPEC unless warranted by depressed oil prices, and it would put more oil on the market when oil supply was threatened by crises or a deliberate cutoff or oil prices rose too high.

The Cold War and Global Oil

America's post–World War II economic boom and the Cold War rivalry with the Soviet Union further increased the region's economic and geostrategic importance to the United States. The fear in the West was that Moscow, or some of its clients in the Middle East, could gain control or influence over oil resources. Thus, a cardinal goal was to prevent this outcome. U.S. policy in various forms aimed to deny Moscow strategic, political, and economic footing in the region. In 1949, American decision makers even created a plan, described in National Security Council directive National Security Council 26/2, to destroy the Gulf oil fields, if necessary, to prevent a Soviet seizure.[24] President Harry Truman started to commit the United States to the task of protecting Saudi security as early as 1947. In 1949, the National Security Council identified the region as "critically important to American security" and called for the United States to "promote pro-Western ties to prevent Soviet penetration of the region."[25]

In line with such Cold War thinking, Washington spearheaded the overthrow of Iran's popularly elected leader, Prime Minister Mohammed Mossadegh. Iran had nationalized its oil assets in 1951 after the shah of Iran was effectively stripped of his powers by the parliament in 1950. That left the Anglo-Iranian Oil Company (later British Petroleum) without portfolio[26] and threatened to make insecure a resource critical to Western fighting capabilities.[27] Washington also feared that Mossadegh was uncomfortably disposed toward the Soviet Union in a period when the Cold War was especially frigid. A U.S.-organized coup put the pro-West-leaning shah back in power in 1953, an act that has embittered Iran until today.

While two world wars drew European states into the region and the Cold War made it more important to the United States, China remained largely uninvolved, although by 1941, it did begin to realize that control of the region by hostile powers could prove very dangerous.[28] Between 1912 and 1949, however, China was far more absorbed with survival and nation building than with global events, much less Middle East politics.[29] The PRC did seek to generate anticolonial sentiment in the region in the 1950s and 1960s and to check Moscow in the 1970s, but it was not until the later 1970s or early 1980s that Beijing, in conjunction with its broader political opening to the world, became more seriously interested in the Persian Gulf.

The Year of Living Dangerously

America's overarching interests in the Persian Gulf have remained largely consistent since the onset of the Cold War: to ensure global access to energy resources and, relatedly, protect regional stability against anti-American forces. For most of the Cold War, rivalry with the Soviet Union posed a real and perceived risk to those interests. Yet it was not until British withdrawal from the Gulf in 1971, precipitated chiefly by Britain's flagging economy,[30] that the United States assumed responsibility for regional security. Reflecting this rising role, President Jimmy Carter described the Persian Gulf in 1977 as "vulnerable and vital . . . to which greater military concern ought to be given."[31]

In the 1970s, the United States entrusted Iran and Saudi Arabia with protecting its interests in the region under Richard Nixon's twin-pillar policy. These states would be the two pillars of America's proxy foreign policy, which allowed Washington to protect regional oil without major and direct intervention into the Persian Gulf. But as we discuss in more detail in the next chapter, the shocks of 1979, one of the most critical years in modern Middle

Eastern history,[32] pushed Washington to develop major military capabilities in the region.

The 1979 Soviet incursion into Afghanistan linked Gulf stability to U.S. global security.[33] Although there is strong reason to believe that Moscow was focused solely on Afghanistan, important decision makers, particularly in Washington, saw the invasion as part of a grand, chess-like scheme and feared that Moscow might even invade the Persian Gulf. Washington was not unreasonable in worrying about the Afghanistan intervention because it occurred at a time of Western vulnerability in the Middle East. In the midst of such tumult, the U.S. framework for Gulf security collapsed in 1979 when the shah of Iran, who had largely supported U.S. security interests in the Middle East even if uneasily, was replaced by the virulently anti-American Ayatollah Khomeini.

The overthrow of the pro-Western shah of Iran in 1979 undermined the main pillar of Nixon's policy. Contrary to popular perception and to his determined stance in the Iran-Iraq War, Iran's spiritual leader was not militarily oriented. In contrast to the shah, whose military expenditures were extraordinary, Khomeini severed the extensive arms relationship with Washington, shut down U.S. military facilities on Iranian soil, and even spurned Soviet arms offers. In addition, he executed or imprisoned many of his top officers and placed much less trust in Iran's regular, better-trained military than in the ideologically motivated Revolutionary Guard. Although Khomeini used force internally, he asserted that even the export of Islam was to be conducted nonmilitarily. However, the Iranian Revolution threatened to spread throughout the oil-producing Middle East, where it could target Arab monarchies viewed as corrupt, illegitimate, and lackeys of the United States.

From Washington's perspective, the Afghanistan intervention presented the West with the possibility that Moscow would exploit U.S. vulnerability in the Middle East by invading the Gulf,[34] which lay just beyond Afghanistan. Writing in the aftermath of the invasion, the U.S. ambassador to Moscow, George Kennan, stated that since World War II, there had not been "as far-reaching a militarization of thought and discourse in the capital."[35]

The invasion shocked President Carter, who described it as "an unprecedented act," a "radical departure from the policies or actions that the Soviets have pursued since the Second World War,"[36] and "the most serious threat to the peace since the Second World War."[37] Appearing not to believe that Moscow could do something so provocative, Carter asserted that his opinion of the Soviets had "changed more drastically in the last week than in the previous two-

and-a-half years"[38] and sent Leonid Brezhnev a message on the presidential hotline claiming that the invasion "could mark a fundamental and long-lasting turning point" in superpower relations.[39] In Carter's view, a "successful take-over of Afghanistan would give the Soviets deep penetration between Iran and Pakistan, and pose a threat to the rich oil fields of the Persian Gulf area."[40]

Suspicious of Soviet motives in Southwest Asia, as Britain had been of imperial Russia's motives in the nineteenth century, Washington was primed for action. On January 23, 1980, the Carter Doctrine was enunciated shortly after the invasion, and in the wake of the aftermath of the Iranian Revolution. It asserted that "an attempt by any outside force to gain control of the Persian Gulf region will be regarded as an assault on the vital interests of the United States of America, and such an assault will be repelled by any means necessary, including military force."[41]

The Dictator and Would-Be Regional Hegemon

To make matters worse, in July 1979, after a decade as the de facto dictator of Iraq under President Ahmed Hassan al-Bakr, Saddam Hussein became president. Saddam Hussein's rise to power added another destabilizing dimension to the regional picture—one that would shape events thereafter. Saddam's rise, which coincided with Iran's tempestuous Revolution, was a prerequisite for the Iran-Iraq War. In September 1980, Iraq invaded its neighbor Iran, confronting Ayatollah Khomeini's Islamic Revolution, and triggering one of the century's bloodiest wars with more than 1 million casualties. Neither side ultimately won, which is what many in the world wanted, but Hussein was not finished. He would sow the seeds of future conflicts that would culminate in his ignominious demise. Even at the point of his capture in 2003 in a spider hole, appearing as if he were a vagrant, he reasserted that he was president of Iraq, only to do so again when put on trial in 2004.

Elevating the American Commitment

While the Carter Doctrine committed the United States to protect the Gulf against external threats, the Reagan doctrine elevated the commitment. It called for U.S. support to anticommunist resistance movements in Soviet-allied nations in Africa, Asia, and Latin America. President Ronald W. Reagan stated in October 1981 that there was "no way" the United States could "stand by" and allow threats against Saudi Arabia to stop its flow of oil.[42] This statement and others like it became known as the Reagan Doctrine, a U.S. commitment to protect Saudi Arabia against external and internal threats to the Persian Gulf and against domestic threats to the regime. The United States made a tacit agreement to protect the Saudis in the 1940s, and the Carter Doctrine reinforced a commitment to protect the free flow of oil from threats outside the region; now Reagan was elevating the U.S. commitment one more notch. Saudi Arabia would become the linchpin of U.S. security in the Gulf.[43] In 1982, Reagan's famous "evil empire" speech clearly pitted good against evil in the Cold War struggle, underscoring the embedded and not even implied image that he and so many others had of the Soviet Union. He saw the Soviet intervention in Afghanistan as further evidence of this evil and sought an opportunity to deal Moscow a major blow.

The U.S. national security strategy issued in 1987 by President Reagan underscored that American goals included "maintaining regional stability, containing and reducing Soviet influence, preserving the security of Israel and our other friends in the area, retaining access to oil on reasonable terms for ourselves and our allies, and curbing state-sponsored terrorism."[44]

Regional Wars

The bloody and lengthy Iran-Iraq War set the stage for even more war. Two years after that war ended, Saddam invaded and annexed oil-rich Kuwait and was in a position to invade Saudi Arabia. The invasion took the world by surprise, despite Saddam's reputation for brutality and opportunism.

Regional and great powers were stunned by Iraq's annexation of Kuwait, an anachronism in modern world politics that harked back to World War II German tactics. Neither Washington nor Beijing was focused on the Middle East in 1990. America was focused on the Eastern European revolutions and on the events in the Soviet Union that led to its demise. Beijing was also embroiled in the aftermath of its own domestic democracy movement, which could have threatened regime survival or at least legitimacy, and the Soviet Union was destabilized and on the verge of disintegrating.

By July 30, 1990, Iraq had eight divisions, 100,000 well-trained troops, and 350 tanks poised on the Kuwaiti border, in formation for extensive operations. On August 2, 140,000 Iraqi troops and 1,800 tanks roared into Kuwait, spearheaded by two Republican Guard divisions: the Hammurabi and the Medina. What had been viewed as mere brinkmanship in late July in an effort to scare the Kuwaitis into making some key economic and territorial concessions turned into a full-blown invasion using Iraq's best forces. The rest is history.

The United States sent a massive force to protect Saudi Arabia in Operation Desert Shield and then to kick Iraqi forces out of Kuwait in Operation Desert Storm. The U.S.-led alliance of twenty-eight members grew to thirty-seven by war's end and included more than half a million soldiers with a 10,000-soldier brigade from the Arab Gulf states, 7,000 Kuwaiti soldiers, and 15,000 Syrian troops who fought only on Kuwaiti soil. On the European side, the British sent 43,000 troops and significant military equipment, while France sent 16,000 soldiers. By January 1991, an incredible half of all U.S. combat forces worldwide would be deployed to the Gulf theater.

In 1991, at the end of the 1991 Gulf war, Washington faced difficult choices regarding war termination. Rather than march on Baghdad or even continue the campaign long enough to destroy Saddam's Republican Guard divisions, the United States and its allies chose to end the ground war at 100 hours. Invading Baghdad was quite possible, but the administration never seriously considered it. It was widely believed that Saddam would be hard to find; that such an operation would have entailed unacceptable potential casualties; and that even if it were successful, finding an alternative Iraqi regime to lead a post-Saddam Iraq would be hard. Moreover, the U.N. mandate that governed U.S.-led operations did not allow such action, and America's Arab allies, some of whom would not even fight Iraq during the war, would have opposed it. U.S. decision makers were concerned that Washington would have been acting without international support and wanted to avoid getting stuck in the Gulf.[45]

The administration of George W. Bush obviously saw Iraq differently, although the times had changed as well, chiefly due to the September 11 terrorist attacks. The Iraq war of 2003 was a choice that America certainly did not have to make,[46] and it has paid dearly for it.

The United States did not intend to maintain a massive military force in Iraq. Rather, it sought to withdraw or at least significantly reduce this force once Iraq became more stable. No American leader could have sensibly said that the United States should occupy Iraq permanently. In fact, the Bush administration expected to rebuild Iraq without great trouble and then to bring U.S. troops home. The occupation lasted far longer because it was poorly planned and ran into unexpected problems, not because the U.S. administration wanted to stay in Iraq.[47]

The outcome of the Iraqi invasion was far more disastrous than President Bush and his administration expected,[48] which was blindsided by postwar problems in Iraq,[49] and especially by the subsequent massive insurgency. In fact, two months before the invasion, Bush reportedly told Prime Minister Tony Blair of Great Britain that it was "unlikely there would be internecine warfare between the different religious and ethnic groups."[50] It is not that the administration did not plan for postwar Iraq. That is a myth or misunderstanding. But as noted charitably by Douglas Feith, a former Defense Department official in the Bush administration, aspects of postwar planning were put in motion, but "the crippling disorder we call the insurgency was not anticipated with any precision, by either intelligence analysts or policy officials."[51]

In January 2007, Bush announced a new approach to the war in Iraq at a time when the insurgency appeared to be escalating out of control and Democrats in Washington were criticizing him for not securing Iraq so that American troops could come home. Rather than withdraw, Bush decided to ramp up U.S. efforts. The new approach, called the "surge," aimed at beefing up the U.S. counterinsurgency strategy. To bolster this approach, Bush ordered the deployment of more than 20,000 soldiers into Iraq. He also extended the tour of most of the army troops in country and some of the marines already in the Anbar Province, which faced the most critical unrest that the Bush administration aimed to quell and reverse so that a unified, democratic federal Iraq that could govern itself could emerge. The surge changed the focus for the U.S. military toward helping Iraqis secure key neighborhoods, protect the local population, build their own forces, and achieve reconciliation among political and ethnic factions.[52]

While the surge proved successful in helping to restabilize Iraq, the withdrawal of American forces allowed the so-called Islamic State to strengthen and for Iraq to descend back into serious instability. The Sunni Islamic State first appeared around 2003 in response to the U.S. invasion of Iraq. Its goal was to check Shiite government domination in Iraq; reestablish Sunni power, which declined with the fall of Saddam Hussein; and establish its version of an Islamic caliphate. It later split from al-Qaeda and rivaled it for jihadist supremacy in the Muslim world, in part by enriching itself through stealing weaponry, drawing monies from oil-rich donors,[53] smuggling, seizing oil facilities, extortion and taxes, and other crimes such as bank robberies and counterfeiting. To be sure, the Islamic State is quite different from al-Qaeda in its etiology. However, as a former deputy CIA director put it, the Islamic State shares al-Qaeda's goals but does not want to follow the guidance of Ayman al-Zawahiri, who took over the reins of al-Qaeda after bin Laden died, or bin Laden before him,[54] and it is more prone to beheadings than is al-Qaeda. They certainly share a similar view of an imperial, oil-stealing United States that seeks to undermine Muslims. This is ironic because the Islamic State has stolen oil in the region in order to fund its enterprise and reward its fighters. It has seized refineries and other oil facilities and sold stolen oil, among other things.[55] So far, the Islamic State has either not seriously targeted or failed to target the American homeland, though it has inspired or even planned much smaller attacks; that could change over time, especially if the United States attacks ISIS more strongly on the ground. In such a case, ISIS may decide to retaliate with a larger terrorist attack in the United States if it has the capability to do so.

To be sure, it would have been hard to predict the rise of such a barbaric organization. However, in general, the George W. Bush administration mis-estimated the challenges of rebuilding an entire nation in the heart of the Arab world where the United States was not well liked and where it would not get much support even from its regional allies, who saw the democratization drive as a threat to their own autocratic regimes. This should not have come as a great surprise. History is littered with outsiders coming to the Middle East only to be attacked and driven out. The British had suffered that fate in Iraq earlier in the twentieth century.

Serious plans for withdrawing American forces were unveiled by June 2006. They were premised on the notion that Iraqi security forces would be prepared to keep the order in Iraq, but they clearly signaled American intent to with-draw its forces from Iraq at some time. In any case, American policy would be determined chiefly by the question of whether Iraq could maintain domestic stability if American forces withdrew rather than by a calculation of how the United States could dominate Iraq for the long run. In fact, President Obama campaigned for the presidency on getting U.S. forces out of Iraq based on a lesser benchmark than domestic stability. He wanted to scale down the American commitment under almost any circumstance, and, like at least half the country and decision makers, he thought that invading Iraq in the first place was a large error. His reelection was based in part on a promise to withdraw the United States from Iraq and Afghanistan, and he fulfilled that pledge.

The shock of the Iraq misadventure did not fundamentally alter America's goals in the region, though it did alter its tactics, making it largely more reluc-tant to commit heavy ground forces against the Islamic State or to bomb Iran's nuclear facilities. In September 2013, President Obama underscored the con-tinuity of America's interests in the Persian Gulf. He stated before the United Nations that Washington aimed to secure "the free flow of resources through key shipping lanes; the defense of our homeland against the pervasive and persistent threat of terrorism and extremism; and the prevention of the proliferation of weapons of mass destruction."[56] American presidents largely agree on the importance of those goals.

The United States and Iran

The American-led invasion of Iraq and subsequent problems in stabilizing Iraq have left Iran a more influential power in the region, but while this outcome has emboldened Iran's foreign policy in the Middle East, it did not prevent Iran from negotiating on its nuclear program. Iran and the P5 +1 nations (the five permanent members of the United Nations Security Council, including the United States, plus Germany) signed an accord on Iran's nuclear program in July 2015. For some time, it even appeared as if the U.S. Congress would reject it and mount a potential campaign to overturn a promised veto by President Obama, but that failed.

However, the effect of the accord will remain an open question for some time—and quite likely for many years. Will Iran abide by the agreement? Will a new American administration overturn or amend it? How will the Arab Gulf states react to an agreement? If the agreement sticks, can Iran be stopped from developing nuclear weapons after provisions of the agreement expire in ten to fifteen years? And will Iran's foreign policy change?

It is far too early to offer any developed assessments or predictions, but a few comments are worth making to frame the issue. In some respects, we are likely to see continuity amid uncertainty in the foreseeable future.

First, the agreement with Iran focuses on the nuclear dimension but not on the other facets of Iran's foreign policy. Iran has viewed the Persian Gulf as its backyard for at least decades, and that is unlikely to change any time soon. Tehran will continue to exert its influence in the region and will not likely decrease its support for Shiite movements from Iraq to Lebanon. Indeed, in summer 2015, the U.S. State Department, which is not known for being biased against Muslim countries, found that Iran remains a large threat that must be understood.[57]

Second, in terms of relations with America, the agreement may improve U.S.-Iranian relations. However, that will require that Iran not push its regional agenda too strongly and that Washington continue to try to bridge relations with Iran, as unpopular as that would be at home and in the region. Neither outcome is likely in the absence of regime change in Iran, but stranger things have happened. Even if a rapprochement can be launched in the next decade, the national interests of the two countries will continue to collide on important issues, as has been the case in U.S.-Russian and Sino-American relations.

Third, the agreement will boost Iran's economy through greater trade and by allowing it to sell more oil and attract various forms of foreign investment. However, it's unwise to exaggerate Iran's potential economic gains. Iran's archaic regulatory system, dubious legal system, and dilapidated infrastructure, not to mention questions about whether the nuclear deal can stick over time, will pose challenges for Iran and outside investors at least in the shorter run.

Fourth, China and Russia will benefit the most, but it will take years to figure out just how much they will gain compared to other countries. America will likely remain hamstrung by its own prohibitions on trade with Tehran, but those may be lifted in the longer run. In that time, Iran may also prove itself more interested in American and Western energy interaction, partly because of American technologies, than in that of China and Russia.

Fifth, the stronger Iran gets, the more likely other nations will try to balance and check it. The potential for it to cheat on the accord will not eliminate fears of its potential nuclear prowess, even if it lowers them. America will have to cooperate even more with Sunni Arab countries and Israel to offset the agreement with Iran. What this means is that while Iran will grow stronger, it will also face more pressures from others, which checks its power.

All in all, the nuclear accord with Iran is a major development, but it is not likely to become a tectonic shift in the region unless Iran actually does develop nuclear weapons down the road.

The Future of Oil

All of these costly wars and conflicts in the region, plus the rise of the American oil boom, have led many to argue that Washington should diminish its role in the Persian Gulf. That's an enticing idea, but for several reasons, it will not be easy to escape the importance of the Persian Gulf in the future.

First, global oil demand is rising. The International Energy Agency (IEA), the global watchdog for energy-consuming states, expects global oil demand to reach 96.7 mbd by 2020 or up by around 7 mbd at present.[58] It has also projected that nearly 80 percent of the increase in global oil and gas output through 2030 will come from national oil companies in the Persian Gulf[59] and conventional oil fields,[60] not from unconventional shale oil, which has been at the center of the American oil boom.

Second, the Persian Gulf, far more than any other region, will serve as the principal source of supply to meet rising demand over the next two decades. This is because it holds the greatest proven reserves of oil, which will last around seventy-five years at current rates of production. That is especially true for China, which will not be able to meet its growth targets and perhaps maintain domestic stability without cheap sources of energy. But it is also true, if somewhat less so, of other countries, including the United States.

The third reason has to do with the American energy surge. Both the American oil and natural gas booms have been achieved largely due to new discoveries of "tight oil" and natural gas using hydraulic fracturing and horizontal drilling. "Tight oil" refers to oil found within reservoirs with very low permeability, including shale. Permeability is the ability for fluid, such as oil and gas, to move through a rock formation.

American oil production rose sharply from 5 mbd in 2008 to over 7.45 mbd in 2014,[61] up to over 9 mbd in 2015. The boom is so major that American oil output may exceed that of the biggest oil producers, Saudi Arabia and Russia,[62] and the increase alone is far higher than what Iran exported to the rest of the world before it faced American-led sanctions over its nuclear aspirations.

In our view, however, the boom's likely benefits for American and global oil security are exaggerated.[63] Many observers, for instance, don't fully appreciate that the boom will peak sooner than they expect. It will be a giant force in the oil patch until its postpeak period. Estimates vary about when the boom will peak, and that will depend on many factors, but the Energy Information Administration (EIA) has the peak in one scenario at around 2020.[64] In that scenario, it will produce only 1.1 million barrels more than was being produced in America in 2007. Even if technological breakthroughs allow for greater oil exploration and the OPEC states cannot continue to tolerate lower oil prices and are forced to cut their production, thus giving the American boom ballast, the boom's peak and postpeak period will be quite different in impact from its current prepeak.

Fourth, America's oil boom is a massive development in global energy, but no matter how much additional oil the United States is able to pump in the years to come, the global oil market is just that: global. The price of oil is set on global markets. Even if the United States received no oil from the Persian Gulf, any serious disruptions of oil from that region would raise the price of oil (and derivatives like gasoline) for all Americans. An American withdrawal would make it harder to prevent or contain such disruptions, because Washington has played the role of regional gendarme since the British relinquished that role in 1971. While being less dependent on Middle East oil and less oil dependent overall is positive, the oil boom is not likely to allow Washington to diminish its regional commitment any time soon. If it's a misconception that America gets most of its oil from the Persian Gulf, it's also questionable to think that the region will be much less important to the United States if it gets little or even no oil from there.

Fifth, China is a key driver of global growth on which all of the major economies depend, and it needs Persian Gulf oil. The United States is less dependent on Gulf oil than are many other industrialized states, such as China.[65] America is dependent on oil to run its giant economy, but increasingly less so on oil imports. China is heading in the opposite direction. It is becoming much more oil dependent, importing about 5.3 mbd out of total demand of 9.9 million and rising, as millions more join the middle class and become consumers of vehicles and other goods.

In particular, as Figure 2.1 shows, U.S. dependence on Persian Gulf oil imports has stayed fairly steady, contrary to rising perceptions that imports have decreased substantially, though they started to head downward after 2013. Meanwhile, Beijing's Middle East imports have increased to over 50 percent. Unlike the United States, which gets most of its oil from Latin America, China gets little from there. Saudi Arabia is becoming much more vital to China, and

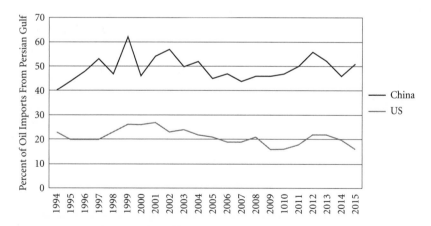

FIGURE 2.1. Persian Gulf Oil Imports, United States versus China, 1994–2015.
SOURCE: U.S. data from Petroleum & Other Liquids database, U.S. Energy Information Administration. China data from *Chinese Statistical Yearbook* (Beijing: Customs General Administration of the People's Republic of China, various years).

were it not for economic sanctions against Iran, Iran would have played a larger role, as may now be the case given the Iran nuclear deal of July 2015.

The upshot is that the Persian Gulf will remain crucial to China's growth and that of other global economies. And since America is dependent on their growth, the stability of the Gulf will be central to America's global economic health, regardless of how much oil it obtains from the region.

All that, however, does not mean that America and its allies should not pursue a more rigorous strategy to decrease consumption of fossil fuels. However, until that happens and even after it is initiated, the Persian Gulf will remain vital to the global economy.

Conclusion

The rise of the oil era set the stage for what would become an increasingly more involved American role and position in the Persian Gulf. However, this escalation of involvement was slow and gained traction only in the 1970s when Washington assumed responsibility for Persian Gulf security from Britain. In particular, the 1979 Iranian Revolution undermined the U.S. regional position and, when combined with the perceived Soviet threat in Afghanistan, forced the United States to strengthen its capabilities in the region.

This chapter has provided a broad sketch of the American narrative in the region, embedded in the fascinating dynamics of the global oil era, that is necessary for understanding more specific features of America's evolution in the region. In this respect, we move on to providing insight into how U.S. diplomatic and security relations and interactions with key regional states have changed over time. The following chapters turn to that feature of the American experience.

3   A New Security Framework

THE EVOLUTION of the standing of any country in any region or issue area is a highly complex phenomenon to assess. We seek to offer panoramic sketches that are appropriate to meeting the goals of this book and are anchored in data analysis. On that score, the United States has expanded, in some cases dramatically, its diplomatic, military, and economic capabilities in the region and ties to regional states in the post–Cold War period. America's diplomatic position has undergone extraordinary change, and although it faced some serious problems, it became stronger from 1991 to 2015, though it fluctuated in that time period. The U.S. ability to project forces to the region and sustain them while in the region increased significantly from the 1980s, as did its defense cooperation with the states of the Gulf Cooperation Council (GCC), and with Iraq in the post-2003 invasion period, even amid rising domestic instability that threatened to tear Iraq asunder.

The Political Aspect of America's Role

We begin by exploring U.S. diplomatic relations with Saudi Arabia, Iran, and Iraq from the 1970s, but especially between 1991 and 2015. Of course, volumes could be written on these subjects and have been.[1] But the goal here is not to provide a historical account. Rather, it is to provide a sense of the trajectory of U.S. relations and to inform the analysis of oil security that follows, especially in chapter 10.

In brief, America's diplomatic position has changed dramatically, but on the whole, it has become stronger, not weaker, over time. U.S.-Saudi relations have weakened since September 11, but relations with Iraq have evolved from hostility and war under Saddam Hussein to a more cooperative, though still dysfunctional, level since then. In contrast to China and Russia, U.S.-Iranian relations have remained largely torturous since the 1979 Iranian Revolution, albeit the nuclear accord of 2015 between the U.N. Security Council and Iran may possibly change that trajectory.

Beyond diplomatic relations, U.S.-Saudi interaction in the security field has strengthened in a major way in the post–Cold War period, despite recurring political differences and what appearances might suggest. U.S.-Iraqi security relations have also improved in the post-Saddam period, even as Iraq struggles with massive instability, the rise of the Islamic State, sectarian strife, and increased Iranian influence.

U.S.-Saudi Diplomatic Relations

Since World War II, both the United States and Saudi Arabia have sought to protect the free flow of oil to the world market.[2] During the Cold War, this goal was threatened by the Iranian Revolution, the Soviet invasion of Afghanistan, and the Iraq-Iran war. Those events cemented relations despite various differences in culture, religion, world outlook, and regional issues such as the Arab-Israeli conflict.

U.S.-Saudi relations were roughly cooperative throughout the early and mid-1970s, but they were aggravated seriously in 1978–1979 by a number of events. Saudi leaders lost confidence in Washington after the Soviets scored gains in Angola, Ethiopia, and South Yemen and after America's perceived failure to save the shah of Iran. In some American quarters, doubts arose about Saudi stability after Islamic zealots seized the Grand Mosque at Mecca and serious Shiite demonstrations erupted in the oil-rich Eastern Province. The December 1979 Soviet intervention in Afghanistan, however, made Riyadh more important to Washington, and the Iran-Iraq War (1980–1988) made Washington more important to Saudi Arabia, despite Riyadh's desire to keep America at arm's length. These developing common interests benefited U.S.-Saudi relations throughout the 1980s and prepared them for Iraq's invasion of Kuwait in August 1990.

America had grown stronger not only in the Gulf but also globally, which influenced its relations in the Gulf as well. The demise of the Soviet Union led some actors, including Saddam Hussein in his famous speech of February 24,

1990, which contributed to his rise as a key leader in the Arab world, to refer to the United States as a regional hegemon.[3]

The United States launched Operation Desert Shield in early August 1990, which was aimed at protecting Saudi Arabia from Kuwait, and then Operation Desert Storm on January 16, 1991, which evicted Iraq from Kuwait. The Gulf crisis strengthened U.S.-Saudi cooperation. The House of Saud agreed to host over a half-million U.S.-led forces and shouldered more than 50 percent of the war costs,[4] and Washington demonstrated its commitment to Saudi security.[5] Riyadh was initially nervous about requesting American support after Iraq's invasion, partly because it questioned American staying power and did not want to offend its own domestic constituents by allowing non-Muslims into the holy land of Mecca and Medina. However, the crisis gave both states invaluable political and military experience, and made the Saudis more likely to stand firm with the United States against aggressors.[6]

Following the 1991 war, the Clinton administration pursued its dual-containment policy of both Iraq and Iran. That made Saudi Arabia more important to Washington,[7] even if Riyadh was reluctant to support overt U.S. military operations against Iraq that could provoke domestic Saudi opposition. In the mid-1990s, Washington continued to try to assure the GCC states of what Secretary of State Warren Christopher referred to as an enduring American "ironclad commitment" to their defense.[8] At the same time, by the spring 1995, Washington stepped up its push for better pre-positioning capabilities in Saudi Arabia. The dual political and military approaches enhanced interstate reciprocity and further strengthened relations. While divisive issues remained, both sides recognized their common interests in checking a revisionist Iraq and a potentially ascendant Iran. Riyadh became more confident in U.S. initiatives, partly because Washington's power at the global level was increasing, and Washington became better able to depend on Saudi Arabia, partly because of its more assertive regional position and role. Moreover, as U.S.-Saudi relations improved, it became more difficult for the Soviets, Iraqis, and Iranians to disrupt improvements in U.S.-Saudi relations or to wean, to the extent possible, the Saudis out of the American orbit.[9]

This set of mutual interests and cooperation would be severely tested in the wake of the September 11 terrorist attacks, which caused the greatest crisis in U.S.-Saudi relations since the 1973–1974 oil embargo. In the words of the Saudi ambassador to the United States, Adel al-Jubeir, the revelation that fifteen 9/11 hijackers were Saudis was "a disaster," which turned Saudi Arabia into an "enemy in the minds of many Americans."[10] To repair relations, Crown Prince Abdullah, the de facto regent of Saudi Arabia until he actually become king in 2005, met with President Bush in April 2002,[11] promising to cooperate on terrorist financing issues in what was reportedly a tense meeting.[12]

Saudi support for the U.S.-led campaign against Iraq in 2003 signaled elements of ongoing cooperation after 9/11. Riyadh granted America use of Saudi bases near the Iraqi border and the command and control center at Prince Sultan Air Base, despite Abdullah's assertion that the invasion "would not serve America's interests or the interests of the world."[13]

The ongoing effects of 9/11 and the 2003 Iraq War also pushed the two countries to downplay visible military cooperation. In part, this was due to the unpopularity of the war in Saudi Arabia and the broader Muslim world. The Iraq War worsened distrust of the United States and anti-Americanism in the broader Arab world, especially in Iraq, where 90 percent polled said they distrusted the U.S.-led coalition.[14] Another poll conducted by political scientist Shibley Telhami found that in 2000, more than 60 percent of Saudi citizens expressed confidence in the United States, whereas by 2004, less than 4 percent had favorable views.[15]

In April 2003, the United States announced the withdrawal of all its combat forces from Saudi Arabia, ending more than a decade of military presence. Explaining its action, Washington argued that the region was now safer with a new regime in Iraq,[16] an idea echoed by the Saudis publicly.[17] But while the House of Saud felt that domestic criticism of the American presence would decrease, they remained concerned that the withdrawal might hurt U.S.-Saudi relations,[18] even as the two states continued their understanding that Washington's forces could reenter Saudi Arabia and use its facilities built over the past several decades should the need arise.

Relations were helped by the perhaps too optimistic conclusions of the 9/11 Commission report, released in July 2004. It concluded that Saudi Arabia had been "a problematic ally in combating Islamic extremism," but the commission found "no evidence" that the Saudi government or senior Saudi officials individually funded al-Qaeda.[19] In April 2005, Bush and Abdullah reconvened at Bush's Crawford, Texas, ranch,[20] and, wary of the ongoing negative effects of 9/11, underscored a shared interest in regional security.[21] Later that year, the two governments inaugurated a cabinet-level strategic dialogue to expand cooperation in six areas of mutual interest: counterterrorism, military affairs, energy, economic and financial affairs, education exchange and human development, and consular affairs.[22]

In May 2008, Bush visited Saudi Arabia to commemorate the seventy-fifth anniversary of U.S.-Saudi relations and signed the memorandum of understanding on civil nuclear energy cooperation, pledging that America would assist Saudi Arabia in developing civilian nuclear energy for use in medicine, industry, and power generation.[23] Riyadh joined two key Bush administration initiatives: the Global Initiative to Combat Nuclear Terrorism and the Proliferation Security Initiative. However, despite these initiatives, the post-9/11 fallout remained an ongoing problem, partly due to highly negative public perceptions in both countries. James Smith, U.S. ambassador to Saudi Arabia, summed up the ongoing dynamic when he called for the necessity of "taking down walls" erected after 9/11.[24]

To add to tensions, the Saudis increasingly worried that Iran was gaining influence with the U.S.-backed government of Nouri al-Maliki in Iraq. Maliki had been a prominent Shiite leader in the anti-Saddam guerrilla movement aided by Iran and Syria. He took office on May 20, 2006, succeeding the Iraqi transitional government that had ruled as a caretaker, pending formation of a new government. From 2006 until his tenure ended as prime minister in 2014, he developed close relations with Iran, with some believing that Iran called the shots in Baghdad. Voicing perhaps exaggerated Saudi frustration with U.S. policy, Prince Saud, the minister of foreign affairs, stated in September 2005, "We fought a war together [with the United States] to keep Iran from occupying Iraq after Iraq was driven out of Kuwait. Now we are handing the whole country over to Iran without reason."[25]

Beyond Iraq, Saudi fear of Iran's ambitions was reflected in a leaked cable in April 2008 in which Abdullah urged the Bush administration to "cut off the head of the snake" by militarily destroying Iran's nuclear program—something that was not in the cards in Washington, which preferred the flawed negotiated outcome that was achieved in 2015 over another possible war in the region. Further emphasizing a key strain of Saudi thought, Abdullah complained that "some say the U.S. invasion handed Iraq to Iran on a silver platter; this after we fought Saddam Hussein," noting that he had "no confidence whatsoever in [Iraqi Prime Minister] Maliki" and adding, "I don't trust this man. . . . He is an Iranian agent."[26]

The election of Barack Obama initially improved bilateral relations. Abdullah thanked "God for bringing Obama to the presidency," which he said created "great hope" in the Muslim world.[27] White House counterterrorism adviser John Brennan met Abdullah in March 2009. In a leaked embassy cable regarding the meeting, Abdullah said that it was "critically important to restore America's credibility" in the world and that the differences between the two states did not "cut to the bone," and Brennan stressed that intelligence-sharing cooperation between the two sides had never been better.[28] Obama's first visit to Saudi Arabia in 2009 and Secretary of State Hillary Rodham Clinton's meeting with Saudi foreign minister Prince Saud al-Faisal later that year sought to shore up ties further.[29] Clinton affirmed shared interests on Iran and terrorism, stating that the "U.S. commitment to Saudi Arabia's security was unwavering," while the Saudis underscored common interests and goals.[30] In June 2010, Abdullah visited America and reaffirmed the depth of mutual relations amid continuing strife over competing views.[31]

The Arab Spring came as a shocking sea change in the politics of the Middle East, straining relations. Obama's eventual support for the overthrow of President Hosni Mubarak of Egypt, a longtime U.S. ally, raised questions in Riyadh about America's reliability and its commitment to Saudi security. According to one thinker, the Saudis saw it as "a betrayal of a key ally."[32] In January 2011, Abdullah urged Obama not to humiliate Mubarak and warned that he would step in to provide funds to Egypt if America withdrew its aid to Egypt, which totaled $1.5 billion annually.[33]

Relations deteriorated even more over the U.S. handling of Syria's civil war and Iran's nuclear program. Riyadh urged the United States to overthrow Syria's President Bashar al-Assad, who was aligned with its rival, Iran. Nor did the kingdom appreciate a preliminary agreement that America and members of the UN Security Council concluded with Iran. They believed that Iran was untrustworthy and that trying to destroy its nuclear capability was preferable to a nuclear agreement that Iran could evade secretly. In October 2013, Saudi Arabia rejected a seat on the Security Council, a reaction that many interpreted as underscoring "the depth of Saudi anger" over a weak and conciliatory" Western stance on Syria and Iran.[34] Al-Faisal tried to play down the imbroglio: "It's only natural that our policies and views might see agreement in some areas and disagreement in others. That's perfectly normal in any serious relationship that spans a wide range of issues."[35] During Secretary of State John Kerry's visit in November 2013, the Saudis suggested that U.S.-Saudi discord was less over objectives than tactics, and Kerry agreed,[36] but this was partly for show. For his part, Kerry described the U.S.-Saudi relationship as encompassing a wide range of bilateral and regional issues and "shared security" concerns.[37] While there was truth to that notion, it was also apparent that relations remained beset by the lagged effects of 9/11 and, much more important, a slate of issues related to the broader Arab Spring, Syria, and Iran.

The disagreement over the U.S. stance on Iran continued to strain the bilateral relations through 2015. In May 2015, Saudi King Salman refused President Obama's invitation to a GCC summit and pulled out of a GCC summit hosted at Camp David aimed at building Arab support for a nuclear deal with Iran.[38] However, in an effort to improve bilateral relations, King Salman met with President Obama in September 2015 in what was the first visit by a Saudi head of state to the United States since King Abdullah's visit in September 2010. During the visit, King Salman expressed his support for the Joint Comprehensive Plan of Action between Iran and the U.N. Security Council plus Germany signed in July 2015.[39] In the joint statement, the two leaders stressed "the importance of continuing to bolster their strategic relationship" and affirmed the need "to continue the effort to maintain security, prosperity and stability in the region and in particular to counter Iran's destabilizing activities."[40] Prior to the visit, U.S. officials announced that they were finalizing a $1 billion arms agreement with Saudi Arabia to reassure the kingdom about the Iran nuclear deal and U.S. commitment to the kingdom.[41] Following the visit, Adel al-Jubeir, the Saudi foreign minister, stated that King Salman "is satisfied with [President Obama's] assurances"[42] regarding the Iran deal, adding that the kingdom believed "this agreement will contribute to security and stability in the region by preventing Iran from acquiring a nuclear capability." In private, the Saudis could not have been happy about this deal, but they probably realized that it would not be blocked, making diplomatic niceties the order of the day.

U.S.-Iran Diplomatic Relations

In contrast to China and Russia, which expanded their diplomatic ties to Iran in the post–Cold War period, U.S.-Iranian relations have alternated between tense and openly hostile since the revolution. That may change if the nuclear deal with Iran in 2015 endures and helps to moderate Iran's view of the United States and vice versa, but that is certainly in question.

In 1984, the Reagan administration designated Iran a sponsor of international terrorism, and subsequent presidents held to that line. In 1995, as part of its policy of dual containment, the Clinton administration increased pressure on Iran by imposing sanctions that banned U.S. trade and investment with it. In 1996, Congress enacted the Iran and Libya Sanctions Act, which broadened the sanctions to include penalties on foreign companies' investment in Iran's

energy sector to reduce Iran's income and impede its ability to sponsor terrorism and acquire weapons of mass destruction (WMD). Relations improved
after the election of relatively moderate President Mohammad Khatami in
1997. Reciprocating Khatami's outreach, Secretary of State Madeleine Albright
stated in June 1998 that the United State "can develop with Iran, when it is
ready, a road map leading to normal relations," and in 2000, she announced
modest easing of certain economic sanctions on Iran.[43] Despite these overtures,
Ali Khamenei, Iran's Supreme Leader, did not share Khatami's sentiment. After
a brief thaw, relations reached a new low when President George W. Bush defined Iran, Iraq, and North Korea as part of an "axis of evil" in his January 2002
State of the Union speech.[44] Iran's clandestine nuclear program, revealed later
that year, reinforced suspicions that Iran sought nuclear weapons and could
not be trusted.

The two countries did discuss Iraq- and Afghanistan-related issues from
late 2001 until May 2003 in Geneva in what constituted "the first confirmed direct dialogue between the countries since the 1979 revolution."[45] But relations
were further hurt by the election of Mahmoud Ahmadinejad in June 2005, a
Holocaust denier who called for Israel's destruction and failed to cooperate
with the International Atomic Energy Agency (IAEA) on Iran's nuclear program. In response to Iran's defiance of various Security Council resolutions
urging it to suspend its uranium enrichment, Washington escalated calls for
international sanctions, and Bush warned about a possible world war if Iran
developed nuclear weapons.[46]

Sanctions pressure on Iran dramatically increased following President
Obama's election in 2009, although Obama also promoted far more engagement than had Bush. For example, at his speech in Cairo in 2009, Obama
reached out to Iran by conceding that during the Cold War, the United States
"played a role in the overthrow of a democratically-elected Iranian government," further stating that "any nation—including Iran—should have the right
to access peaceful nuclear power" if it adheres to requirements of the 1970
Treaty on the Non-Proliferation of Nuclear Weapons (NPT).[47] However, bilateral tensions escalated when Iran cracked down on protesters who were re-
belling over Iran's presidential elections in 2009, which were widely viewed as
rigged, and when Tehran continued to stonewall on its nuclear program. In response, the Obama administration orchestrated and gradually escalated broad
international economic pressure on Iran while keeping an offer of sanctions
relief in exchange for a negotiated deal.

Iran elected the relatively moderate Hassan Rouhani to the presidency in June 2013. Pressed by a rapidly deteriorating economy, Iran sought new negotiations. In September 2013, Obama and Rouhani had the first direct conversation between the presidents of the two countries since 1979. The phone call was followed by an interim nuclear agreement between America and its allies and Iran reached on November 2013, culminating in the historic deal of July 2015 to limit Iran's nuclear ability in return for lifting international sanctions.[48] Nonetheless, relations remained bedeviled due to Iran's development of ballistic missiles, rising power in the post-Saddam Gulf, influence in Iraq, support for the Syrian regime, and ties to Hezbollah and Hamas.

Illustratively, despite the nuclear deal, Khamenei described any potential U.S. expectations of Iran curbing its missile development as "stupid and idiotic."[49] This was underscored in August 2015 when Iran's defense minister, Hossein Dehghan, stated that Iran "will design and produce any missiles that we want proportionate to threats,"[50] and with subsequent missile tests. Khamenei repeatedly appeared to be highly skeptical of the nuclear agreement and U.S. intentions, while at the same time not trying to undermine relations too much.

U.S.-Iraqi Diplomatic Relations
America's relationship with Iraq after 2003 has been far better than its relationship with Iraq under Saddam Hussein, despite enormous strains. It is worthwhile offering a brief sketch of key points in the evolution of U.S.-Iraqi relations.

During the Cold War, Iraq had been Moscow's main ally in the region, but the United States indirectly supported Baghdad during the Iran-Iraq War to counter the Iranian threat. Iraq's invasion of Kuwait in 1990 was a watershed event. The U.S.-led coalition expelled Iraq from Kuwait in 1991, and America and its allies, chiefly Britain and France, kept Iraq politically, economically, and militarily contained until the U.S.-led invasion of Iraq in 2003.

Containment initiated after the 1991 Gulf War escalated under Clinton's policy of dual containment in the 1990s. In addition to sanctions and enforcement of no-fly zones, it included efforts to overthrow Saddam. Martin Indyk, special assistant to the president for Near East and South Asian Affairs and the architect of dual containment, described Iraq in 1993 "as a criminal regime, beyond the pale of international society and, in our judgment, irredeemable."[51] CIA efforts to undermine Saddam expanded in 1996 and then escalated in October 1998 after Iraq stopped cooperating with international inspectors. In response to this noncooperation, the Clinton administration expanded containment by signing the Iraq Liberation Act, which explicitly called for regime change, tightened the no-fly zone, and even bombed Iraq in December 1998 in Operation Desert Fox. In February 1998, President Clinton had voiced his frustration with Iraq's defiance of UN inspectors, asserting that "Iraq admitted, among other things, an offensive biological warfare capability, notably, 5,000 gallons of botulinum, which causes botulism; 2,000 gallons of anthrax; 25 biological-filled Scud warheads; and 157 aerial bombs. It is obvious that there is an attempt here, based on the whole history of this operation since 1991, to protect whatever remains of his capacity to produce weapons of mass destruction, the missiles to deliver them, and the feed stocks necessary to produce them."[52]

Against this general backdrop of tension and suspicion, the events of September 11, 2001, contributed to the American decision to invade Iraq. In his speech to the United Nations on September 12, 2002, President Bush urged Saddam Hussein to comply with sixteen U.N. resolutions passed between 1991 and 2002, all of which Iraq had defied.[53] In his January 2003 State of the Union speech, two months before the invasion of Iraq, Bush asserted that a "brutal dictator, with a history of reckless aggression, with ties to terrorism, with great potential wealth, will not be permitted to dominate a vital region and threaten the United States."[54]

History has shown that Iraq lacked WMD and ties to terrorism; nevertheless, such misconceptions drove American-led action. On March 20, 2003, the U.S.-led 125,000-strong force invaded Iraq and removed Hussein from power. The force increased in size to an additional 30,000 U.S. forces into Iraq in 2007, aimed at U.S-led nation-building involvement that lasted until December 2011. In accordance with the November 2008 security agreement, the official conclusion of the U.S. combat mission in August 2010 and Iraq's decision in October 2011 not to extend legal protection to U.S. troops despite the U.S. appeal,[55] America decreased its force presence to 47,000 in 2010 and withdrew the last troop contingent in December 2011.

The Strategic Framework Agreement signed in December 2008 was designed to normalize and buttress the U.S.-Iraqi relationship. The United States cooperated with Iraq on a number of political issues. It worked with Maliki and his Sunni and Kurdish opponents "to narrow areas of disagreement" and "facilitate serious discussions on revenue sharing" between the Iraqi Kurdistan region and central government.[56] Washington also worked to promote Iraq's regional integration and strategic independence under both Maliki and his successor, Haider al-Abadi, who tried much harder than Maliki to integrate Sunnis into the Iraqi government.

In mid-2014, the U.S. deployed 3,100 military personnel to advise and train the Iraqi Security Forces and began conducting airstrikes to help the Iraqi government defeat the Islamic State.[57] Termed Operation Inherent Resolve, the effort to defeat the Islamic State escalated in June 2015, with the United States announcing the deployment of an additional 450 military trainers and advisors to Iraq.

While America's relationship with Iraq has improved from past decades, it could easily transform into an adversarial one depending on the course of Iraq's domestic politics and U.S.-Iranian relations. Even so, it could not be much worse than U.S. relations with Saddam Hussein. In fact, Iraq would still be less threatening absent Saddam's great military capability and reckless foreign policy behavior. Iraq could also break down as a country into its three historical parts: Mosul in the North, Baghdad in the center of Iraq, and Basra in the South. Iraq's sovereignty is in serious question. Indeed, the Kurds in the North have a high level of autonomy, which almost creates a state within a state. It will take better leadership in Baghdad, more effective interaction between Baghdad and the Kurds, and a good plan of coordination to help keep Iraq functioning as one sovereign state, even if it retains that titular role.

U.S. Military Capabilities and the Persian Gulf

While America's diplomatic relations underwent enormous change, so did its overall security position. From 1980, its military capabilities in the region, force projection, and security cooperation with regional states strengthened substantially, though with notable fluctuations. This represents one of the most significant changes in the region.

The United States began to expand its navy at least as early as the presidency of Theodore Roosevelt, who understood that expansion required major sea power. But it would take the United States many more decades to develop sea-power reach into the Persian Gulf, not to mention other facets of its forward military position.

Washington maintained modest capabilities in and around the region after World War II, but that changed with the 1979 Iranian Revolution, Soviet invasion of Afghanistan, and the Iraq-Iran War. Washington accelerated development of the rapid deployment force (RDF), secured access to military facilities in the Middle East, upgraded the U.S.-operated military base at Diego Garcia in the Indian Ocean, and urged efforts to develop the Saudi military infrastructure for the entry of U.S. forces. These actions helped the United States in its rivalry with Moscow in the Persian Gulf and would later play a critical role in reversing Iraq's invasion of Kuwait in August 1990. As Secretary of Defense Harold Brown stressed, the RDF was not a response to internal matters in the Gulf but was intended "to offset Soviet forces."[58] The largest comparative increase in the fiscal year 1981 budget was in airlift and sealift, which reflected the commitment to the RDF.[59] Beyond playing a role in its funding, the Afghanistan invasion motivated the growth in the RDF's size and configuration and gave it an anti-Soviet role, particularly with respect to Gulf defense.[60] The size and planning of the RDF was based on an actual, albeit unlikely, Soviet invasion of the Gulf.

In 1981, in a crucial and signal development, the United States agreed to sell the Saudis airborne warning and control systems aircraft and high-performance fighter jets, and Riyadh consented to building a nearly $200 billion extensive defense infrastructure able to accommodate a rapid and massive deployment of U.S. forces.[61] This unprecedented agreement was motivated mainly by the Iranian threat in the region and by Moscow's perceived threat at the global level. The agreement established the bedrock of U.S.-Saudi strategic cooperation. When Iraq invaded Kuwait, these facilities served in Operations Desert Shield and Desert Storm. Without them, such operations would not have been possible.

By the late 1980s, all of the GCC states provided assistance to the United States in the region and jointly participated in military exercises with the United States. This security cooperation, along with a developed military infrastructure in Saudi Arabia, proved critical in the 1990–1991 Gulf War by enabling a massive and rapid deployment of U.S.-led forces.

In the post–Cold War era, Washington expanded its military presence and security cooperation with the Arab states. Before the 1991 war, the GCC states insisted on keeping U.S. forces "over the horizon"; after the war, their willingness to grant the United States access to their military facilities considerably increased. America concluded defense agreements with Oman in 1991, Bahrain and Kuwait in 1991, Qatar in 1992, and the United Arab Emirates (UAE) in 1994. Although Saudi Arabia preferred not to advertise its security relationship with America to minimize domestic criticism, it allowed the U.S. Air Force access to its air bases, while Kuwait granted access to numerous facilities, including Ali Al Salem Air Base, and agreed to house U.S. RDFs.[62] Bahrain provided access to military facilities and expanded joint military training and exercises. By 1995, the U.S. Fifth Fleet had established a permanent headquarters, and the country became home to U.S. Marine Forces Central Command, Destroyer Squadron Fifty, and three combined maritime forces.

After the liberation of Kuwait, the United States reduced its military presence in Saudi Arabia to fewer than a thousand military personnel stationed in 1993. Following the removal of Saddam Hussein's regime in 2003, it relocated almost all of the 5,000 troops deployed in the kingdom along with its Combat Air Operations Center to neighboring Qatar, leaving 200 to 300 U.S. military personnel and a contingent of contractors in Saudi Arabia in support of long-standing U.S. training programs. During the 1990s, Qatar had invested over $1 billion to construct the massive Al Udeid Air Base for U.S. use, and in 2002, that came in handy to serve as CENTCOM forward headquarters.

The cutting-edge Combat Air Operations Center serves as a regional hub for the command and control of airpower throughout twenty regional countries, hosting U.S. Air Force, Army, Navy, Marine Corps, and coalition partners. Although Qatar subsidizes much of the U.S. presence, the United States invested over $457 million for its military infrastructure in Qatar between 2003 and 2011, including construction of a new air force and special operations facilities.[63]

The move to Qatar was crucial, and the two countries expanded other types of cooperation as well. The UAE allowed use of ports, pre-positioning of an armored brigade, and aerial refueling, while Oman granted the United States access to air bases at Masirah, Seeb, and Thumrait for its air force strategic bombers.

The following sections of this chapter sketch the evolution of U.S. military capabilities in terms of key bilateral relations. This further underscores the rise of such capabilities over time, even amid serious political differences with regional countries.

U.S.-Saudi Security Relations

Washington significantly expanded security cooperation with Saudi Arabia in the 1980s, as we have suggested, and in the post–Cold War period. Although the two countries did not conclude the formal Defense Cooperation Agreement (DCA) after the 1991 war, Saudi Arabia allowed the United States to increase its access to air and seaports and establish the state-of-the-art Combined Air Operation Center at Prince Sultan Air Base.[64] Reluctantly, Saudi Arabia also allowed America to use its bases to fly strike missions against Iraq in 1996 and

1998 and in support of Operation Enduring Freedom in 2001 and Operation Iraqi Freedom in 2003.

Despite the diminished military presence in Saudi Arabia, and strained political relations in the aftermath of the 9/11 terrorist attacks, security cooperation continued to broaden during the 2000s, especially in counterterrorism and collective regional defense. The two sides worked to coordinate operations against al-Qaeda in the Arabian Peninsula.[65]

Beginning in May 2003, the kingdom became a target of a series of terrorist attacks. In November 2003 and in 2004, terrorist attacks in Saudi Arabia escalated, with targets including Saudi Arabia's oil infrastructure and the U.S. consulate in Jeddah. Although terrorist attacks against U.S. facilities had occurred in the kingdom during the 1990s, "attacks against non-U.S. targets did not begin until May 2003."[66] The 9/11 Commission report observed, "As in Pakistan, Yemen, and other countries, [Saudi] attitudes changed when the terrorism came home."[67] Before the September 11 attacks, the Saudi government had resisted cooperating with America in trying to cut off al-Qaeda's funding sources, although its cooperation improved in some measure after terrorist attacks in the Saudi kingdom in 2003.[68]

Since 2003, the kingdom has created new entities and laws designed to combat terrorist financing in coordination with American agencies. Cooperation expanded further after 2005 when Washington boosted its training and technical assistance to Riyadh for counterterrorism. In subsequent years, the U.S. Department of State praised improvements in Saudi cooperation but also noted that Riyadh needed to do far more to monitor fundraising activities in the kingdom and Saudi charitable activities abroad.[69] That was diplomatic talk for Riyadh's failure to take more serious measures to check terrorist impulses within its borders.

Indeed, the U.S. Treasury Department, which was more critical of the Saudis, politely underscored that Riyadh was serious about fighting al-Qaeda but still remained the primary location in the world from which more money was going to terror groups.[70] Importantly, the House of Saud remained highly reluctant to prosecute violators of its own rules of conduct regarding the use by terrorists of charity monies. In a 2014 report on terrorism, Washington praised Saudi Arabia for its continued efforts to "maintain a robust counterterrorism relationship with the United States" and for joining and taking military action in support of the Global Coalition to Counter the Islamic State.[71] Security cooperation increased further in 2015 when Saudi Arabia began to launch a U.S.-

backed air campaign aimed at halting the advance of Houthi forces in Yemen that were backed by Iran.

While cooperation on counterterrorism has been checkered, though it has improved over time, cooperation on Saudi internal security has broadened. The Office of the Program Manager–Ministry of Interior (OPM-MOI) has facilitated U.S. assistance in the areas of critical infrastructure protection and public security, including border protection, civil defense capabilities, and coast guard and maritime capabilities.[72] The OPM-MOI, which the CENTCOM 2013 posture statement sees as vital,[73] has coordinated the development of Saudi Arabia's 35,000-strong facility security force for the protection of critical energy infrastructure, including oil and gas facilities, diesel plants, power generators, and future nuclear plants, from attacks by militants. The initiative complements a long-standing U.S. military training mission to Saudi Arabia established in 1953 that has managed the modernization and development efforts of the Saudi Arabian National Guard since 1973. Saudi Interior Ministry spokesman General Mansour al-Turki asserted that the initiative was important due to a "new threat to oil installations from terrorists that has to be confronted. . . . We can't just rely on a security system that was built some time ago for a different kind of risk."[74] The improvement in internal security cooperation was reflected clearly in the sharp rise in the number of Saudi military officers who have trained in America: it increased seven-fold to 700 officers from 1998 to 2008.[75]

American Security Relations with Other GCC States
U.S. security cooperation with Bahrain expanded in the 1980s and then in the post–Cold War period as well. In addition to hosting U.S. naval headquarters, Bahrain participated in the U.S.-led coalition in 1991 and hosted 17,500 U.S. forces and 250 U.S. combat aircraft at Shaikh Isa Air Base. From 1991 to 1998, Bahrain agreed to host the regional headquarters for U.N. weapons inspections in Iraq and the U.S.-led multinational interdiction force that enforced a U.N. embargo on Iraq from 1991 to 2003. In 2001, the two states renewed the DCA for another ten-year period, and despite domestic opposition, Bahrain provided support to the U.S.-led wars in Afghanistan and Iraq. It allowed the United States to fly combat missions from its Shaikh Isa Air Base in both operations, deployed its U.S.-supplied warship and its ground and air assets in support of the U.S. missions, and hosted over 4,000 U.S. military personnel during Operation Enduring Freedom (2001–2003). Bilateral security cooperation was

underscored in September 2014 when Bahrain joined the U.S.-led, anti–Islamic State coalition, flying airstrikes on Islamic State positions in Syria.[76]

The already close defense relationship strengthened further in March 2002 when President Bush designated Bahrain a "major non-NATO ally," qualifying it for arms normally sold only to member countries of the North Atlantic Treaty Organization (NATO). Bahrain also became the largest GCC recipient of U.S. grant security assistance, and America initiated the expansion of its naval facilities in Bahrain to permit larger U.S. ships to dock and expanded the Shaikh Isa Air Base, which hosts U.S. aircraft.[77] The U.S. headquarters in Bahrain coordinated the operations of over thirty U.S. warships performing support missions in the 2003 Iraq War, antiterrorism missions against al-Qaeda, and maritime narcotics interdictions across the Arabian Sea.[78]

In May 2011, President Obama,[79] as well as U.S. Secretary of State Hillary Clinton, criticized Bahrain for cracking down on protesters in the period when the Arab Spring was set in motion around the Middle East, but security cooperation remained largely unaffected. America temporarily halted defense transfers and security assistance to Bahrain, but resumed them in June 2015, and in August 2011, the DCA initially signed in 1990 was renewed for another ten years. Moreover, the two sides continued to expand military capabilities in reaction to regional threats, leading to the increase of the U.S. military presence from 6,500 personnel in 2013 to about 8,300 in 2015.

For their part, U.S.-Kuwaiti security ties were largely absent during the Cold War but expanded in the 1980s when America reflagged Kuwaiti oil tankers during the Iraq-Iran War. The 1990–1991 Gulf crisis was a watershed because it is hard to imagine the forceful reversal of Iraq's invasion without the United States. Kuwait contributed over $16 billion to compensate for Operations Desert Shield and Desert Storm, and between 1992 and 2003, U.S. forces used Kuwaiti facilities to enforce a no-fly zone over southern Iraq. In 2001, the two countries renewed the 1991 DCA, and they continued to engage in joint military exercises, training of Kuwaiti forces, pre-positioning of U.S. military equipment, and joint access to a range of Kuwaiti facilities.

The U.S. presence in Kuwait increased significantly as a result of the U.S.-led 2001 Afghanistan and 2003 Iraq wars. The 2003 U.S.-led invasion of Iraq further deepened ties with Kuwait, unlike in the case of Saudi Arabia, which became far more sensitive to domestic criticism of the American presence after the U.S.-led invasion of Iraq in 2003. Kuwait agreed to host about 25,000 U.S.-led support forces and 250,000 invasion forces, along with massive volumes of equipment, while contributing $266 million annually to support the increased U.S. presence on its territory.[80]

Closer bilateral ties were underscored in April 2004 when the Bush administration designated Kuwait as a major non-NATO ally of the United States.[81] After America's withdrawal from Iraq in December 2011, its presence in Kuwait fell to 13,500 U.S. troops, allowing the United States to retain at least some combat power close to both Iraq and Iran. Kuwait has remained eager to maintain a significant U.S. military presence and to receive U.S. military training.[82]

U.S.-Qatari relations have also expanded in the post–Cold War era. Official diplomatic relations were established in 1973 but remained stillborn until after the 1991 Gulf War. In 1992, the two countries signed a defense agreement that spearheaded cooperative defense exercises, equipment pre-positioning, and base access agreements. Qatar also served as the forward command center for CENTCOM personnel during the Afghanistan and Iraq War.

Security relations expanded further in 2003 when the United States moved its massive Combat Air Operations Center to Qatar from Saudi Arabia, and such relations continued to develop. As one indication, in 2011, Qatar's forces and fighter jets participated in NATO-led operations over Libya, and America and Qatar signed a new ten-year defense cooperation agreement in December 2013.

As with the other GCC countries, U.S. security relations with the UAE have expanded in the post–Cold War period. The two countries signed the DCA in 1994, which, with UAE subsidization, permits the United States to pre-position equipment and grants it better naval and air force access.[83] Under the DCA, the UAE allowed the United States to upgrade its airfields at Al Dhafra Air Base and use them in support of Operation Iraqi Freedom in 2003 and the war in Afghanistan to which the UAE has committed around 250 troops since 2003.[84] Notably, in 2012, the UAE became home to the new Integrated Air Missile Defense Center, which serves as a key training facility for U.S.-GCC cooperation on missile defense. Building on the May 2015 Camp David summit aimed at reaffirming the U.S.-GCC strategic partnership, the United States increased cooperation with the UAE on maritime security, military preparedness, arms transfers, cybersecurity, and counterterrorism.

Oman was the first GCC country to grant Washington military access in a 1980 defense agreement, which has been renewed several times since then. It hosted U.S. forces during every U.S. military operation in and around the

Gulf since 1980. Under the renewed 2000 defense agreement, the United States invested $120 million to upgrade an air base at Musnanah.[85] Oman hosted around 4,300 U.S. forces, mostly air force, during Operation Enduring Freedom, which ousted the Taliban in Afghanistan, and a force of 3,750 during Operation Iraqi Freedom. However, since 2004, the U.S. military presence in Oman has dropped to a small U.S. Air Force contingent, and Oman has sought to relocate all U.S. military personnel to the offshore and sparsely inhabited Masirah Island.

U.S.-GCC Security Framework

Judging from media reports of America's relations with Muslim countries in the region, we would assume that they were in serious decline. Although serious problems have emerged, cooperation has strengthened in some important areas. Indeed, complementing bilateral security arrangements, Washington has also improved GCC-wide cooperation in the post–Cold War period through a variety of institutionalized security frameworks. They aim to boost GCC capacity to face regional threats. In his March 1995 congressional testimony, Assistant Secretary of Defense for International Security Affairs Joseph Nye described one such initiative as "a three-tier cooperative approach" with the GCC countries.[86] This framework consisted "of strengthening local self-defense capabilities, promoting GCC and inter-Arab defense cooperation, and enhancing the ability of U.S. and coalition forces to return and fight effectively alongside local forces in a crisis."[87]

In 1998, the Clinton administration introduced the Cooperative Defense Initiative (CDI) to reaffirm its commitment to Gulf security and increase defense cooperation with the GCC states. The CDI focused on meeting threats from weapons of mass destructions, including chemical and biological weapons. As part of the CDI, CENTCOM sponsored a variety of exercises with the GCC and regional states, with the first exercise taking place in May 2000 in Bahrain.

The Bush administration launched a Gulf Security Dialogue (GSD) in May 2006 to revive and expand U.S.-GCC security cooperation and promote more robust cooperation among the GCC states themselves to meet common threats.[88] Under this framework, the United States has broadened its engagement with the GCC countries in six areas: GCC defense capabilities and interoperability; regional security issues, such as the Arab-Israeli conflict; counterproliferation; counterterrorism and internal security; critical infrastructure protection; and Iraq. While promoting multilateral cooperation and integrated engagement, the interagency dialogue complements, but does not replace, the existing bilateral arrangements between the United States and individual GCC countries, such as military-to-military coordination programs. GSD discussions have been held with each country semiannually.

Not surprisingly, efforts to foster intra-GCC and integrated GCC-U.S. security cooperation have faced significant challenges. As in the case of past initiatives of this sort, including an attempt to create a serious GCC RDF, the GCC countries had different views of the security threats and how to address them.[89] For its part, the U.S. Government Accountability Office noted in 2010 that GSD "has not succeeded in enabling multilateral cooperation among Gulf countries because these countries prefer bilateral discussions with the [United States] on security concerns."[90] GCC states hardly move in lockstep. Oman, for example, did not join GCC forces in crushing protesters in Bahrain 2011, nor did it join in airstrikes in Syria or in Yemen in 2015, and it has been closer to Iran than any GCC country.

The GSD continued under the Obama administration, which emphasized the multilateral aspect of security cooperation while focusing chiefly on the development of a Gulf missile defense system to deter and protect the region against potential missile attacks from Iran. In March 2012, the Obama administration launched the U.S.-GCC Strategic Cooperation Forum in Riyadh, aimed at deepening multilateral cooperation and coordination. Secretary of State Hillary Clinton praised the initiative's focus on ballistic missile defense and interoperability, as well as on counterterrorism and border security,[91] as did Secretary of Defense Chuck Hagel.[92] Obama designated the GCC eligible for foreign military sales as a bloc in 2013, which further enhanced regional ballistic missile defense through multilateral procurement and shared systems,[93] and he also expanded the authority of the U.S. Air Force to conduct integrated air and missile defense training at the U.S.-UAE Integrated Air and Missile Defense Center in the UAE.[94]

In May 2014, during Hagel's meeting with ministers from the six GCC countries in Saudi Arabia, Saudi Crown Prince Salman affirmed the need for coordination to meet "persistent threats to the region's security and stability."[95] Hagel noted that despite Iran's diplomatic engagement being a "positive development," the United States and GCC states "continue to share concerns about Iran's destabilizing activities throughout the region . . . [including Iran's] sponsorship of terrorism, its support for the Assad regime in Syria and its efforts to undermine stability in GCC member nations. . . . That is why we are committed to continuing to work together to reinforce GCC defense and capabilities." During the meeting, the GCC ministers and Hagel agreed on the need "for more cooperation in three areas: more integrated air and missile defense coordination; closer maritime security integration; and expanded cybersecurity cooperation,"[96] and subsequent meetings focused on exchanging best practices on counterterrorism and border security within which cybersecurity became an increasingly prominent topic.[97] In May 2015 President Obama and the GCC heads of delegations met at Camp David and expanded cooperation in maritime security, military preparedness, arms transfers, cybersecurity, and counterterrorism.[98]

U.S.-Iraqi Security Relations

Despite its troop pullout from Iraq in 2011, the United States kept over 16,000 political and security-related personnel in Iraq, about 50 percent of whom were contractors.[99] This includes the Office of Security Cooperation-Iraq (OSC-I), which is "the largest U.S. security cooperation office in the world," staffed with more than 3,500 largely civilian U.S. security and support personnel. By the end of 2013, that presence dropped much further. Since the U.S. withdrawal, OSC-I staff have continued to administer arms sales to Iraq, as well as train, mentor, and otherwise cooperate with the Iraqi military and the government on counterterrorism and naval and air defense and through joint exercises.[100] Moreover, the two countries cemented a five-year memorandum of understanding providing for training, counterterrorism cooperation, the development of defense intelligence capabilities, and joint exercises.

As Sunni unrest in Iraq continued to escalate in 2013, partly due to a spillover from Syria's civil war, Washington and Baghdad discussed options to further enhance security cooperation. This was underscored during Maliki's meeting with President Obama and Secretary of Defense Hagel in November 2013, when he sought greater access to U.S. intelligence and expedition of arms sales to deal with al-Qaeda–affiliated groups threatening Iraq. As security conditions deteriorated in early 2014, the Obama administration boosted security cooperation with Iraq, resuming an active military role and presence in Iraq with a stated goal of defeating the Islamic State.[101]

Since August 2014, the United States has conducted airstrikes on Islamic State positions, and U.S. Special Forces have played increasingly more important roles in conjunction with the Iraqi military and the Kurds in fighting the

Islamic State in Iraq. However, U.S. foreign policy in Syria, which failed to end the Syrian Civil War or contain President Assad, was complicated in 2015 with Russia's intervention. It may take some time to understand how Moscow's intervention will affect relations between Baghdad and Washington and between Russia and other powers in the region.

Arms Sales

Since the Cold War, the United States has used arms sales, military training, and other security assistance to further its national security objectives in the region. As Figure 3.1 illustrates, these efforts accelerated in the post–Cold War period and particularly in the past decade during which U.S. arms sales to the GCC states dramatically increased. The Gulf crisis of 1990–1991 exemplified the threats that the GCC states faced in the region, and their memory of the Iraqi invasion was a key cause of their arms purchases for the rest of the decade. After the 2003 invasion of Iraq, Iran's growing power and the Obama administration's increased focus on burden sharing spurred greater sales. America saw such sales in part as a way to balance Iran.[102]

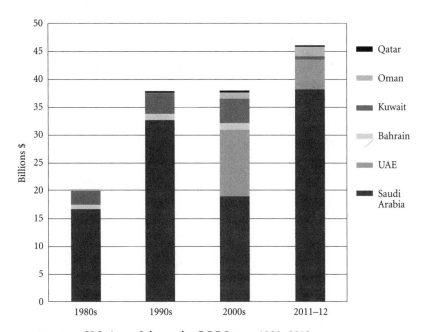

FIGURE 3.1. U.S. Arms Sales to the GCC States, 1980–2012.
SOURCE: Data compiled by the authors from various Congressional Research Service reports by Richard F. Grimmett.

TABLE 3.1. U.S. Foreign Military Sales Agreements to the Persian Gulf States (U.S. Dollars in Thousands)

Country	FY 1950–2004	2005	2006	2007	2008	2009	2010	2011	2012	FY 2005–2012
Saudi Arabia	67,129,439	724,613	802,972	1,635,990	6,257,289	2,837,882	2,026,968	3,364,301	34,733,840	52,383,855
Qatar	18,462	18	0	26	17,352	194,828	17,106	1,175	37,518	268,223
UAE	912,687	26,574	761,995	1,627,834	653,060	7,559,603	501,642	1,532,937	3,850,990	16,514,635
Bahrain	2,062,220	26,241	89,823	203,349	75,919	95,629	88,010	105,065	25,759	709,795
Kuwait	9,103,598	95,992	657,608	82,132	523,379	298,019	1,071,604	409,424	178,372	3,316,530
Oman	1,049,385	45,687	17,224	38,588	28,501	86,060	11,709	139,384	1,462,768	1,829,921
Iran	10,715,417	0	0	0	0	0	0	0	0	0
Iraq	13,152	80,724	0	1,049,611	2,350,423	901,437	817,788	1,841,331	1,497,011	8,538,325

SOURCE: Compiled by the authors from the U.S. Department of Defense Security Cooperation Agency's Historical Fact Books and Fiscal Year Series, September 30, 2012.

The data paint a stark picture. As Table 3.1 demonstrates, U.S. arms sales from 2005 to 2012 in many cases exceeded or were nearly equal to total U.S. arms transfers to these states in the previous more than five decades. From 2007 to 2010 alone, the six GCC states' arms and training services agreements accounted for nearly 30 percent of all U.S. foreign military agreements in that period. While U.S. arms sales to Iran ceased after the Islamic Revolution in 1979, Iraq, a major purchaser of Soviet advanced weaponry during the Cold War, has become a beneficiary of U.S. foreign military sales (FMS) since 2005.

American arms sales to the GCC states have been driven in part by the multilateral initiatives already discussed in this chapter. From 2007 to 2013 alone, they totaled more than $75 billion and nearly equaled in worth the sales made in the previous fifteen years.[103] Between 2004–2007 and 2008–2011, U.S. arms agreements with the GCC countries increased more than eightfold.

The arms agreements have focused on development of the GCC's air, naval, asymmetric warfare, counterterrorism, and, particularly, missile defense capabilities. In line with the U.S. goal to build an integrated regional defense and broaden burden sharing,[104] several GCC states purchased missile defense systems, and others expressed a similar interest. The UAE and Qatar have bought U.S. Terminal High Altitude Area Defense, the most sophisticated missile defense system in the world. During Hagel's visit to the region in late 2013, the United States finalized an agreement for F-15, F-16, and advanced munitions that Hagel described as "the most advanced capabilities we have ever provided to this region."[105]

Saudi Arabia has been the largest customer, "with active and open cases valued at approximately $97 billion" as of March 2014.[106] Its arms agreements with the United States increased ninefold between 2008 and 2011 compared to 2004 to 2007. In October 2010, Washington announced $60 billion worth of military aircraft to the kingdom in what would be the largest U.S. arms sale in history, and in September 2015, it finalized an additional $1 billion arms agreement in support of Saudi war efforts against the Islamic State and Yemen.[107] Other GCC countries have also considerably increased their arms purchases. For instance, from 2007 to 2010, the UAE agreed to procure U.S. defense articles and services through the foreign military sales program totaling $10.4 billion, which is more than any other country in the world except Saudi Arabia.[108] Although Oman has traditionally relied on British-made defense articles, it has increasingly procured U.S. systems to modernize its arsenal and enhance interoperability with U.S. forces (see Table 3.1). Notably, in May 2013, during Secretary Kerry's visit to Oman, the two countries agreed on the sale of the Terminal High Altitude Area Defense system.[109] Qatar has increasingly become another nontraditional buyer of U.S. arms. Although France has supplied most of Qatar's arsenal for decades, Qatar has also shifted in the past decade toward advanced U.S. attack and transport helicopters and air and missile defense, which should benefit U.S.-GCC security cooperation[110] and create ongoing interdependencies and synergies that will strengthen the U.S. position in Saudi Arabia.[111]

Iraq has also emerged as an important purchaser of U.S. arms in the post-Saddam era following the lifting of U.N. sanctions on the country, albeit it is unclear to what extent such purchases actually contributed to the fighting capabilities of Iraq's forces given their poor initial showing against the Islamic State. Nonetheless, such sales do indicate a level of security interaction between Baghdad and Washington.

OSC-I managed hundreds of U.S. foreign military sales, including the sale of thirty-six F-16 combat aircraft and associated training, parts, and weaponry, with a total price tag of about $6.5 billion.[112] In 2013, Iraq agreed to purchase the U.S. Integrated Air Defense System and Apache helicopters with a price tag of around $10 billion for use against the Islamic State,[113] and such cooperation increased especially after the rise of the Islamic State threat. Washington also has supplied Iraq with numerous other weapons, including Hellfire missiles and unarmed surveillance drones for use against Islamic State targets, and trained Iraqi counterterrorism units; equipped Iraq's most elite military forces; and enhanced interoperability with U.S. forces and regional partners.[114]

Conclusion

America's ability to deploy to the Gulf rose from a negligible level in 1980 to a major capability by 1990. It has fluctuated since then, but at a far higher level than in 1980. Significant improvements in U.S. sealift capability have provided for unprecedented movement of equipment and supplies, though they are not at the highest postwar level. Prior to 1980, America's only permanent facility in the Gulf had been a defense fuel supply station in Bahrain; since then, it has established massive access throughout the region, which has provided tremendous military firepower. America withdrew most of its presence from Saudi Arabia in 2003 due to political sensitivities, but it has renewed and, in the majority of cases, expanded its access to critical installations in all the remaining GCC countries, and it could redeploy to Saudi Arabia should conflict arise without maintaining a costly and unsustainable presence.[115]

Despite serious political tensions in U.S-Arab state relations, security co-operation has remained a cornerstone of those relations in the post–Cold War era. The 2003 war removed the Iraqi threat, but the terrorist threat and ascendancy of Iran have provided a new logic for U.S.-GCC security cooperation.[116]

The Obama administration's increased focus on burden sharing and interoperability with the GCC states drove unprecedented arms sales to them and bilateral security arrangements aimed in part at checking Iran. Cooperation in nontraditional security areas such as counterterrorism, critical infrastructure protection, and cyber domains has increased dramatically since the mid-2000s, as cooperation in traditional areas such as missile defense has also significantly expanded. The Iran nuclear accord has given such efforts even more ballast as a way of balancing against Iran that GCC states fear will become stronger due to the Iran nuclear accord. Beyond balancing, Washington also has aimed to establish its commitment to these states, partly due to the accord, which has raised questions about its traditional role of supporting them against Iran and intermittently against Iraq and other threats.

4 The United States, Economics, and Energy

SECURITY COOPERATION represents the bedrock of America's relations with regional states, but its economic position has also developed in the post–Cold War period, particularly since the mid-2000s. This dimension of great power involvement in the region is underemphasized compared to security factors, but it deserves more consideration not only because economic strength is an important part of overall capabilities, but also because economic ties sometimes strengthen other dimensions of power, including in the security area. Such ties can also affect the propensity for cooperation or conflict in the region and with the great powers, and they influence oil security. The better that economic relations are, the more robust is oil security, all other things equal. This is not only because it suggests better security cooperation in provisioning oil but also greater interdependence between America and China and regional states.

A General View of U.S.-Arab State Economic Interaction

At a general level, America has enjoyed unprecedented trade volumes and commercial cooperation with GCC states (Figure 4.1). In particular, the value of U.S.-Saudi trade more than tripled in the decade following the 9/11 terrorist attacks, and energy cooperation expanded at both the governmental and private sector levels. In fact, as of 2003, more than 700 U.S.-affiliated companies operated in the GCC countries, and the U.S. private sector investment in the GCC economies constituted half of the world's investment in the GCC.[1]

Since about 2005, the GCC countries have also dramatically expanded their investment in America and the West in general through their sovereign wealth funds (SWF). Rising oil prices helped raise these investments to $1.6 trillion in 2012, up from $1 trillion in 2007, and they accounted for more than 32 percent of overall global SWF assets.[2] Illustratively, Saudi Arabia, which holds the highest volume of SWF in the GCC at around $690 billion reportedly, placed 80 percent of its portfolio in U.S. Treasury bonds in 2013 despite political disagreements over regional issues.[3]

American Bilateral Economic Relations

This section explores key changes in U.S.-regional state economic interaction, which not only provide insight into its economic capabilities but also into an arena of interaction that has global importance. It focuses on U.S. bilateral ties with individual GCC countries and Iraq. We start with the most critical relationship: Saudi Arabia.

U.S.-Saudi Economic Relations

U.S.-Saudi trade increased considerably in the post–Cold War era, making Saudi Arabia the main U.S. trading partner in the Gulf. During the 1990s, the value of bilateral trade stagnated but then rose by more than 350 percent between

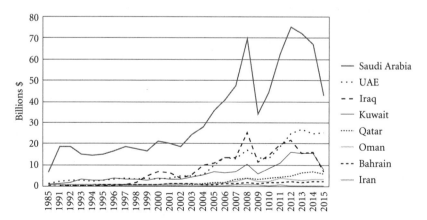

FIGURE 4.1. Total Trade between the United States and the Persian Gulf States, 1985–2015.

SOURCE: Created by the authors with data drawn from U.N. Commodity Trade Statistics Database (New York: United Nations, various years), and *UN International Trade Statistics Yearbook* (New York: United Nations, various years).

2000 and 2014 to over $75 billion,[4] partly facilitated by the signing in 2003 of the Trade and Investment Framework Agreement and Saudi Arabia's admittance into the World Trade Organization in 2005, following twelve years of negotiations with Washington.

American oil imports from Saudi Arabia have decreased in recent years due to increased U.S. domestic oil production, but high oil prices since 2002 enhanced the value of bilateral trade. While U.S. oil imports from Saudi Arabia account for the bulk of the total bilateral trade, U.S. exports to Saudi Arabia also increased considerably, rising by 300 percent between 2003 and 2014 alone.[5] According to David Hamod, president of the National U.S.-Arab Chamber of Commerce, the increase in U.S. exports was largely attributable to unprecedented infrastructure development in the GCC states.[6]

In 2009, Riyadh launched a five-year, $400 billion project to build infrastructure, expand energy production, and boost economic growth,[7] and it announced plans to invest $150 billion over the next two decades to upgrade its utility-related infrastructure.[8] Washington has intensified trade-related engagements with Saudi Arabia through a variety of business dialogues and trade visits in order to boost investment by U.S. companies in these projects amid increasing competition from China, Russia, and Europe.[9] And American companies have increasingly pursued energy and nonenergy opportunities.[10] U.S. foreign direct investment in Saudi Arabia increased by more than 17 percent between 2011 and 2012, with over 150 U.S. companies starting businesses there in 2012.[11] In addition to these new entrants, giants such as General Electric have continued to maintain multiple long-standing joint venture projects in the kingdom engaged in power generation, electrical and medical equipment service, information services, and other services for more than seven decades.[12]

Despite strained political relations, U.S.-Saudi commercial links continued to intensify. In September 2013, U.S. Commerce Secretary Penny Pritzker underscored that by 2012, trade in "both directions hit an all-time record high," surpassing the prerecession levels for the first time.[13] Despite these successes, America has lost market share to other countries, most notably to China. In 2000, U.S. exports represented nearly 20 percent of total Saudi imports, but that dropped to 13.5 percent by 2007.[14] In contrast, China's total share of the Saudi market in the same period more than doubled from 4.1 percent to 9.6 percent. Similarly, in 2000, 20 percent of Saudi exports went to the United States, but by 2007, the figure had dropped to around 15 percent.[15]

U.S.-GCC Economic Relations

Beyond U.S.-Saudi relations, it is interesting to assess America's relations with the GCC as a bloc. The United States has expanded economic relations with all GCC states and in recent years with the GCC as a bloc, partly due to the Bush administration's 2003 Middle East free trade area initiative, one dimension of a broader reform plan aimed at promoting democracy in the Middle East.[16] Washington expanded its economic ties in the region further by concluding the U.S. Free Trade Agreement with Oman in 2009 and Bahrain in 2006. Under the Obama administration, the United States and the GCC also signed the Framework Agreement for Trade, Economic, Investment and Technical Cooperation in September 2012 to expand on bilateral economic arrangements.

America imports little oil from the UAE, but it has become the top U.S. export partner in the Arab world. In 2014, bilateral trade reached nearly $25 billion, with U.S. exports accounting for almost 90 percent.[17] American exports to the UAE, mostly transportation equipment and electronic products, increased from around $1 billion in 1991 to more than $11 billion in 2006, reaching over $24 billion by 2013 before slightly dropping to $22 billion in 2014. As with other GCC countries, the UAE's infrastructure boom has continued to attract U.S. foreign direct investment, which increased by nearly 34 percent between 2011 and 2012 alone.[18] America also continues to be an important destination for the UAE's investment. A representative of the Abu Dhabi Investment Authority (ADIA), one of the biggest sovereign investment funds in the world, stated in 2010 that "between 35% and 50% of ADIA's assets are being invested in the U.S., [while] between 25% and 30% are invested in Europe."[19]

While U.S. trade ties with all of the smaller GCC states have expanded at varying levels, Qatar and Kuwait have seen the largest increases.[20] U.S. exports to Kuwait increased by more than 70 percent between 2003 and 2014, and U.S. imports have been up by 455 percent for the same period.[21]

U.S.-Iraqi Economic Relations

The removal of U.N. sanctions on Iraq after the fall of the Saddam Hussein regime has boosted U.S.-Iraqi economic ties. That must be considered, along with security cooperation in fighting groups like the Islamic State, when assessing these sometimes stormy relations. Positive economic relations are a bright spot in a bilateral relationship that has been vital not only to dealing with Iraq's problems but also with other issues like Syria and Iran.

Bilateral trade, based on U.S. imports of Iraqi oil, increased from near zero in the 1990s to over $20 billion in 2012 before dropping to $16 billion in 2014 as a result of increased U.S. domestic oil production. Meanwhile, U.S. companies in the energy, defense, information technology, automotive, and transportation sectors became increasingly active in Iraq. In 2013, the bilateral Trade and Investment Framework Agreement between the United States and Iraq came into effect, which has promoted strong economic ties and efforts to integrate Iraq into the global economy.

The Energy Dimension

As we suggested in the Introduction, we are treating energy relations and ties differently from trade. This is because energy relations have their own important dynamics and, in fact, suggest more intense and involved interaction than does nonenergy trade alone. Having said that, it is important to consider several dimensions of America's position and ties in the energy arena.

The Oil Trade

As Figure 4.2 shows, American oil imports from the Gulf as a total have decreased from around 2000, including with the advent of the U.S. shale oil boom around 2007–2008. That is a positive development for U.S. security, even if the American economy is fundamentally affected by global oil markets. Consumers

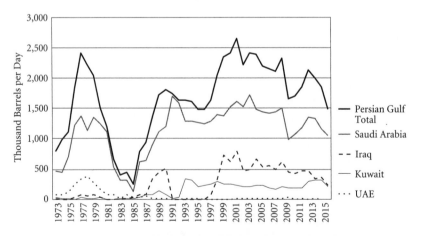

FIGURE 4.2. U.S. Crude Oil Imports from the Persian Gulf, 1973–2015.
SOURCE: Created by the authors; data drawn from the U.S. Energy Information Administration, Petroleum & Other Liquids statistical database.

roughly pay the market price for oil, which can be affected by various global events and developments, regardless of where we get our oil.

While American oil imports from the Gulf have decreased due to the U.S. oil boom, the share of oil imports from the region as a percentage of the overall U.S. oil imports has risen in recent years after it temporarily decreased in 2009–2010 (Figure 4.3). This is partly because the major shale oil fields of the Bakken in North Dakota and the Eagle Ford in Texas produce light oil, while many U.S. refineries are designed to process heavier crude from the Gulf. In fact, America's largest refinery in Texas, which is jointly owned by Royal Dutch Shell and Saudi Aramco, has seen greater demand for Gulf oil in the face of the U.S. shale boom.

American Energy Companies

It is important to look at the role of international energy companies. American national interests and those of its oil companies are different, but they are often related. Oil companies are nationalized in the Persian Gulf, as they are in China and Russia. Although American firms are privatized, they interact with these nationalized companies and, in turn, with the governments that largely run them. While these companies are private, they are also subject to U.S. governmental regulations and foreign policy restrictions and can benefit from Washington's influence and foreign policy decisions. Moreover, U.S. companies benefit from U.S. economic welfare in general and in the region.

American energy companies have enhanced their already established position in the region, although China has made major strides, as we discuss in Chapter 6.

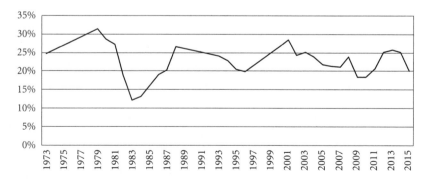

FIGURE 4.3. U.S. Oil Imports from the Persian Gulf as a Percentage of Total U.S. Oil Imports, 1973–2015.
SOURCE: Created by the authors; data drawn from the U.S. Energy Information Administration, Petroleum & Other Liquids statistical database.

Chevron discovered oil in Saudi Arabia in 1938 as the Standard Oil Company of California. That formed the basis for the Arabian-American Oil Company, which transformed into Saudi Aramco. Chevron has been the only major energy company to have a continuous upstream presence in Saudi Arabia for over seventy years, conducting exploration and production on behalf of the Saudis.[22] Chevron and Saudi Arabia have also expanded partnerships in Saudi downstream, such as in petrochemicals and related marketing and retail.

For its part, ExxonMobil has remained one of the largest foreign investors in the kingdom and buyers of Saudi Aramco crude. For over three decades, it has participated in petrochemicals manufacturing, refining, and other petroleum operations in Saudi Arabia through three major joint ventures: Samref, a refining joint venture with Saudi Aramco, and Yanpet and Kemya, two manufacturing joint ventures with Saudi SABIC.[23] In March 2007, ExxonMobil joined forces with Saudi Aramco and China's Sinopec to expand a refinery in China's Fujian Province. This $5 billion deal represented the first fully integrated refining, petrochemicals, and fuels marketing project with foreign participation in China.[24]

Chevron and ExxonMobil have also been active across the Gulf. They have operated for more than three decades in the UAE's oil production and downstream. Notably, ExxonMobil inaugurated a world-scale petrochemical complex in Qatar in 2003, its first joint venture with Qatar Petroleum; that was followed in 2009 by a center of excellence in renewable power and energy efficiency[25] and a May 2013 agreement with Qatar Petroleum International for construction of a $10 billion natural gas export terminal in Texas.[26] In 2000, ExxonMobil opened its office in Kuwait and since then has provided a variety of technical services to Kuwait.[27]

It is also worthwhile noting that U.S.-regional trade has increased in non-hydrocarbon-related areas. That is suggested by a 2008 memorandum of understanding on civil nuclear energy cooperation in which America will assist in developing Saudi civilian nuclear energy for use in medicine, industry, and power generation.[28]

The American Oil Boom, High Technology, and a Saudi Fracking Revolution?

Beyond the regular forms of energy interaction with American and global companies, the House of Saud has launched its own fracking boom. This boom may make the Saudi energy sector more reliant on American oil majors and service contractors, at least in the short run, and it could result in longer-run synergies. That is an advantage that America enjoys over Russia, China, and other nations around the world, even if America's energy companies are private entities. The technology of its companies is in particular demand.

In 2011, several years after America's boom was in full swing, Saudi Aramco launched its own unconventional gas program in the northern region. Two years later, it was ready to commit new shale gas production to a 1,000 megawatt power plant.[29] Ali al-Naimi, Saudi minister of petroleum and mineral resources, estimated that the kingdom possesses about 600 trillion cubic feet of shale gas reserves,[30] which would place Saudi Arabia fifth in the world in total unconventional reserves.[31]

Saudi Aramco, in its 2014 annual report, spoke of its unconventional gas program as "continuing to gain momentum,"[32] and al-Naimi added that "the kingdom has made promising shale gas discoveries and acquired the technologies to produce it at a reasonable price."[33] Notably, in early 2015, Saudi Aramco raised the amount earmarked for its own boom from an original $3 billion to $10 billion.[34]

The Saudis have also established a global research network of eleven total technology offices and research centers housed in North America, Europe, China, and at home in Saudi Arabia.[35] Saudi Aramco's vice president of upstream technologies said that "R&D and innovation underpin our intent to emerge as a truly global, integrated energy and chemicals company by the end of the decade."[36] On September 19, 2014, Saudi Aramco inaugurated the Aramco Research Center in Houston Texas, a major hub for the American oil and gas industry.[37] The center is operated by the Saudi Aramco U.S.-based subsidiary Aramco Services Company (ASC). According to ASC, the objective of this facility is to conduct unconventional upstream energy research in exploration, drilling, field development, and project management.[38] The Saudis, who have been endeavoring to expand their own unconventional program, are looking to gain American expertise through direct and indirect recruiting efforts specifically aimed at U.S. shale workers.[39]

To be sure, IOCs are closed out of upstream production, and Riyadh appears to want to gain technological expertise so that it can launch its own boom in earnest. But its desire to do so also opens up possibilities for American energy companies.

The Iraq Factor

U.S.-Iraqi energy relations are in flux, but in the post–Saddam Hussein era, America and its companies have forged energy ties with Iraq that were not possible before. Iraq was closed to American investment in earlier decades, but since 2003, Washington has helped rebuild Iraq's energy sector, investing $4.6 billion in the power sector and $2.1 billion in the oil sector, while also providing ongoing energy capacity-building programs.[40] These efforts brought four export platforms online south of Basra in 2012, each with the capacity to export 900,000 barrels per day.[41] America continued to cooperate with Iraq on energy issues after the U.S. withdrawal in 2011 through the Joint Coordination Committee on Energy established in 2008 as a part of strategic framework agreements.

Notably, American service oil company Halliburton joined Shell to develop the Majnoon oil field, one of the world's largest, and other U.S. service oil companies such as Baker Hughes, Schlumberger, and Weatherford also have large stakes in Iraq. In 2010, ExxonMobil, with junior partner Royal Dutch Shell, signed an agreement with Iraq to rehabilitate and redevelop the 8.7 billion barrel West Qurna Phase 1 in southern Iraq.[42] From 2011 to 2013, ExxonMobil was also awarded six production-sharing contracts in Iraq's Kurdistan region.[43]

Regardless of America's penetration, most of Iraq's energy contracts have gone to non-U.S. companies. The national oil companies of China and Russia have performed better in Iraq than America's privatized companies.[44] In one of the biggest auctions held anywhere else in the 150-year history of global oil, contracts to exploit Iraq's oil were awarded in 2009. Five of Iraq's six major oil fields went to European, Russian, and Asian oil companies.[45] The one major U.S. contract went to ExxonMobil for refurbishing the West Qurna oil field, which, due to its enormous and almost untapped potential, is crucial to Iraq's goal of increasing oil production. Two of the most lucrative of the multibillion-dollar oil contracts went to Russia and China, which had strongly opposed the U.S. invasion. Although it is true that the oil services companies Halliburton, Baker Hughes, Weatherford International, and Schlumberger won smaller lucrative drilling subcontracts, America performed poorly despite being in effective control of Iraq, with tens of thousands of troops deployed and extraordinary economic costs absorbed.

The Impact of the American Oil Boom

The American oil boom is a major development in global energy. It is worthwhile focusing additional attention on it and what it means for relations with Gulf states, in particular Saudi Arabia.

On the positive side, the Saudis have sought American energy boom technology. As the kingdom's highly productive fields age and the demand for energy grows, Saudi Arabia and Kuwait are turning to heavy oil that is harder to get out of the ground with the help of Western IOCs. For instance, in 2012, Saudi Aramco and U.S. Chevron began exploring a project with heavy oil in the Wafra oil field. Since the collapse in oil prices in 2015, Saudi Aramco has been also wooing fired U.S. shale workers to Saudi Arabia as the country seeks to increase its capacity in the unconventional sector.[46]

The U.S. energy boom has also attracted significant Saudi investment in America for projects such as expanding refining capacity[47] and petrochemical production.[48] This may yield the U.S. government some benefits and influence, even if has limited control over American companies that are at the forefront of the energy boom. However, while yielding benefits, the American energy boom has evidently unsettled some key Saudi leaders.

In November 2013, Saudi billionaire and influential businessman Prince Alwaleed Bin Talal warned that the increased shale oil output in the United States poses a significant threat to the kingdom's economic stability, asserting that new shale discoveries "are threats to any oil-producing country in the world... It is a pivot moment for any oil-producing country that has not diversified."[49] His view was contested by the Saudi deputy oil minister who said that world economic growth would be "sufficient to handle growth from all sorts— shale oil, shale gas, tight oil and including renewables,"[50] as well as by Saudi oil minister Ali al-Naimi, who stated in January 2014 that Riyadh "welcomes this new source of energy supplies that contribute to meeting rising global demand and also contribute to the stability of the oil markets."[51]

Judging from media reports, one would think that the Arab oil producers generate most of the world's daily production, but they produce about one-third or less of it, with OPEC as a whole contributing around 40 percent of the world's daily oil. That is still a major amount, and so whatever OPEC states, and especially Saudi Arabia, do matters a great deal.

The Saudis have played the role of swing producer—a role in which Riyadh uses its massive oil capabilities to check prices that not only rise too high but also fall too low. In mid- to late 2014, the Saudis decided not to play this role. Instead of cutting oil production in order to fend against lower oil prices, Saudi Arabia's oil company cut its oil prices for Asia, Europe, and the United States. In November 2014, the Saudis continued an incarnation of this unusual strategy when OPEC met to consider oil production cuts. OPEC uncharacteristically failed to decrease oil production, leading some to conclude that OPEC's power and capability were now in eclipse.[52] These actions contributed to a fall in oil prices to the mid-$60s on the New York Mercantile Exchange (NYMEX) by December 2014, with the possibility of an even greater plunge.

Riyadh switched its strategy probably to protect market share, which was threatened by a variety of developments, including the American oil boom and possible overproduction of oil by other big oil producers. It may well have gambled that lower oil prices could hurt American shale oil output because U.S. shale oil is far more expensive to extract than is Saudi oil.[53] Challenging the Saudi position, Iran's oil minister, Bijan Namdar Zanganeh, asserted that the Saudi-led approach would do little to check the U.S. oil boom.[54] Riyadh has also been concerned that the American boom will make it less important to Washington, allowing America to decrease its commitment to the Persian Gulf and possibly to develop closer relations with Iran, especially given the 2015 nuclear deal with Iran. Such concerns probably give the Saudis added incentive to try to undermine the American oil boom.

We must also consider dynamics among non-American oil producers. Prince Turki, who has been Saudi Arabia's ambassador to the United States, stated that the "kingdom is not going to give up market share at this time to anybody and allow—whether it is Russia, Nigeria, or Iran or other places—to sell oil to Saudi customer"; he added that the Saudis and other producers would consider adjusting production only if other members of OPEC adhered to the group's quotas.[55]

The Saudis certainly preferred not to cut production if other major oil producers could not share the burden.[56] In fact, even if they could have dragooned others into agreeing to serious production cuts, the Saudis still may have preferred to drive prices lower. That is because Riyadh feared that others would fail to carry out these cuts[57] and instead would take Saudi market share. By refusing to support cuts, the Saudis signaled other OPEC members (and states outside OPEC like Russia) that they would have to join in serious cuts in the future or face the pain of lower oil prices.

In essence, Riyadh must have considered whether it would obtain more revenue now and in the future with lower market share and higher oil prices or with higher market share and lower oil prices, and what the probability would be of achieving either strategy. It chose the latter strategy.

The 2014 switch in Saudi strategy may also have been aimed at weakening Iran, which Riyadh fears.[58] Iran certainly saw it that way. Government spokesman Mohammad Baqer Nobakht asserted in October 2014 that "some so-called Islamic countries in the region are serving the interests of America and [other] arrogant powers in trying to squeeze the Islamic Republic."[59] Iran seeks to undermine the House of Saud and competes with its brand of Islam in the region, and Riyadh sees Iran's nuclear aspirations, despite the nuclear accord with the U.N. Security Council, as a major national security concern. Lower oil prices hurt the Iranians, who depend on much higher oil revenues to meet their budget targets at home than do the Saudis. To add to the drama, the Russian newspaper *Pravda* ran an article asserting that Washington and Riyadh were in collusion to push oil prices downward in order to hurt Russia.[60] Such coordination is highly unlikely, although Riyadh may have sought to pressure Moscow to cut its own production.

We saw that the U.S. oil boom has some positive effects, but what are negative effects of Saudi concerns about the boom? First, it is possible that OPEC's decision, and that of Saudi Arabia, will trigger a longer-term oil price war—a race of pain tolerance and not just a one-year affair. In such a case, all OPEC producers will feel pain, though it will vary from state to state. Meanwhile, many American companies will feel pain. If this continues for some time without positive diplomatic efforts to contain U.S.-Saudi tensions, that could damage relations.

Of course, market forces may have a mitigating effect. Falling oil prices may pressure the Saudis, OPEC, and American producers to cut oil production repeatedly in the effort to push oil prices higher.

Second, if Riyadh feels especially threatened by the boom, the Saudis will be less likely to cooperate with American oil companies. That negative dynamic could spill over into state-to-state relations.

Third, the boom has accentuated an age-old question in U.S. relations with the Arab Gulf states about U.S. commitment to their security. Will the boom allow Washington to diminish its commitment to the Gulf? That is doubtful but possible.

Conclusion

Logic would suggest that America's political differences with the Gulf states over major questions such as Iran's nuclear program and the fate of Syria's President Bashar Assad would spill over into economic interaction. Yet that assumption is revealed to be faulty by virtue of a panoramic view of these relations. If we take the long view, which is far more telling and accurate than any snapshot, data clearly show that American trade volumes and commercial cooperation have grown with GCC states in the past decade or more and took off with Saudi Arabia in the decade following the 9/11 terrorist attacks when political tensions were high. Similarly, since the mid-2000s, the GCC countries have built up their sovereign wealth funds and invested their monies in the United States more than in any other country. Such interactions add support to U.S. relations with regional states. All of the actors are aware of the multifaceted nature of their mutual relations, and that feeds into their interest in maintaining positive relations and avoiding major political and economic conflicts.

America's position in the energy arena has also improved with the GCC states and certainly yielded more new opportunities with Iraq than had existed under Saddam Hussein, even if other countries, such as China, have performed well in Iraq, and in some ways better than the United States and its energy companies. For its part, the American oil boom has created both benefits and potential costs for U.S. energy companies and for the U.S. government. The effect of the boom on U.S.-Saudi relations will depend on numerous factors, including varying levels of Saudi threat perception. The more the Saudis see the boom as a threat in any time period, the more negative will be its effect on U.S.-Saudi relations. But such perceptions may be tempered by the broader context of interdependent relations that militate against severe disruptions in relations.

II THE ROLE OF CHINA AND RUSSIA

5 China's Steep Ascent in the Persian Gulf

F EW OTHER ISSUES have received more attention than the rise of China in world politics, and for good reason. China's economy grew faster than any other economy at nearly 10 percent from 1978 to 2011. And it has remained an energy-consuming powerhouse, even after slowing down to a lower level of growth in recent years. We have heard repeated predictions that China's economy will surpass that of the United States by 2020 or 2025 and that the Chinese will develop the leverage to challenge America seriously and alter the rules that govern international relations.[1] Whatever one thinks of such predictions, it is certainly interesting to examine to what extent Beijing's global rise at the global level is also reflected in regions of the world such as the Persian Gulf, especially given that its role there and in energy is likely to become even more important.[2]

Indeed, the Chinese may or may not generally follow the notion by Confucius that "to go beyond is as wrong as to fall short," but in the area of energy, China appears willing to risk going beyond so as not to fall short. If China in the past represented the inscrutable East in foreign imagination, its objectives have become clear: it is driven to secure its energy needs in order to ensure economic growth. That desire makes it far less interested in undermining America's efforts to protect oil security, even as it tries to check the United States, especially when it appears to flex its muscles excessively, as in the case of the 2003 Iraq war.

This chapter and the next demonstrate that in the post–Cold War period, and particularly over the past decade, China has unprecedentedly expanded diplomatic, economic, and, though to a much lesser degree, security capabilities across the region, making it an important player in the Gulf. This chapter focuses on the rise of China's diplomatic position, as well as on changes in its security position. The PRC has developed good relations with all of the Persian Gulf states, including the members of the GCC, Iran, and Iraq. Since the 2000s, these relations have expanded in tandem with increasing trade and energy cooperation.

China and Persian Gulf Energy

Despite 2,200 years of political history, the PRC is a relative newcomer to the Persian Gulf region. It was not until the mid- to late nineteenth century that isolationist China developed some interest in the Persian Gulf.[3] In sharp contrast to European powers and Russia, China's interests and involvement in the region remained rather limited. In the first half of the twentieth century, China remained largely insulated from great power rivalry and eschewed colonial possession. It was preoccupied with its own nation building rather than with global events, let alone Middle East politics.[4]

For most of the Cold War, China avoided Gulf politics, although in the 1950s and 1960s, it sought to generate anticolonial sentiment in the region. While the United States and the Soviet Union were engaged in serious rivalry, China was barely into its industrial move and opening to the rest of the world. That would be launched in 1978 when the Chinese leadership, under Deng Xiaoping, implemented a policy of modernization and steered away from Marxist ideology to allow greater trade and commercial relations globally. This opening helped pave the way for the PRC's political penetration of the Middle East and for greater Chinese interest in regional dynamics.[5] Even so, while the United States was trying to stave off perceived Soviet gains in the Persian Gulf in the 1970s, the communist Chinese regime was still obsessed with trying to prevent its own predicted demise, and in that effort, it launched post–Mao reforms.[6]

It has only been since the end of the Cold War that China has dramatically increased its role and interest in the region, chiefly due to its overriding concern for economic growth.[7] While a major oil producer in its own right and a net oil exporter until the early 1990s, China has been a net importer of oil since 1993. In the 1980s, it had sufficient oil to run the domestic economy. But in that decade, industrialization expanded so quickly that China's oil fields, which would eventually be depleted, could not meet demand. Fueled by a booming economy, China's energy demand has skyrocketed, making it the world's second largest oil consumer behind the United States.[8] Indeed, in a span of only one decade, 2000 to 2010, China's oil consumption increased by 90 percent, or 4.3 mbd.[9]

The combination of rising oil demand and decreasing domestic oil production from depleted oil fields has resulted in increasing dependence on imports of foreign oil. In 2000, oil imports accounted for 29 percent of China's oil needs; by 2014, China imported nearly 60 percent of its oil consumption, or 6.2 mbd. With oil demand increasing by around 12 percent each year since 1980, the IEA projects that China's oil imports will increase to 80 percent by 2035.[10]

Skyrocketing oil consumption made China the world's second largest net oil importer in 2009, and in October 2013, it surpassed the United States as the world's largest importer of foreign oil. China's use of natural gas has also increased rapidly in the past fifteen years, making it a net importer of pipeline and liquefied natural gas (LNG).[11]

The political workings of the Chinese government are byzantine and opaque, but it is fair to say that Beijing's increasing dependence on foreign oil imports has made the Middle East critical to its energy security for several reasons. First, since 1996, more than half of China's imported oil has come from the Middle East, particularly the Persian Gulf. Specifically, oil imports from only four countries—Saudi Arabia, Iran, Iraq, and Oman—accounted for more than 70 percent of China's imports from the Middle East in 2014.

Second, China has no alternative to Middle East oil because the region holds nearly two-thirds of the world's proven crude oil reserves. It appears that global oil production will increasingly be concentrated in the Persian Gulf region.[12] As China's oil demand increases, so will its dependence on the Persian Gulf, despite its dogged efforts to diversify its energy partnerships and oil suppliers.

For China, access to energy resources will affect prospects for regime survival in the upcoming decades.[13] In its Tenth Five Year Plan (2001–2005), the Chinese government acknowledged explicitly, and for the first time publicly, that securing overseas oil supplies is essential to its continued economic growth and modernization.[14] That view has only become more prominent since then.

Third, rising energy dependence on oil exposes China to the risk of oil supply disruptions and oil price volatility on the global energy market—neither of which China can control. A disruption of China's supply of oil or skyrocketing prices could damage the economy and engender domestic unrest, possibly endangering the power of the regime. Consequently, trying to hedge against the vagaries of economic globalization, part of the PRC's strategy has been to penetrate the Gulf politically and economically while relying on the American security framework.

China's Strategy and Performance

In 2003, China formalized the so-called going-out strategy, an effort to mitigate any possible shortages of oil.[15] As part of this strategy, it has focused on developing diplomatic relations with regional states; selling arms partly for monetary reasons but also for greater influence in regional security affairs; and, as the next chapter will demonstrate, expanding its economic position in the region.

Diplomatic Relations

China's diplomatic successes in the region were aided by improving Sino-American relations in the 1970s, implementation of an "open and reform" policy in 1978, and the subsequent end of China's support for revolutionary movements. In 1970, China and Iran reestablished diplomatic relations, which had been broken off in 1949 following the establishment of the PRC, but it was not until the early 1980s that these relations improved significantly.[16]

In the 1980s, arms sales to Iran, Iraq, and Saudi Arabia became China's primary link to the region. It was not until 1990 that Beijing successfully established formal diplomatic relations with all Persian Gulf countries. Kuwait was the first Arab Gulf state to form diplomatic relations with China in 1971, followed by Oman in 1978, the UAE in 1984, Qatar in 1988, Bahrain in 1989, and Saudi Arabia in 1990. Despite the establishment of formal relations, it has been only in the past decade that these relations have broadened and deepened into unprecedented levels.

Sino-Saudi Diplomatic Relations   In the post–Cold War era and particularly in the past decade, China has dramatically expanded its diplomatic ties to Saudi Arabia, which were first established in the 1930s but cut after the establishment of communist China in 1949. Formal diplomatic relations were established in 1990, but it was not until 1998, when King Abdullah, then crown prince, visited China—the highest-level Saudi visit ever.[17] This was followed by President Jiang Zemin's first visit in 1999. Underscoring the centrality of mutual energy interests, the two countries signed a strategic oil partnership in which Saudi Arabia agreed to open selected portions of its upstream energy sector to Chinese investment in return for China's opening its downstream and oil refinery sector.[18]

After about 2005, the frequency of high-ranking visits notably increased and focused more on energy cooperation. In January 2006, King Abdullah chose Beijing for his first state visit as a king, before making an official visit to any Western country.[19] It was the first visit by a Saudi king to China since 1990. During the visit, the two sides signed five agreements on cooperation in the areas of oil, natural gas, and minerals,[20] and Abdullah expressed interest in further bilateral cooperation in economy, energy and infrastructure, and cultural exchanges with China.[21] President Hu Jintao reciprocated the visit in April 2006 and was honored as one of the few foreign leaders ever to address the Shura, the Saudi consultative council that advises the king and cabinet.[22] During the visit, several energy agreements were signed that, according to King Abdullah, were intended to "write a new chapter of friendly cooperation with China in the twenty-first century."[23]

In response to the severe earthquake that hit China in May 2008, Saudi Arabia became the biggest donor to China in material.[24] In February 2009, President Hu traveled to Saudi Arabia for the second time, aiming to elevate the bilateral ties. During the visit, Hu asserted that "China attaches great importance to bilateral relations with Saudi Arabia and is ready to work with the Saudi side to deepen pragmatic cooperation."[25] In January 2012, Premier Wen Jiabao traveled to Saudi Arabia to discuss oil cooperation, as well as Iran, Syria, Iraq, and the Israeli-Palestinian peace process. Wen's visit, which came amid Washington's pressure on China to reduce its imports of Iranian oil, was part of his six-day tour through the region. During the visit, Wen called for strengthening cooperation with Saudi Arabia on major issues.[26] In May 2013, Xi underscored the importance of Saudi relations "no matter how the international situation changes," and suggested that China would not support an Iranian nuclear program that could pose a threat to the Gulf region.[27] The relations were further strengthened in March 2014 when Crown Prince Salman traveled to China for a four-day visit, the first visit of the crown prince to China.[28]

Sino-Iranian Diplomatic Relations   China and Iran share a long history of cultural, economic, and diplomatic ties, dating back to their precolonial empires.[29] Diplomatic ties were cut in 1949 following the formation of the PRC, reestablished in 1970, and elevated in the early 1980s on the anvil of mutual interests regarding the Iran-Iraq War (1980–1988), arms sales, nuclear cooperation, and balancing the superpowers.[30] Prior to the 1979 Iranian Revolution, bilateral relations were limited, partly due to the U.S. pressure on Iran to limit its economic and diplomatic ties with communist China.

The significance of the relationship has been reflected in mutual high-level visits. In June 1985 and May 1989, Ali Khamenei, president of Iran, met with Chinese leader Deng Xiaoping during his visit to China.[31] High-level visits continued during the 1990s. However, realizing that Chinese military assistance to Iran was straining Sino-American relations and possibly China's economic growth, Beijing diminished its cooperation with Iran on its nuclear and missile programs in 1997.[32]

The early 2000s witnessed the resumption of high-level cooperation between the two countries. Iran's president, Mohammad Khatami, visited China in June 2000, and in January 2001, Vice President Hu Jintao reciprocated. Relations received a boost when China joined the World Trade Organization in late 2001, which diminished U.S. leverage over Beijing, and by the revelation of Iran's uranium enrichment program in 2002, which led to Iran's gradual international isolation and thereby opened opportunities for China to fill the economic and diplomatic vacuum.[33] Beijing, however, had to carefully balance its ties with Iran and America so as not to anger Washington too much. Chinese presidential and prime ministerial visits to Iran ceased after the two visits made by Hu Jintao as vice president in January 2001 and Jiang Zemin as president in April 2002. Upon the election of Ahmadinejad as Iran's president in June 2005, the Chinese president did not travel to Iran and instead visited Abdullah of Jordan, who became king in August 2005. Beijing preferred to interact with Iran in the regional security forum of the Shanghai Cooperation Organization.[34] China's rising demand for energy and Iran's increasing isolation fueled cooperation, though amid serious differences.

In September 2014, two Chinese warships docked at Iran's naval port to conduct joint naval exercises in what was the first visit to Iran by Chinese naval ships.[35] A Chinese fleet commander, Rear Admiral Huang Xinjian, said the visit was intended to "deepen mutual understanding, and to enhance exchanges between our two countries' navies."[36]

In anticipation of the nuclear deal and lifting of sanctions against Iran, a senior delegation from Iran traveled to China in April 2015 to discuss China's existing investment in oil and gas projects in Iran. In July 2015, China praised the Iran deal as carrying a "win-win spirit."[37]

Sino-Iraqi Diplomatic Relations   The U.S.-led invasion of Iraq in 2003 paved the way for an unprecedented expansion of China's relations with post-Saddam Iraq. Sino-Iraqi diplomatic relations were established in 1958 but remained frosty until mid-1975, with Iraq leaning toward Soviet Union as opposed to China. Thereafter, China became more concerned about "Soviet designs in the region, and that made Iraq more important to China, while the Iran-Iraq war would make China more important to Iraq as an arms supplier."[38] International sanctions imposed on Iraq following the 1991 Gulf War further hindered an expansion of Sino-Iraqi relations.[39] China had condemned Iraq's invasion of Kuwait but assumed a neutral stance by abstaining from the U.N. Security Council's vote authorizing the use of force against Iraq. Later in the 1990s, China joined France and Russia in calling for the lifting of sanctions against Iraq, hoping to score energy contracts that had been in abeyance. In the lead-up to the 2003 war, China voted in favor of U.N. Resolution 1441, giving Iraq the last chance to comply, but in 2003 China joined Germany, France, and Russia in opposing the U.S. invasion.

It was not until the establishment of the Iraqi Interim Governing Council following the 2003 U.S.-led invasion that the two countries began to expand bilateral relations. The relations intensified in 2007 when Iraqi's president, Jalal Talabani, made the first official visit to China by an Iraqi president since the two countries established diplomatic relations in 1958.[40] Iraqi leaders encouraged Chinese companies to bid for oil contracts, and Hu committed to support and participate in the country's reconstruction process in the fields of energy, education, technology, and health.

In January 2010, China also agreed to write off 80 percent of Iraq's $8.5 billion Saddam Hussein–era debt in an effort to cultivate its business interests in the country and strengthen bilateral ties, and Beijing also granted Iraq $6.5 million for public health and development programs.[41] The deal was preceded by Iraq's award of two lucrative oil tenders to the state-run China National Petroleum Corporation (CNPC). Bilateral relations were further enhanced following U.S. withdrawal from Iraq in 2011. In April 2011, several Chinese companies cancelled or reduced Iraq's remaining debts.[42] Then in July 2011, Prime Minister Nouri Al-Maliki paid a visit to China, in what was the first visit of an Iraqi prime minister to China in over fifty years, and the two sides signed two agreements to build long-term cooperation in the oil and gas sector, electricity, and other fields.[43] The relations continued to develop under the new Iraqi leadership, with Prime Minister Haider al-Abadi visiting China in December 2015. During the visit, the two countries issued a joint statement upgrading their relationship to a strategic partnership that would provide "a solid foundation" for future bilateral relations.[44]

Broader Relations   China's diplomatic ties with the smaller GCC states have also expanded. In 1981, the PRC established diplomatic ties with the GCC bloc itself, and by 1996, the GCC and China established regular annual consultations to support increased economic and trade cooperation. In January 2004, China and the Arab League established the Sino-Arab Cooperation Forum to promote cooperation in political, trade, energy, and cultural affairs. On the occasion of the fifth ministerial meeting in May 2012, Vice Foreign Minister Zhai Jun asserted that the forum had "remarkably enhanced the overall level of China-Arab friendly cooperation."[45] The sixth ministerial meeting in June 2014, which marked the tenth anniversary since the launch of the Sino-Arab forum, was, according to Foreign Minister Wang Yi, "a significant move initiated by the Chinese government" and aimed to "build upon past achievements to shape the future."[46]

It is worthwhile taking a brief look at China's diplomatic trajectory with each GCC state. Of all GCC states, Kuwait and China enjoy the longest diplomatic relationship, established in 1971. Officials from both countries have made frequent visits since 1989. Kuwait had been China's largest supplier of preferential official loans, providing China with $620 million in loans on favorable terms between 1982 and the end of 2001. In 1991, Kuwait sought to sign a security agreement with China similar to the ten-year agreement that it had signed with the United States earlier that year, while also pledging its support to any efforts that China undertakes to guard its national sovereignty, including preventing Taiwan and Tibet from declaring independence.[47]

The relations intensified following the Kuwaiti prime minister's visit to China in 2004, during which the two countries signed three agreements on economic and technology cooperation, oil, and natural gas. In September 2008, China's foreign minister visited Kuwait and hailed cooperation with Kuwait and the GCC.[48] For his part, the Kuwaiti emir made his first visit to China in May 2009 during which Wen Jiabao sought to expand cooperation in trade, energy, infrastructure, and finance,[49] and expressed Beijing's eagerness to advance relations with the GCC.[50] The visit culminated in six signed agreements and memorandums of understanding in the fields of energy, education, communication, sports, and finance.[51] In April 2014, officials from the countries vowed to boost bilateral economic ties, with China calling for enhanced cooperation in constructing the Silk Road economic belt between the two regions.[52] In August 2014, state-run Kuwait Petroleum Corporation (KPC) and the China International Untied Petroleum and Chemicals Company signed the biggest-ever oil contract in KPC's history that will almost double crude oil deliveries over a decade.[53]

China and Bahrain expanded bilateral relations in the second half of the 2000s. Bahraini Prime Minister *Khalifa* visited China in May 2002, touching off myriad lower-level visits.[54] In May 2006, when Chinese Assistant Foreign Minister Li Zhaoxin visited Bahrain, Al Khalifa praised China's efforts at developing relations with all GCC member states and Arab countries,[55] as did other high-level Bahraini officials in September 2011.[56] Bahraini King Hamad visited China in September 2013, praising the visit as a "historic success."[57]

Officials from China and the UAE also initiated increasingly more important diplomatic exchanges.[58] In January 2012, Wen Jiabao's visit to Saudi Arabia, UAE, and Qatar was the first ever paid by a Chinese premier to the UAE and Qatar. Vice President Xi Jinping assessed the deal as marking "a new stage of China-UAE relations."[59] During the visits, the two sides agreed to increase bilateral trade and energy business and expand cooperation in banking, military industry, and energy.[60] In March 2012, Xi Jinping met with the UAE's crown prince in Beijing to strengthen the bilateral strategic partnership, launching subsequent visits aimed at developing cooperation in the areas of economy, energy, and culture.[61]

Wen's January 2012 visit to Saudi Arabia, UAE, and Qatar, in what constituted the first visit ever paid by a Chinese premier to Qatar, coincided with a 45 percent increase in Sino-Qatari trade within just one year.[62] During the visit, Wen emphasized the importance of energy to Sino-Qatari relations, stating that "establishing a long-term, stable and comprehensive partnership with Qatar on natural gas is an important topic between us."[63] Wen's visit was reciprocated by Qatar's prime minister later the same year. In November 2014 President Xi Jinping and the emir of Qatar, Sheikh Tamim Bin Hamad al-Thani, announced the establishment of a strategic partnership aimed at boosting economic ties and mutual support on issues involving sovereignty and territorial integrity.[64]

The PRC has also sought to enhance relations with Oman, as illustrated in 2010 when China's top political adviser visited Oman to promote "mutual trust and [cooperation] in trade, energy and culture" and "inject new vitality to bilateral relations."[65] During the visit, the two countries signed four agreements on cooperation in the economic, trade, and cultural areas, and Oman's deputy prime minister noted that Oman views China, its largest trading partner, as a major strategic partner.[66]

It is important to stress that although China needs the Gulf states much more than before, the opposite is not untrue. That means that a synergy of overlapping interests has developed. For example, GCC states and Iraq increasingly see China as a possible alternative to Washington at some level, which, if it continues, could yield the PRC greater ability to soft-balance against the United States. The American energy boom has accelerated concerns about

America's commitment to regional security. Moreover, unlike America, which pushes democracy in the region, China is uninterested in influencing domestic politics. Beijing is not as politically radioactive domestically in the Gulf as America, given its hegemonic narrative and support of Israel.

The Security Dimension
China's diplomatic successes in the region have created some potential for security gains, but Beijing's capabilities are not strong.

China's Limited Military Capability   In contrast to the United States, and to some extent Britain, France, and Russia, the PRC has never had military bases, access agreements, and pre-positioning sites in the area or access to regional facilities.[67] Moreover, although all of China's imported oil from the Persian Gulf is delivered by tanker, Beijing is decades away from being able to project serious naval and air projection capabilities to influence developments in the region and to be able to protect the 7,000 miles of sea-lanes between Shanghai and the Strait of Hormuz in the Persian Gulf.

To be sure, China's growing need for energy, especially from the Gulf, has motivated it to improve the military means to protect its transport sea lanes, from Chinese seaports all the way to the Persian Gulf region and the Horn of Africa.[68] And some leaders in Beijing have argued for a much stronger military capability for protecting China's sea-lanes and oil interests. As political scientist Tom Christensen points out, at the global level, China has "long sought to affect the psychology of a militarily superior US and its regional allies by posing potentially costly military challenges to forward deployed US forces."[69]

However, while Beijing has an interest in increasing its military reach into the Persian Gulf, its actions so far have not been significant. Consider several of these actions. In February 2013, China and Pakistan concluded an agreement that grants China the operating rights to the Gwadar port facilities in western Pakistan, along the Arabian Sea and near the Strait of Hormuz.[70] In 2012, China rejected Pakistan's offer to build a naval base in Gwadar, preferring to keep it nonmilitary; nevertheless, the Gwadar deal signals Beijing's growing interest in the Persian Gulf.[71] It will allow China to monitor maritime traffic and naval activities in the Gulf and Indian Ocean and provide China with a transit terminal for crude oil imports from Iran and Africa to China's Xinjiang region.

In September 2014, China held joint naval exercises with Iran that involved Chinese warships for the first time ever in the Persian Gulf, which were involved in the PRC's role in antipiracy outside the Gulf region. This exercise was meaningful. It sent a strong political message that Iran was important to China for energy reasons and that Beijing could play some role in the Gulf, even if dwarfed by America's vaunted position. China's role is minor, but when combined with its arms sales to Iran, it suggests a potential for greater mutual security cooperation, especially if the lifting of sanctions on Iran holds over time. Some observers have also interpreted this move to be a counterbalance to America's "pivot to Asia" policy, which aimed chiefly at bolstering Washington's alliances in the region, partly to contain China.[72] However, it would take a more elaborate and repeated set of actions by China to reach that conclusion.

The role of China's navy in sustained multiyear antipiracy operations in the Gulf of Aden puts it near oil supply routes to Asia. These activities, which include port calls in the Persian Gulf, marginally boost Beijing's strategic position and underscore its interest in some influence in the Gulf. Such strategic actions augment the PRC's growing diplomatic and economic clout in the region.

It is conceivable that the PRC could substantially improve its military position near the region in the coming decades. For example, China's ties to Saudi Arabia have improved over time on the anvil of its 1999 strategic oil partnership. While the Saudis have so far declined to engage in more significant strategic cooperation with Beijing at the risk of straining relations with Washington, that could change if Saudi-American relations decline significantly and America is perceived to be less committed to Gulf security and Saudi stability. Iran may also become more forthcoming to a larger Chinese role in the future. While such developments are possible, they are not likely to change the regional balance of power for a long time, even if they do transpire.

Arms Sales   The PRC's performance in the area of arms sales is uneven in the region, with gains achieved mainly with Iran. In fact, while America's arms sales to regional states increased dramatically, China's declined in the post–Cold War period.

In the 1990s and even more so in the 2000s, energy cooperation became the fulcrum of Sino-Gulf relations, but during the 1980s, arms sales were central. China entered the Gulf arms market during the Iran-Iraq War, with arms sales to both parties totaling over $12 billion. These sales provided China with hard currency to modernize its own military program.[73] Although the PRC developed a limited arms trade with Saudi Arabia and some of the smaller Arab Gulf states, its arms link to Iran has been the most developed and worrisome to the United States.

In 1985, China and Iran concluded an agreement under which China would sell Iran missile technology, and in 1986 China sold Iran Silkworm antiship missiles. This raised concerns in Washington because Iran could use missile technology to obstruct oil tanker traffic in the narrow Strait of Hormuz. This is a bottleneck 34 miles wide, through which around 40 percent of the world's seaborne oil exports flows each day, a number that is projected to increase to 60 percent by 2030 as global oil demand rises and oil reserves fall.[74] China sold Iran tactical ballistic and antiship cruise missiles, including C-802 and Silkworm missiles that Iran deployed against Kuwaiti shipping in 1987.[75] Under American pressure, China discontinued sales of the sophisticated missiles to Iran, but it continued to assist Iran in military modernization efforts, with Chinese design and technology being detected in the Iranian short-range Oghab and Nazeat missiles and the long-range Shahab 3.

The PRC's arms sales to the Gulf states fell significantly after peaking in 1988 largely because Western suppliers dominated the market with more competitive military hardware.[76] Indeed, after the Iran-Iraq War, arms sales to the region dropped by about 40 percent, although the Middle East remained China's most lucrative arms market, accounting for over 50 percent of China's total arms exports.[77] Between 1994 and 1997, China's arms agreements in the Middle East accounted for around 3.5 percent of region's total agreements.[78] By 2001, the arms agreements with the region had fallen to around 2.2 percent and then increased to approximately 4 percent of the region's total agreements from 2004 and 2007.[79] From 2008 to 2011, China's share of the region's total arms agreements decreased to an all-time low of 1 percent.[80]

Despite the substantial drop in China's share of arms transfers in the 1990s, such sales remain troubling to Washington, especially in the case of Iran, which has remained the primary recipient of China's arms. Between 1985 and 1996, China supported Iran's nuclear program with various types of nuclear technology, assistance in uranium exploration, mining, the use of lasers for uranium enrichment, training of Iranian nuclear engineers, and establishing the Esfahan Nuclear Research Center, which has been critical in the development of Iran's nuclear program.[81] In 1997 China ceased nuclear assistance to Iran to placate Washington, but the United States has continued to suspect Chinese companies of providing dual-use technology to Iran, possibly without the knowledge of the Chinese government.[82]

Moreover, an unclassified Pentagon review from 2010 revealed that both China and North Korea had assisted Iran "in developing and expanding its missile program," and in January 2011, David Albright, president of the Institute for Science and International Security, noted that while the United States and Europe had developed export-control networks to prevent sales of dual-use materials to Iranian companies, "a large amount" of dual-use technology in China continued to reach Iranian buyers.[83] The PRC also reportedly helped Iran develop the antiship cruise missile Nasr, which bears resemblance to the Chinese C-704, and in 2010 assisted in establishing a plant for manufacturing the Nasr.[84] China has been also alleged to have transferred ballistic missile technology to Iran through North Korea.[85]

While U.S. arms sales to the GCC members and particularly Saudi Arabia have increased dramatically, the PRC had trouble penetrating Saudi Arabia's arms market. During the 2000s, the kingdom bought only $800 million worth of arms from China, which sharply contrasts with over $50 billion Saudi Arabia spent on American arms imports between 2004 and 2011.[86] In January 2012 and again in August 2014, the two countries signed an agreement to jointly develop nuclear energy to meet the kingdom's rising energy demands, raising suspicions that Saudi Arabia may be positioning itself for developing nuclear weapons to counter Iran's nuclear program.[87]

Conclusion

Events in the Middle East made it harder for the administration of President Barack Obama to focus on the "pivot to Asia" strategy, though Washington has pivoted to some extent. Beijing has launched its own pivot—toward the Persian Gulf. That pivot has occurred politically; more modestly in a security sense; and, as the next chapter shows, far more profoundly in terms of trade and energy. Beijing's diplomatic penetration has generated some potential that it would also gain in security capabilities in the region, but compared to Washington, China lacks the military infrastructure in the region and the force projection to the region that is crucial for influencing events. Beijing appears committed to improving its force projection, but that will take many years, and perhaps decades, to execute seriously.

We must also consider a countervailing effect. As China has risen in the region, it has competed with Washington economically and might do so in the future at the security level. At the same time, it has become more interested in preserving oil security, which cannot easily be achieved if the United States is weakened in the region. A weaker or more distant America may not as effectively protect oil supplies and moderate oil prices. That would pose a threat to the PRC's economy and one that might well outweigh the benefits of any serious rivalry with Washington in the region, certainly in the coming years, if not much longer. China therefore may well be limited in just how aggressive it can be in challenging the United States. In this sense, interdependence can serve as a stabilizing force.

6 Global Oil and
China's Economic Penetration

THE PERSIAN GULF has become critical to China's grand plan to reinvent itself economically and to ascend the world stage as a great power—one possibly on par with the United States in the future.[1] So far, we have shown how Beijing has improved its political position in the region, and to some extent its security standing, but how has China's economic position changed in the Persian Gulf?

The major evolution of China's diplomacy has helped catapult it economically in the Persian Gulf. Beijing's trade and energy cooperation has skyrocketed in a very short period of time, and it has also exercised nascent elements of mercantilism, which we discuss in this chapter. The Chinese narrative has differed sharply from that of the United States. Most important, the rise of the PRC's diplomatic and economic profile has not been accompanied by a regional military presence or meaningful security cooperation. But its enhanced economic position represents a profound change in the region. Moreover, growing interdependence with regional states has given China an interest in not taking actions to generate regional instability that could annoy these states and might threaten oil security. All things equal, the more China needs the region for oil and trade, the more secure is oil.

Broad Patterns in Sino-GCC Economic Interaction

The data are indisputable and quite telling: growing economic interdependence between China and the Gulf has been reflected in increasing trade, mutual investments, and a multitude of joint ventures and construction projects (Figure 6.1).

China's share of GCC trade increased from less than 2 percent in 1992 to over 11 percent in 2012.[2] Similarly, although the European Union (EU) remains the biggest GCC trading partner, its share of GCC trade decreased from 24 percent in 1992 to 13 percent in 2012. Between 2010 and 2013 alone, GCC trade with China grew more rapidly than with any other significant trade partner, at a rate of 30 percent for export and 17 percent for imports.[3]

These changes reflect a larger shift in the trade pattern that began in the 1990s and accelerated in the 2000s. In 1980, North American and Western European countries accounted for almost 85 percent of all GCC trade, but by 2012, Asia had become the GCC's largest trading partner, accounting for around 57 percent of GCC total foreign trade. In 2013, trade with the GCC states represented 70 percent of all Sino-Arab trade.[4]

China may become the GCC's most important economic partner by 2020,[5] especially given that American and European oil demand is projected to remain flat or decrease due to alternative energy sources, increased energy efficiency, and the shale oil boom. The American energy boom is also driving Persian Gulf countries closer to China and not just vice versa. American oil imports from the Gulf will continue to drop as long as the boom is in motion. Arab oil producers are looking to Asia for a growing market, and China has

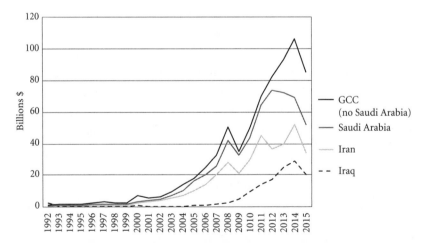

FIGURE 6.1. Total Trade between China and the Persian Gulf States, 1992–2015.
SOURCE: Created by the authors with data drawn from U.N. Commodity Trade Statistics Database (New York: United Nations, various years).

the deep pockets to help build infrastructure in the Middle East. In addition, Western countries are increasingly focused on climate change problems and sustainable energy practices. Some in Saudi Arabia see a "wave of hostility from some western countries under the guise of energy security, protecting the environment and fighting global warming."[6] Whatever one thinks of this Saudi perception, it makes China more palatable as a partner than it was in the past because Beijing is not viewed as pushing a climate change agenda.

The GCC and China, however, are concerned with more than the free flow of oil from the Persian Gulf. The oil-rich GCC states have also become a growing export market for Chinese goods and a bidirectional flow of foreign direct investment (FDI) has also been growing.

Sino-Saudi Economic and Energy Relations

The PRC's economic ties with Saudi Arabia developed recently but have grown immensely. To put this in perspective, when the two countries reestablished diplomatic relations in 1990, energy played a minuscule role, and bilateral trade totaled only $296 million. By 2014, trade between the two countries stood at $70 billion, up from $43 billion in 2010, as Saudi Arabia became China's largest trading partner in the Middle East. Saudi Arabia has been China's top crude oil supplier for the past decade. Oil lies at the center of the bilateral trade relations, which has also gained critical importance in terms of security. The House Saud has repeatedly reassured Beijing of precisely what it wants to know: that it can rely on Saudi oil to fuel China's continued economic growth.

The rise in oil trade is astonishing. While in 1995, Saudi oil accounted for only 2 percent of China's oil imports, by 2002 Saudi Arabia became China's largest supplier of crude oil, supplying around 20 percent of China's oil every year since then. In absolute terms, China's oil imports from Saudi Arabia grew twenty-four times in only a decade, increasing from only 50,000 barrels per day (bpd) in 1999, to 455,000 bpd in 2005, surpassing 1 mbd in for the first time in 2009, reaching 1.2 mbd in 2012 though decreasing to 993,000 bpd in 2014.[7] In 2009 China surpassed the United States as Saudi Arabia's number one oil customer while U.S. imports from Saudi Arabia fell below 1 mbd for the first time in twenty years (Figure 6.2).[8]

Energy relations took off in the late 1990s. In 1998, the two countries concluded their first oil contract, and Saudi Aramco opened a subsidiary office, Saudi Petroleum Ltd., in Beijing to oversee sales and marketing, despite the low volumes of oil that China was importing.[9] During Jiang Zemin's visit to Saudi Arabia in

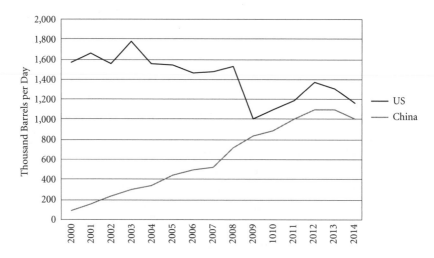

FIGURE 6.2.   Saudi Arabia's Oil Exports to China and the United States, 2000–2014.

SOURCE: U.S. data obtained from U.S. Energy Information Administration, Petroleum & Other Liquids database. Chinese data from *Chinese Statistical Yearbook* (Beijing: Customs General Administration of the People's Republic of China, various years).

1999, the two countries fostered a strategic oil partnership that allowed China to invest in the Saudi market, excluding upstream oil production and exploration,[10] and key Saudi business leaders asserted that the PRC would become a premier energy growth partner.[11] They, along with Saudi energy officials,[12] repeatedly reassured China about guaranteed oil supplies to Beijing,[13] while Sinopec chairman Fu Chengyu underscored that "China needs energy to fuel its economic growth," and the kingdom "needs a reliable market."[14] But as Khalid al-Falih, the president and chief executive of Saudi Aramco noted, it would be a mistake to see these relations "exclusively through the narrow lens of energy supply security ... because increasingly they have diversified beyond that arena."[15] Sino-Saudi economic relations have gradually become more multifaceted, extending to industrial collaboration and cross-investments within and beyond the oil industry.

The 1999 strategic oil agreement has facilitated mutual cross-investments and joint ventures in refining, petrochemical sector, infrastructure projects, and petroleum technical service cooperation. In 2001, Saudi Aramco, ExxonMobil, and Sinopec agreed to build a refinery in Qingdao in eastern Shandong province and expand the capacity of a petrochemical plant in Quanzhou in Fujian province. As part of the deal, China allowed Saudi Aramco to open 600 gas stations in the province in exchange for a thirty-year supply contract for 30,000 bpd of Saudi oil. The refinery, which opened in November 2009 and in which Aramco invested some $750 million, triples the capacity of the Fujian plant to process Saudi heavy crude oil from 80,000 bpd to 240,000 bpd.[16] The two countries also concluded an agreement under which Aramco would supply the Fujian government with 30,000 bpd of oil for the next thirty years, thereby securing a long-term outlet for its crude.[17] Meanwhile, Chinese companies have also sought to acquire and expand their foothold in Saudi Arabia's downstream and upstream. For instance, in 2004, China's oil company Sinopec secured a ten-year contract with Saudi Aramco to explore the natural gas field in Saudi Arabia's al-Khali Basin, an area that Saudi Arabia has opened to foreign firms for the first time in twenty-five years.[18]

The energy cooperation intensified after King Abdullah's visit to China in 2006, the first ever by the Saudi monarch to China. During the visit, the two countries signed five new energy cooperation agreements, including a memorandum on oil, natural gas, and mineral cooperation. The kingdom also agreed to help China build its own strategic petroleum reserve on Hainan Island.[19] Largely thanks to this deal, China's strategic oil reserves reached an estimated 91 million barrels by November 2014.[20]

When President Hu Jintao reciprocated the visit in 2009, the two countries signed five additional agreements expanding economic cooperation, including the first major nonhydrocarbon deal worth $1.8 billion under which the China Railway Construction Cooperation would build a high-speed rail between the holy cities Mecca and Medina.[21] The same year, Saudi SABIC was awarded a contract to help develop a $3 billion petrochemical complex at Tianjin, and in 2011, Aramco and CNPC's subsidiary, PetroChina, signed an agreement under which Aramco would develop and supply 200,000 bpd oil refinery in China's Yunnan province. Aramco will supply oil through a $2 billion oil and natural gas pipeline from Myanmar, halving shipping time from Saudi Arabia to China.[22] In 2010, Saudi Aramco's board of directors unprecedentedly chose China for their meeting, further signaling growing energy links.[23] In 2012, Aramco opened Aramco Asia in Beijing, and during Wen Jiabao's visit to Saudi Arabia the same year, Sinopec was awarded its first major investment in Saudi Arabia's oil sector to build an oil refinery in Yanbu.[24] The 400,000 bpd refinery shipped its first diesel cargo in January 2015.[25]

China would like to gain a foothold in the kingdom's oil upstream, but Chinese NOCs have so far been able to provide only engineering and maintenance services and natural gas development assistance, as the kingdom sought to keep its upstream closed to foreign investment.[26] Similarly, despite increased energy cooperation, the Yanbu refinery is the only downstream project China has secured in Saudi Arabia so far.

For its part, China has been eager to attract Saudi investment to its refining industry to secure a stable supply of Saudi oil, while Riyadh has sought to invest in China's oil industry to solidify its status as a major oil provider to China. As part of its economic diversification strategy, Saudi Arabia strives to expand sales of refined products in China and gain access to China's downstream. Over the past two decades, Saudi Aramco has developed from principally an oil and gas producer to an integrated company with significant refining, shipping, and distribution assets. Similarly, Saudi Basic Industries Corporation boosted regional sales and marketing infrastructure with offices in China and Asia at large.[27] In 2009, SABIC's CEO, Mohammed al-Mady, noted that "SABIC's growth in China has no limits, especially when the Chinese market is currently the world's biggest for petrochemical products."[28] Despite the increased investment in petrochemicals and oil refining over the past decade, the extent of the investment and collaboration on refining and other energy projects remains small. A refinery in Fujian, a joint venture between Sinopec and Saudi Aramco, and Sinopec's Yanbu refinery in Saudi Arabia were the only two up-and-running plants in 2015.[29]

Although oil-related cooperation drives Sino-Saudi economic interaction, the two countries agreed to cooperate in renewable energy during Premier Jiabao's visit to the kingdom in 2012.[30] Saudi Arabia aims to diversify energy sources to decrease domestic oil consumption, which has been annually growing by 7 to 8 percent, and it plans to invest $100 billion in sixteen nuclear reactors by 2030. China will contribute in areas such as development and maintenance of nuclear power plants and research reactors, as well as the supply of nuclear fuel components. The Saudi atomic and renewable energy body has already signed nuclear cooperation deals with countries able to build reactors, including the United States, France, Russia, South Korea, and Argentina.[31]

While Sino-Saudi trade relations and economic cooperation increased unprecedentedly in the post–Cold War period and in the past decade in particular, such interaction faces limits. China's trade with Saudi Arabia accounted for less than 2 percent of China's total trade in 2014. At the same time, while Saudi Arabia's exports to China consist mostly of oil, chemicals, and plastics, the PRC's exports to Saudi Arabia consist of low-value goods. In contrast, U.S.

exports to Saudi Arabia are dominated by high-tech goods. Mutual trade is booming, but as Yang Guang of the Chinese Academy of Social Studies notes, neither Saudi Arabia nor China sees "attracting capital as their chief goal. . . . Both are seeking technological know-how. However, neither has the expertise the other wants."[32]

The United States, not China, has remained Saudi Arabia's largest source of coveted FDI, representing more than 25 percent of all FDI in the kingdom. Saudi Arabia's share of China's total global outward investment between 2005 and 2013 was only 2.2 percent.[33] Gulf capital flows into China are hampered by Chinese capital controls, which have impeded the Gulf's sovereign wealth funds from building large portfolios in China. China also has much higher investment stakes in the U.S. energy sector than in Saudi Arabia. Between 2005 and 2014, China's investment in the U.S. energy sector totaled nearly $16 billion ($36 billion in Canada's energy sector), compared to $8 billion in the Saudi energy sector.[34] There have been other limits to economic cooperation too. Although Riyadh guaranteed China a reliable oil supply, the kingdom keeps its upstream closed to foreign investment. That prevents China from securing stakes in equity oil. Such stakes are valuable because they would allow Chinese NOCs to bypass the global oil market and ship oil from Saudi Arabia directly to China.

The two states have also had differences over key projects. For example, the biggest infrastructure project, a much-heralded Chinese-built railway between Mecca and the holy sites of Mina and Mount Arafat, ended in a dispute. China Railways threatened to sue the Saudi authorities for the losses it made on the investment due to problems over the allocation of land, cost overruns, and workers' riots.[35]

Sino-Iraqi Economic and Energy Relations

By the end of 2014, three years after President Barack Obama officially declared the Iraq War over, Chinese NOCs, mainly CNPC, and not U.S. companies, have been operating three fields in southern Iraq and producing more than 50 percent of Iraqi oil output. That is a major story that underscores Beijing's opportunistic and rising role. U.S.-led forces liberated Iraq at enormous cost, but China, which opposed the ill-advised war, benefited greatly in the oil sector.

Iraq's potential for oil production is enormous given its vast, largely undeveloped reserves. The IEA projects that Iraq will account for 40 percent of global oil supply growth over the next two decades, making it the second largest global oil exporter,[36] and that by 2035, Iraq will produce 8 mbd, with about 80 percent of its future oil exports going to Asia, mainly to China. Nearly a third of the future oil production in Iraq is projected to come from fields that either are directly owned or co-led by Chinese companies.

In the post-Saddam period and particularly since 2009, China's trade and cooperation in energy with Iraq have also expanded unprecedentedly. The U.N. sanctions imposed on Iraq after the 1991 Gulf War deflated Sino-Iraqi trade, but by the end of the 1990s, trade increased as a result of the U.N. Oil-for-Food program. In an effort to ensure long-term access to Iraqi oil, the PRC successfully negotiated several major oil deals with Saddam Hussein's regime. In 1997, CNPC, along with China North Industries Corp., signed a $1.2 billion contract to develop Iraqi's al-Ahdab oil field in southern Iraq, and in 1998 the two sides initiated negotiations for the Halfayad field. However, the realization of the prospective contracts depended on the removal of U.N. sanctions. In 1998, China and Iraq signed the largest oil contract under the Oil-for-Food program, but at the time that the United States launched Operation Iraqi Freedom in 2003, Iraqi oil accounted for less than 1 percent of China's total oil imports.[37]

Before the 2003 invasion, Iraq's oil industry deteriorated under U.N. sanctions. After sanctions ended, the industry experienced a slow but checkered recovery, and Iraq eventually overtook Iran as OPEC's second-largest oil producer. Since 2012, Iraq has been producing oil at the highest rate since Saddam Hussein seized power in 1979, and in 2013 it surpassed Iran in oil exports to China. Between 2009 and 2013, Iraq's exports to China more than tripled, to account for more than 8 percent of China's total oil imports. Iraq may challenge Angola as China's second largest oil supplier behind Saudi Arabia.[38]

In serious need of investments after a decade of the Iran-Iraq War and then U.N. sanctions, Iraq opened its upstream to foreign companies. Since 2009, Chinese companies have gradually become top players in the Iraqi oil sector. Although all oil contracts and negotiations were suspended following the U.S.-led invasion of Iraq in 2003, China's CNPC renegotiated the $3 billion oil service contract for the major al-Ahdab oil field signed under Saddam—Iraq's first oil contract to a foreign oil company since Saddam's overthrow.[39] In Iraq's first oil field auction in June 2009, China's CNPC, in partnership with British Petroleum, also won a contract to develop Iraq's biggest oil field in Basra from 985,000 bpd to 2.85 million bpd within seven years at a cost of $15 billion, which would make it the world's second largest oil field behind

Saudi Arabia's Ghawar.[40] In December 2009, the CNPC, in a consortium with France's Total and Malaysia's Petronas, secured a contract to increase production of the Halfaya oil field from 3,100 bpd to 535,000 bpd.[41] Moreover, in May 2010, China National Offshore Oil Corporation (CNOOC) and Turkey's TPAO were awarded a contract to raise production at the Maysan complex of fields located along Iraq's border with Iran from 100,000 bpd to 450,000 bpd.[42] In addition, China's Sinopec, along with ENI, Oxy, and Kogas, won the bid for increasing capacity of the Zubair field to 1.125 million bpd.

China's projects in Iraq could potentially increase the PRC's access to almost 1.9 mbd, turning Iraq into the PRC's largest supplier of crude oil by 2020. Foreshadowing China's even greater role in the Iraqi energy sector, PetroChina in August 2013 confirmed it was negotiating with ExxonMobil to codevelop the Iraqi West Qurna 1 oil field which holds oil reserves worth $50 billion.[43] The deal materialized in December 2013 when PetroChina bought a 25 percent share for $590 million from ExxonMobil, further increasing its stake in one of Iraq's largest oil fields to 32.7 percent in May 2014 when it bought another 7.7 percent for an additional $442 million.[44] The deal makes the Chinese company the biggest single foreign investor in the Iraqi oil industry. The company has also been holding talks with Lukoil OAO Holdings, Russia's second-biggest oil producer, over joint development of the currently stalled West Qurna-2 project after Norwegian oil company Statoil ASA sold its 18.75 percent stake in 2012.[45] Lukoil head Vagi Alekperov told Reuters in January 2013 that an "attractive partner for us would be China, where there is stable demand growth."[46]

While Lukoil still continued to be the sole operator as of July 2015, holding a 75 percent stake, Iraq's cabinet approved a $526.6 million drilling deal with China's Zhongman for the West Qurna-2 oil field in May 2015.[47] Due to its enormous and almost untapped potential, the West Qurna field is crucial to Iraq's goal of increasing oil production from about 3 mbd to 12 mbd by 2017, surpassing Russia's production of 10 mbd and rivaling Saudi Arabia's 12.5 mbd. In July 2015, Anton Oilfield Services Group (Antonoil), a top oil field services provider in China, was awarded a $140 million contract for work on more than 160 wells.[48]

Chinese state-owned companies have invested more than $2 billion a year to rehabilitate Iraq's oil sector, while also sending hundreds of workers to post-Saddam Iraq.[49] In 2013, China built an airport near the Iranian border to ferry its workers to Iraq's southern oil fields. The three Iraqi oil fields, al-Ahdab, Halfaya, and Rumaila (along with Majid-e-Suleiman and North Azadegan oil fields in Iran), are a cornerstone of China's CNPC growth plans; it aims to almost triple its foreign production from 1.5 mbd in 2009 to 4 mbd in 2020, to make up for falling Chinese domestic production from mature fields.[50]

China's expanded role in the Iraqi oil industry has been facilitated by its willingness to accept poor contract terms. The Iraqi Oil Ministry offers foreign operators as little as $2 per barrel produced. Since Chinese national oil companies, unlike Western IOCs, are not accountable to shareholders, they can tolerate minimal profits.[51] For instance, the CNPC-Total-Petronas consortium accepted a remuneration fee of only $1.40 per barrel, and CNOOC-TPAO agreed to develop the Maysan fields for a fee of $2.30 per barrel.[52] Meanwhile, other companies, such as ExxonMobil, have moved to secure separate deals with Iraq's semiautonomous Kurdish region, whose terms are more generous but which the Iraqi central government considers illegal.

China has expanded its commercial activity in Iraq well beyond its sizable role in Iraq's oil and gas sector. For example, in 2010, China's Shanghai Electric started work on a $1 billion power plant project in Iraq.[53] The power plant is projected to increase Iraq's electricity capacity by 1,320 MW. In December 2013, China Communications Construction Company was awarded a $156 million sewage treatment project.[54]

Of course, security, political, and infrastructure constraints in Iraq have impeded and will likely continue to stymie its progress, making such predictions far too rosy. And the evolution of the role of the Islamic State in Iraq within the context of sectarian strife adds another major wild card that should give any optimist serious pause.

Economic and Energy Relations between China and Small GCCs

Trade with other GCC countries has also increased substantially in the post–Cold War period and particularly in the last decade. The UAE is China's greatest nonhydrocarbon trade partner in the Persian Gulf. In 2012, China's exports to the UAE accounted for 75 percent of total Sino-UAE trade, primarily made up of Chinese textiles and machinery. Trade between the two countries increased from only $608 million in 1992 to $10 billion in 2005, reaching over $55 billion in 2014, making China Dubai's second largest import partner, with Dubai securing the position of China's twelfth largest export market.[55] The presence of Chinese companies in Dubai increased from 18 in 2005 to around 3,000 in 2014, with some of the companies serving the local market and others using Dubai as a regional base.[56]

Sino-Qatari trade also rapidly expanded from $77 million in 1992, to $1 billion in 2007, reaching over $10 billion in 2014. China's increasing demand for natural gas accounts for most of the increase, with China's imports accounting for nearly 90 percent of total Sino-Qatari trade in 2014. While in 2008, 80 percent of China's LNG imports was sourced from Australia, Qatar had overtaken Australia as China's largest supplier in 2012, accounting for 34 percent of LNG imports.[57] After 2005, the two countries expanded cooperation in the energy sector. In late 2009, Qatargas set up a representative office in Beijing to market Qatari gas to other Chinese companies. In May 2010, PetroChina signed a thirty-year agreement with Qatar Petroleum and Shell to jointly develop natural gas in Qatar's Block D.[58] In March 2012, Qatar signed with China a memorandum on promoting bilateral energy cooperation.[59] Sino Petro and China Offshore Oil Engineering Corporation are also engaged in the exploration of natural gas in Qatar.[60]

Qatar has come to play an important role in meeting China's increasing natural gas consumption. Driven by fast economic growth, China became a net importer of natural gas in 2007, and since then, gas imports have increased on average by more than 60 percent annually.[61] China opened its first regasification plant in 2006; by July 2015 it had built eleven LNG receiving terminals, and now it is building eight new regasification plants with a total capacity of 23.8 MT.[62] These projects suggest a further increase in seaborne LNG imports in coming years. Beijing's greater focus on cleaner energy has driven projections that it will triple the use of natural gas to top 300 billion cubic meters by 2020, and nearly a third of that would be imported.[63] While in the long term, the development of China's enormous shale gas reserves could boost domestic gas output, there remain significant technological obstacles and environmental concerns over shale gas extraction in China.

Trade relations with Oman also improved. Trade increased from $455 million in 1992 to $1 billion in 2002, reaching $26 billion in 2014.[64] China's imports of Omani oil account for nearly 90 percent of the overall Sino-Omani trade, and in 2012, nearly 50 percent, or 382,000 bpd, of Omani oil exports went to China.[65] In 2012 and 2013 alone, China's oil imports from Oman increased by 26 percent, reaching 477,000 bpd in 2013 and accounting for nearly 50 percent of Omani's total oil export.[66] This made Oman the third largest supplier to China in 2013, up from seventh in 2012.[67] In 2014, Oman accounted for 10 percent of China's oil imports.[68] China's CNPC also secured 50 percent of an upstream concession in Omani oil sector.[69]

Sino-Iranian Economic and Energy Relations

Sino-Iranian trade relations have expanded significantly since 2000. Iran became China's second biggest trading partner in the Persian Gulf for most of the past decade. While the UAE has been China's largest nonhydrocarbon trade partner in the region, Iran has been one of the Beijing's top sources of imported oil from the region since the early 1990s.

During the 1990s, Germany, Italy, and France were Iran's biggest trading partners, but the Iranian nuclear stand-off and the ensuing international sanctions hurt this trade. In 2003, China was Iran's sixth biggest trading partner, but Beijing gradually filled this vacuum and overtook the EU as Iran's largest oil customer and trading partner in 2007.[70] Indeed, while other countries curtailed activities with Iran, Sino-Iranian trade and investment ties expanded significantly.[71]

Iran has been one of China's top suppliers of crude oil since the mid-1990s, accounting on average for 10 percent of its oil imports, although they have fallen since 2010. Due to sanctions, Iran dropped from being the fourth largest oil supplier to China in 2012 to the sixth position in 2014, but still accounting for 9 percent of China's oil imports.[72] That should change if the lifting of sanctions sticks in the coming years.

China has also established and expanded its role in Iran's upstream. In March 2004, China's state-owned oil company, Zhuhai Zhenrong Corporation, signed a twenty-five-year deal to import 110 million tons of LNG from Iran. In 2004, China's CNPC bought Canada's Sheer Energy subsidiary and gained the rights to develop Masjid-e-Soleyman oil field. In this $80 million project, China plans to bring on stream 25,000 bpd.[73]

China's NOCs have also filled the investment vacuum in Iran's upstream energy sector following the withdrawal of Asian and European energy companies and gradually became the dominant investor in Iran's oil and gas sector. This has made Iran more dependent on Chinese investment and technology.[74] In 2007, China's Sinopec finalized a $2 billion deal to develop the Yadavaran oil field with a goal to bring 300,000 bpd on stream. In 2009, CNOOC concluded a $16 billion deal to develop the North Pars offshore gas field, and that same year, CNPC won a deal to develop northern part of massive Azadegan oil field;[75] in 2010, it replaced Japan's Inpex to develop the entire field on its own.[76]

In 2011, China has also become Iran's largest petrochemicals export market, worth $1.7 billion.[77] Iran has also sought Chinese investment to expand its refining capacity to meet domestic fuel demand because, despite sitting on the second largest oil reserves, it imports almost 40 percent of its fuel needs due to lack of refineries.

While oil trade dominates, Chinese state companies have also built ports, airports, power plants, cement factories, auto industry, shipping lines, and other infrastructure projects, especially in major Iranian cities. For instance, between 2000 and 2006, China built the Tehran metro system, and in 2011 China's Sinohydro Corp. inked a $2 billion contract with Farab Iran Corp. to build the world's tallest dam in Iran's province of Lorestan.[78] Fiber Home Communication Technology won a contract to build broadband fiber optics in Iran, and Hisense Electronic Company has built a factory to produce televisions.

Beijing largely shunned U.S. requests to curb its energy investment in Iran until later in 2010. Beijing instructed its oil companies to slow down on their projects in Iran to avoid U.S. sanctions on its big energy firms.[79] In June 2012, the United States granted and since then has several times renewed eighteen-day exemptions to China on purchases of Iranian oil in exchange for China's lowering its oil imports from Iran. Due to international and U.S. sanction pressure, China decreased imports of Iranian oil by 25 percent between 2011 and 2013.[80] Consequently, Sinopec's work on the Yadavaran oil field had been delayed, and in April 2014, Iran cancelled CNPC's contract to develop the Azadegan oil field, citing unacceptable delays.[81] Similarly, for lack of progress, Iran suspended a CNOOC contract for the development of the North Pars natural gas field in 2011.[82] However, following a deal in July 2015 that limits Iran's nuclear activities in return for lifting sanctions that have more than halved Iran's oil exports since 2012, China NOCs renewed production and started pumping 160,000 bpd at Yadavaran and North Azadegan by the end of 2016.[83]

China also developed economic ties with the GCC. Notably, in 2004, China and the GCC signed the Framework Agreement on Economic, Trade, Investment and Technology Cooperation and launched negotiations on the China–GCC Free Trade Area. These negotiations, however, stalled in 2009, partly due to China's protective policies and specifically its reluctance to open its markets to GCC petrochemical and chemical products.[84] In 2010, China and the GCC launched a Trade and Economic Joint Committee, and in 2011, the two sides discussed the formation of an operations committee to further bolster bilateral trade and investments.

The Rise of a Mercantilist China?

With access to energy being necessary to fuel China's rapid economic development, the PRC has initiated an approach to secure its energy needs, which we have referred to as the "going-out strategy."[85] Some observers see this in purely defensive terms. They believe the PRC aims to address domestic problems caused primarily by overpopulation and resource scarcity and to foster energy and trade cooperation. Under this view, the implementation of this geoeconomic strategy relies mainly on the Chinese government's ability to expand its overseas investment and foster energy and trade cooperation. By increasing the well-being of the Chinese people and developing the domestic economy, China seeks to maintain stability and reshape the world economic order.[86]

Yet while the approach may be largely defensive or not offensive, part of this strategy is also mercantilist in that it seeks to circumvent energy markets. Such an approach, like so much else in China, is government driven and therefore contrasts dramatically with the approaches of Western countries, including the United States, that lack much influence over the behavior of their oil companies and cannot use them as sovereign tools of power. It is interesting that a communist state is so acquisitive in the area of energy. While the tenets of liberalism and capitalism urge individuals to gain property and fortunes, those notions are not the wellspring of China's ideology.

The mercantilist aspect is driven not only by China's rising energy demands and global ambitions, but also by ambivalence about or even mistrust of global energy markets, which are American dominated.[87] Some Chinese decision makers are also insecure about America's domination of the Persian Gulf. At a minimum, the PRC wants a backup strategy for energy security and may also seek to soft-balance against Washington.

As part of this going-out strategy, China has created, funded, and dispatched its NOCs, including Sinopec, CNPC, and CNOOC, to pursue aggressive acquisition of equity oil or agreements in which they would own or have controlling stakes in oil fields. They now increasingly operate abroad and possess equity stakes,[88] for which they often overpay by 10 to 30 percent, as compared to IOCs, while sometimes suffering serious losses.[89] In case of an oil supply disruption, NOC shares in equity oil would allow China to circumscribe the global oil market by shipping oil it owns directly to itself. However, normally, Chinese NOCs sell their equity oil in local or international markets, as does any other company, to avoid transportation costs associated with shipping its equity oil back home. The equity oil that China's NOCs have been able to lock in remains meager as a percentage of total Chinese oil imports but could increase in the future if China feels more insecure.[90]

Besides equity oil, China also pursues a loan-for-oil strategy to lock in oil supplies when buying equity shares is not possible. Loan-for-oil deals rest on promises to sell an agreed amount of oil directly to China instead of selling it on international energy markets or to other countries.

While Beijing has initiated equity stake and loan-for-oil deals mainly in the former Soviet Union, Africa, and Latin America,[91] they have grown in importance in the Middle East[92] and could develop further into a tool of Chinese influence. China's NOCs have acquired growing equity oil stakes and signed long-term crude oil supply contracts in the Arabian/Persian Gulf, anchored by growing involvement in Iran's oil and gas sector and more recently by growing energy and diplomatic ties with energy giant Saudi Arabia.[93]

Riyadh keeps its upstream closed to foreign investment. That prevents China from securing stakes in equity oil. But the House of Saud has guaranteed China a reliable oil supply in their agreements. For its part, Iran is wont to give out equity investment deals in its oil and gas sector due to a constitutional prohibition on foreign ownership of hydrocarbon resources, but it does sign so-called buyback contracts. These contracts allow foreign companies to develop a field to the point where it is ready to begin production and hand it over to National Iranian Oil Company, which then runs it. The foreign oil company receives a guaranteed rate of return, paid in oil.

In Iraq, sectarian violence compelled Western firms to abandon southern Iraq in favor of oil sources in Iraqi Kurdistan; Chinese state oil companies stepped in to take advantage of the region's resources. With state backing, Chinese firms are more risk tolerant and have collectively made China the biggest single player in Iraq's energy industry. China's NOCs now own major stakes in the al-Ahdad, Halfaya, and Rumaila oil fields. Such penetration is likely to translate into some political influence, even if that is not Beijing's direct goal compared to meeting its oil security needs.

To be sure, contrary to what many people think and that the media report, much of the oil that China produces abroad is sold on the open market. That is important to note because it does not fit into a mercantilist profile. However, it is fair to say that Beijing's activities put it in a position to be more mercantilist in the Middle East and elsewhere. Insofar as practices such as buying up global oil assets are aimed at circumventing oil markets in an effort to obtain oil, they can also chip away at the American-favored oil market mechanism and the prevailing order of trading oil in dollars. That may become a problem for the United States and others that support the current market mechanisms. It would signal more rivalrous behavior in the oil patch for obtaining oil outside oil markets in a manner that suggests a self-help alternative to mutually agreed-on market mechanisms.

We should consider one other aspect of China's role in the region, which is tied to its rivalry with Washington at the global level. Oil transactions are usually settled in dollars. However, in a little noticed but crucial development in 2012–2013, Beijing began seriously using its own domestic currency, the yuan, to buy oil from Iran and Russia. This may turn out to be a broader strategy to rival the dollar as an international currency. Beijing's move helped Iran get around global sanctions over its nuclear aspirations. They hinder its ability to accept oil payments in dollars. China's move diminishes American power of control over where Iran can sell its oil by circumventing the U.S.-controlled dollar. Iran can sell its oil to China and receive yuan in return, and use the yuan to buy resources for its economy and nuclear programs. In fact, this is not just theoretical. Iran began selling oil to China, the biggest buyer of Iranian crude, undermining American pressure on Beijing to join a global boycott of Iran over Tehran's nuclear program.[94]

Conclusion

In the post–Cold War era, China has developed and expanded diplomatic ties to all of the regional states, and Sino-Gulf trade and energy cooperation has been on the rise, particularly in the past decade. This dramatic change represents a major development in the international relations of the region and in the PRC's relations with regional states and America.

While the PRC has significantly expanded energy cooperation with all the Gulf states, its energy ties to Iraq and Iran have become especially robust. In fact, while Saudi Arabia and Iran appeared to dominate China's energy interest since the 1990s, China switched its focus from Iran to Iraq in the late 2000s.

In a short period between 2009 and 2014, Chinese national oil became the driving force behind more than 50 percent of Iraqi oil output in that period. China's NOCs have also filled the investment vacuum in Iran's upstream energy sector following the withdrawal of Asian and European energy companies, gradually becoming the primary investors in Iran's oil and gas sector. Iran's relationship with China has changed from one of mutual cooperation in the

1980s into one of lopsided dependence today. By 2007, China had become Iran's top trading and economic partner.

While Iran has become heavily dependent on China economically and politically, Beijing has been willing to offer support only to the extent that would not endanger its U.S. ties and international reputation. China largely disregarded American pressure to curtail its energy investment in Iran until 2010, but as pressure mounted, Beijing gradually instructed its oil companies to slow down on their projects in Iran. This suggests that China will probe and test American resolve in the effort to challenge Washington without going too far.

At the same time that American hegemony has developed in the region, it has also had to face various types of efforts to check it, including soft balancing by China and Russia. Recall that soft balancing has the same end goal as hard balancing, which is to check the strongest states, but it relies on international institutions and other nonmilitary means for balancing rather than the military means and alliances that constitute hard balancing. Yet while China at times has tried to check the United States, the more powerful incentive has been to protect oil security. Since America is central to that effort, Beijing could go only so far in balancing the United States and at times has cooperated on oil security. That is a challenging balancing act that fairly conceptualizes a key dimension of Sino-American interaction in the Persian Gulf and possibly at the global level.

7 Russia: From Cold War to the Modern Era

THE END OF THE COLD WAR generated a seismic shift in global politics and heralded an era of potentially improved cooperation among the great powers. However, that promise was not realized as expected. The end of the Cold War enhanced relations between Moscow and Washington, largely weakened Russia's regional position, and benefited oil security in key ways. Yet it did not spawn a clear break with the past, nor did it render as unimportant Russia's efforts, some dogged and bold, to continue to challenge American national interests in the Middle East. This was the case even before Russia's intervention in Syria in 2015, which sought to prop up the dictatorship of President Assad for various reasons.

Russia has experienced a difficult transition in the post–Cold War period, and the nature and course of this transition remain important to world politics and the Middle East. On the whole, Russia's power and position in the Persian Gulf have eroded substantially in the post–Cold War period. However, the collapse of empire did not altogether undermine Russia, and it proved beneficial in some ways. In the 1970s and 1980s, Moscow's regional position was handicapped by its global ideology, menacing military reputation, atheistic propensities, and poor record in dealing with the Muslim world. This was demonstrated most clearly in its invasion of next-door Afghanistan. The end of the Cold War diminished the importance of these factors.

As this chapter and the next demonstrate, Moscow has remained interested in enhancing its position in the Gulf region in the post–Cold War era and has essayed to develop political, military, and economic ties to the Gulf states. Data suggest that Russia's foreign policy toward and position in the Persian Gulf shifted to include more mercantilist and economic goals. However, it continued to try to challenge U.S. regional hegemony, an action that has raised the costs of hegemony for the United States. In the post–Cold War period, trade and commerce have increased in importance in Russian motivations, and that shift is certainly beneficial to oil security. Indeed, in the Cold war, Russia was devoted to undermining the United States in the region; in the post–Cold War period, Moscow has moderated that tendency, leaving Washington with an assertive but less serious rival focused also on economics in the region.

This chapter first discusses some signs of a shift in Russian motivation. It then explores changes in Russia's strategic and diplomatic position in the Persian Gulf. While the main focus here is on the post–Cold War period, the chapter situates these areas of interaction into some historical perspective as well.

Russia's Shifting Mix of Motivations

While this chapter does not focus on Russia's global foreign policy, signs of change amid continuity appear to be afoot. The continuity is expressed, for example, in Russia's intervention in Georgia and Ukraine, support of Bashar al-Assad's regime in Syria, and Putin's use of energy as a political weapon.

Energy is also salient in U.S.-Russian interaction outside the Middle East. Indeed, the Europeans have been divided over the extent to which Russia, with its huge oil and gas resources, should be isolated for its aggressive behavior in annexing Crimea in 2014, while Washington has pushed for a stronger stance in general. The U.S.-led allies imposed economic sanctions after it annexed Crimea, and NATO and the EU have also taken military steps, including a 2015 agreement to develop a NATO rapid-reaction force, pre-positioning of weapons in front-line countries, and conducting many more exercises.

Despite such tensions and threats, it would be a mistake to believe that Russian foreign policy has devolved back to the Cold War,[1] even if its Ukraine and Syrian interventions suggested as much. Against the backdrop of a muscular approach in Ukraine and Syria, we should also consider a more complicated picture. For some time preceding the rise of global tensions over Ukraine and Syria, Russian leaders referred to the importance of globalization and joining the World Trade Organization. Positive relations with the West were critical to economic development goals. Vladimir Putin aimed to double GDP within a decade when he became president in 2000.[2] In his view, "Now for Russia are important not only quantitative but qualitative parameters of the economy, and sustainable economic growth."[3] In former President Dmitry Medvedev's view, Russia's modernization was not proceeding fast enough given that there "is absolutely no alternative to modernization of the economic or political system."[4]

Putin refocused attention on economic growth in 2011 in his speech at the First Social Business Forum in Moscow,[5] and then again as reelected president in October 2012 during the "Russia Calling" Business Forum.[6] Recognizing that raw materials cannot serve as the only engine of growth, he repeatedly promised an expansion and diversification of foreign trade and industry,[7] and he stressed that "Russia certainly needs modern technology and private investment in development."[8] In April 2012, Putin reiterated his targets, including improving Russia's position in the World Bank's Ease of Doing Business index by 100 places by 2018 from its 120th position.[9] Despite being critically aware of a need for reform, Medvedev admitted that energy revenues would remain critical in the short term.[10] He stressed that nostalgia should not guide foreign policy, and that Russia "needed a post-industrial society,"[11] to become modern."[12]

The decline of empire is one of the defining processes of history and a painful one for imperial states that sometimes seek to regain their caché. Describing British decline, Winston Churchill asserted that the "only times I ever quarrel with the Americans are when they fail to give us a fair share of opportunity to win glory."[13] Putin sought to regain great power status and has been more far more confrontational than his predecessors. That said, Russia's leaders must also operate in a different, more interconnected global environment. They must also operate in a region where Washington has solidified its position over the past three decades, even if its intermittent political problems with regional states created some openings for Moscow. Those realities put some limits on just how far Russia's adventurism can go both globally and in the Persian Gulf and should be better appreciated.

The evolution of Russia's position in the Persian Gulf is characterized by a major expansion in diplomatic, trade, and energy relations, especially since 2000.

Strategic Position

In contrast to China's narrative in the region, it is important first to discuss Moscow's security standing in the region before exploring other elements of its capability. This is because its strategic position deteriorated, and that shaped other elements of its experience. Chapter 2 has already sketched aspects of this devolution, but a few points are worth making.

The Iraq Factor

In the 1970s, the degree of regional influence that Moscow and Washington enjoyed was related to their ability to manage, and sometimes exploit, Iran's rivalry with Iraq at the regional level while simultaneously jockeying in their own rivalry at the global level. Most notably, in the 1970s, Soviet-Iraqi relations were formalized by the 1972 Treaty of Friendship and Cooperation, which established serious strategic relations and gave Moscow a foothold in the region. The treaty provided for the qualified Soviet use of the Iraqi base at Umm Qasr and increased Soviet-Iraqi cooperation. Moscow gained from Iraq's revisionist propensities, its support of progressive forces such as the Dhofar rebels in Oman, and its inclusion in the socialist camp. By the late 1970s, Iraq began to somewhat moderate its policies and turn to the West for economic assistance and for arms. This, however, did not stop it from exploiting the anti-Americanism generated by the Camp David Accords as a means of gaining Gulf and perhaps Arab world leadership. In fact, to Moscow's benefit, Iraq remained opposed to increased U.S. regional influence partly because it fancied itself the sole regional gendarme.

However, the eight year Iran-Iraq War set in motion some developments and accelerated others that forced Iraq to restructure its foreign policy agenda. First, while the war made Iraq dependent on the GCC states for financial and political support, it also worsened the Soviet-Iraqi estrangement that had developed in 1978 as a partial result of the Soviet-inspired Afghan coup in 1978 and Iraq's harassment of the Iraqi Communist Party.

The war also made it more difficult for Moscow to support Iraq's adversaries, Syria and Iran, without losing influence with Iraq and the GCC that supported Iraq. The October 1980 Soviet-Syrian Treaty of Friendship exacerbated already strained Soviet-Iraqi relations, as did the Soviet decision to woo Iran at the war's outset in lieu of mending relations with Iraq. Although Moscow sent some arms to Iraq, it rejected Iraqi requests for a major airlift and at the war's outset reportedly turned back a ship full of tanks that had already reached Iraq.[14] In some respects, this was understandable: the Soviets were displeased with Iraq's attack on Iran, they coveted Iran as the "strategic prize," and they probably felt that the already deteriorated state of bilateral relations left them little to lose. This increased tension, however, was not offset by a clear and immediate improvement in Moscow's relations with Iran as Moscow might have hoped. Rather it underscored its dilemma of courting two antagonists at the same time, a dilemma that Washington avoided by devoting considerably less energy to wooing Iran.

While the war clearly damaged the connection between Moscow and Baghdad, the extent of the damage was not fully clear for several reasons: Iraq's move away from the Soviets predated the war; the war, while pushing Iraq toward the West, also increased Iraq's dependence on Soviet arms; and the U.S.S.R.'s connection with Iran yielded it some leverage with Iraq. Iraq must have realized that the Soviets could potentially influence Iran into accepting a cease-fire in the war.

Third, at the global level, the war improved U.S.-Iraqi relations in the short term, a fact that is hard to fathom given the 1991 Gulf War, and it further exacerbated Soviet-Iraqi relations. Prior to the Iran-Iraq War, Iraq distanced itself from Moscow, yet hardly favored U.S. interests. Despite its improved economic ties to Washington, Iraq still perceived the United States as a military threat. The war at times damaged the relationship, but largely pushed Washington to make efforts to build relations with Iraq, though Iraqi dependence on Moscow complicated this effort. Iraq's view of Washington's role in regional defense also changed. For instance, Iraq called on Washington to end the war, whereas prior to the war, Iraq stridently objected to a U.S. regional presence. In addition, Iraq agreed to reestablish diplomatic relations with Washington in 1984 even at the risk of disappointing the Soviets.

Although Soviet-Iraqi relations reached their nadir after Iraq's invasion of Kuwait, Moscow worked consistently in the 1990s to improve them, only to see them crash with the elimination of Saddam's regime in 2003. Whether Russia's intervention in Syria will translate into more influence in Iraq remains to be seen, but post–Cold War Russia's troubles with Iraq militated in favor of Washington and its broader efforts to protect oil security, because it did not have to worry nearly as much about this alliance as a bulwark against its interests.

Iran and Afghanistan

When the shah abdicated his throne in January 1979, Moscow seriously tried to lure Iran out of the U.S. orbit, only to discover that Ayatollah Khomeini's disdain for the United States did not translate into an affinity for Moscow. Nonetheless, the U.S.S.R. continued to woo Iran, to Washington's chagrin.[15] The Soviet invasion of Muslim Afghanistan hurt Moscow's ability to score any strategic inroads with Iran, partly because it chafed against the religious sensibilities of the Islamic Republic, not to mention the House of Saud, and presented the West with the possibility that Moscow would exploit U.S. vulnerability in the Middle East by invading the Gulf.[16] From Afghanistan, Moscow's troops were about 320 miles closer to the Gulf. The Russians, it was said, had always wanted a warm-water port as well as influence in the region.

While there is strong reason to believe that the Soviet Union was focused solely on stabilizing Afghanistan under a pro-Soviet puppet government, many in Washington described the act as part of a grand, chess-like scheme. The American policy of détente toward Moscow—trying to engage it in order to contain it—was replaced with an outright return to Cold War considerations in Washington.[17]

To be sure, Washington was not unreasonable in worrying about the invasion. The superpowers had a tacit agreement in which Moscow could intervene militarily and control its Eastern Europe sphere of influence, but not beyond this area. The invasion appeared offensive partly because it violated this understanding, was on such a wide scale and brutal, and, as Secretary of State Cyrus Vance saw it, could "set a dangerous precedent for Soviet aggression in other areas."[18] In addition, the Afghanistan intervention took place at a time of Western vulnerability in the Middle East.

The Unraveling: 1979–1991

The Gulf region was unstable not only because the U.S. framework for Gulf security collapsed in 1979 with the fall of the shah of Iran and faced the perceived threat from Moscow in Afghanistan, but also due to perceptions of Soviet political and military gains in Angola, Ethiopia, South Yemen, and Afghanistan. Coupled with Washington's loss of Iran as an ally, those perceived gains damaged U.S. credibility further by suggesting that Washington could not stop Soviet influence from rising. Galvanized by gains on the periphery of the Gulf and by Washington's travails, Moscow even tried to lure Iran into its orbit after the revolution.

Moscow's position began to weaken even before the end of the Cold War as our analysis of Soviet-Iraqi relations has shown, but the change from 1979 to 1991 was stark at a panoramic level. In 1979, the superpowers were locked in dangerous global rivalry. Moscow had some potential to balance during the Cold War chiefly through its alliance with Iraq struck in 1972. That alliance unraveled with the end of the Cold War, as underscored when Russia grudgingly cooperated with the United States against Iraq in the 1990–1991 Gulf crisis. While the U.S. presence has grown, Russia's has fallen in the post-Soviet era. Moscow has removed thousands of military advisers from the Middle East; downgraded ties to Syria, Libya, and Iraq; and virtually lost its position in

Yemen and the Horn of Africa. While Gulf state leaders were highly concerned about the presence of Soviet forces on the periphery of the Gulf during the Cold War, that changed after the Cold War. By contrast, regional states have become acutely sensitive to and aware of U.S. military capability.

The Arms Trade

Moscow's strategic decline has been furthered by diminished arms sales to regional actors. Russia has historically used arms sales and transfers to build influence in the Middle East, but its ability to do so has significantly decreased in the post–Cold War period. Even before that, however, it had difficulty translating arms sales into regional influence. In the 1980s, Gulf states were at least as angered by arms sales to their opponents as they were appreciative of receiving arms from Moscow. While Russian arms transfer agreements in the Near East increased from 1992–1995 to 1996–1999 (4.6 percent to 7 percent of total agreements), the increase was negligible in the Gulf proper as far as actual arms deliveries were concerned.[19]

The Gulf War and the ensuing embargo against Iraq shut down Moscow's most lucrative regional market, and Russian arms sales to Iraq dropped from $4.1 billion from 1988 to 1991 to near zero. Russian arms exports to the region remained concentrated on Iran through the mid- to late 1990s, though even with Iran, they weakened by 2000. Just as the United States has reaped significant export profits from its Saudi connection, Russia's arms sales and transfers to Iran have proved quite lucrative. As a result of Iran's military degradation during the war with Iraq in the 1980s and its inability to purchase modern Western equipment, it turned to Russia for new weapons systems in a number of areas, including air defense, communications systems, and surface-to-air missile (SAM) systems. In a $10 billion arms-for-oil deal, Russia agreed to supply Iran with MiG-29 fighters, Su-24 fighter-bombers, and SA-5 SAMs.[20] Russia also aided Iran in integrating into its air force the 122 Iraqi aircraft that Iran acquired during the Gulf War[21] and sold Iran three Russian Kilo-class submarines whose crews are Russian trained, making Iran the only Gulf state with such capability.

By sometimes presenting itself also as a counterweight to Iran while at the same time offering future suspension of arms deals, Russia's arms link with Iran yielded it some influence with Arab Gulf states. For instance, after its submarine sale to Iran, Russia negotiated an agreement with the UAE in January 1993 that allowed its naval vessels maintenance rights in UAE ports in exchange for pledges to help protect Gulf shipping if necessary. Hence, its ships were afforded a new port in the Gulf, which Russia was eager to exploit. In 1993, Moscow also concluded a bilateral security agreement with Kuwait that covered arms exports and equipment training and was aimed at repelling aggression, a reference to Iraq.[22]

Since the end of the Cold War and particularly in the past decade, Russia has sought to penetrate a lucrative GCC arms market that had been closed to it during the Cold War, but its penetration was largely limited to the UAE.

Iran remains the only significant importer of Russian arms in the Persian Gulf, albeit in 2006, Russia resumed limited arms sales to Iraq. Despite the improved relations with Saudi Arabia, Russia has not been successful in concluding a significant arms contract with the kingdom. In August 2009, Russia was "in a final stage of talks" on the purchase of thirty Mi-171 helicopters that started in 2007, with Saudi Arabia also expressing interest in acquiring Russian weaponry, including S-400 air defense system, T-90 tanks, and BMP-3 infantry fighting vehicles, all worth an estimated $4 billion.[23] Similarly, in February 2010, Russia's first deputy director of the Federal Service for Military and Technical Cooperation reported that the two parties were finalizing an array of agreements on helicopters, armor, and air defense systems with an estimated value of $4 billion to $6 billion.[24] However, in March 2011, the Russian Federal Service for Military-Technical Cooperation reported that "one should hardly expect the signing of large weapons contracts with Saudi Arabia."[25] The service's deputy director, Vyacheslav Dzirkaln, told Interfax-AVN, "Yes, we did plan to sign some contracts but negotiations have dragged on due to various reasons."[26] He added, "There is no any serious progress in the process."[27]

Diplomatic Relations

The economic position and overall influence of outside states is related to their diplomatic standing, status, and access in the region. Improved political relations may allow them to jockey for influence on a range of other issues. Russia has made significant diplomatic strides since the 1990s.

While Moscow's links to Iraq eroded in the 1980s, and with the fall of Saddam, it scored some diplomatic breakthroughs in the region. They were facilitated initially by Mikhail Gorbachev's foreign policy of greater liberalization and aided by the withdrawal of Soviet forces from Muslim Afghanistan in 1989, Moscow's stand against Iraq's invasion of Kuwait in 1990, and the demise of the Soviet Union in 1991. Moscow lacked diplomatic relations with Saudi Arabia,

Bahrain, the UAE, Qatar, and Oman during most of the Cold War.[28] But it established these relations with Saudi Arabia in 1991 and the others in the 1980s. Kuwait was the only Arab state Moscow has maintained diplomatic relations since 1963.

In the 1980s, Russia sought eagerly to reestablish diplomatic relations with Saudi Arabia but succeeded only after the end of the Cold War. The withdrawal from Afghanistan and the fact that Riyadh needed Moscow against Iraq's threat at the regional level were no doubt key factors in generating the diplomatic breakthrough for Moscow. Riyadh agreed to Moscow's request precisely at a time when Gorbachev was weighing how strong an anti-Iraq position his country would take in the first Gulf War. But it would not be until after that war and the fall of the Soviet Union that serious steps would be made on the diplomatic front. In 1992, the Russian Foreign Ministry implemented a new policy toward the Gulf States to create economic and political partnerships that laid the foundation for improved interaction in the 1990s. Prior to that, in 1991, Saudi Arabia provided Moscow with $2.5 billion in assistance; this, however, was not followed up with more investment in the 1990s as had been expected.[29]

Relations improved further after 9/11 when U.S.-Saudi relations reached an all-time low and particularly intensified after 2003 when Crown Prince Abdullah visited Moscow, the most senior Saudi official to visit Russia since 1932. In 2005, Russia became an observer at the Organization of the Islamic Conference and in 2006 formed the Russia-Islamic World Strategic Vision Group.[30] Medvedev repeatedly stated that Russian-Saudi relations were "gaining ever greater dynamics, reflecting cooperation at all levels."[31] In April 2006, Foreign Minister Sergei Lavrov praised intensive dialogue with Saudi Arabia and indicated Moscow's interest in the "development and deepening of mutually beneficial cooperation in various spheres, especially the economy."[32]

Closer ties between Russia and the GCC were particularly underscored by Putin's inaugural tour of Saudi Arabia, Qatar, and Jordan in February 2007— the first-ever trip by a Russian or Soviet head of state to the Gulf. King Abdullah gave Putin the country's highest award, the Abd-al-Azir order, for services to Islam, and the two sides pledged greater cooperation in the energy sector, as well as in economic, commercial, cultural, scientific, technological, and transport sectors.[33] They also concluded several business contracts and aimed to remove obstacles to greater Saudi-Russian trade.

Putin's visit was followed by King Abdullah's first sovereign visit to Moscow in November 2007,[34] which touched off a spate of high-level visits. In July

2008, Medvedev evaluated Russian-Saudi relations as developing dynamically in "trade-economic relations, in cultural ties, and in other fields of cooperation."[35] Such cooperation continued to the point that Abdullah in 2011 sought to advance and develop relations of friendship and cooperation in all spheres between Saudi Arabia and Russia.[36]

While economic relations continued to develop, diplomatic relations have cooled over geopolitical developments in the region. Russia's support for the Assad regime in the Syrian Civil War since 2011, call for a suspension of Saudi airstrikes in Yemen in April 2015,[37] and removal of the self-imposed ban on a delivery of a missile air-defense system to Iran in April 2015[38] have strained relations with the GCC states, particularly with Saudi Arabia, which has advocated for Assad's removal and containment of Iran. Nevertheless, despite the diverging regional policies, bilateral ties continued to deepen, as demonstrated by Salman's visit to Russia in June 2015, during which the two countries signed six deals ranging from defense to greater cooperation in energy development.[39]

Russia's diplomatic relations with the other Gulf states also expanded. Officials from Russia and the UAE have maintained frequent visits since 1992. In 2007, Putin visited the UAE, the first such high-level visit ever in their bilateral relations,[40] which spurred greater cooperation in energy, space, culture, science, education, and media. In September 2013, UAE Crown Prince Mohammed Al Nahyan visited Russia to exchange views on international issues, primarily on the situation in Syria, and discuss prospects for strengthening trade, economic, energy, and investment cooperation.[41] The UAE confirmed in June 2014 that the economic cooperation between the two countries would not be hurt by Western sanctions against Russia.[42]

In 2010, the emir of Qatar visited Russia, and Medvedev awarded the Order of Friendship to the Kuwaiti deputy minister of Awqaf and Islamic Affairs. The same year, Russia signed with Kuwait and Qatar a memorandum of understanding on cooperation in the peaceful use of atomic energy, and in 2008, Russia and Bahrain signed a declaration to further develop friendly relations. December 2008 marked the first official visit in history by the king of Bahrain, Hamad bin Isa Al Khalifa, to Russia, following myriad lower-level visits. In February 2008, Lavrov praised "the expansion of mutually beneficial cooperation in trade, economic and business spheres and development of cultural and educational ties" with Bahrain.[43] In April 2014, the two countries signed a series of agreements designed to enhance trade, defense ties, and investment in spite of U.S. and European economic sanctions on Russia.[44]

The first GCC-Russian strategic dialogue took place in November 2011. The two sides explored security and political issues, as well as areas of strategic importance such as trade, investment, technology, intercultural, and interfaith dialogue.[45] Such relations would have been nearly unthinkable in the 1980s.

Russia's intervention in Syria threatened to upset its relations with the Sunni Arab monarchies in the Persian Gulf, which have sought the removal of President Assad of Syria. However, they may also respect Russian power in Syria, which may mitigate the negative effect on these relations, but that all remains to be seen.

In contrast to steadily improving relations with the smaller Gulf states, the evolution of Russian-Iraqi relations has been tortuous. Moscow helped Iraq during the 1990s when Iraq was isolated under U.N. sanctions, but it distanced itself from Iraq in the post-Soviet era, partly in order to maintain good relations with the GCC and the West. In the first Gulf War, 1990 to 1991, Russia joined the U.S.-led alliance against Iraq, albeit quite reluctantly. Moscow sought to arrange a face-saving withdrawal for Saddam, but when that was rejected by President George H. W. Bush, it sided with Washington to evict Iraq from Kuwait.

Russian political and economic influence in Iraq rapidly declined after the U.S.-led invasion in 2003, but Moscow sought to improve relations with the new Iraqi authorities, partly in order to protect its economic contracts and interests. Moscow agreed to write off 80 percent of the Iraqi debt to Russia, which in 2007 amounted to $13 billion, though Putin added, "We assume that the interests of our companies will be taken into account."[46] In April 2009, Prime Minister Nouri al-Maliki became the first Iraqi leader to visit Russia since 1981.[47] Bilateral ties were enhanced by Lavrov's visit to Baghdad in May 2011[48] and Iraqi Prime Minister Haider al-Abadi's visit to Moscow in May 2015, during which he stated that Iraq "highly appreciates the relations with Russia. . . . We are set to develop ties in all the areas, including the military and technical cooperation, economic cooperation and the oil and gas sphere."[49] Prior to the visit, Lavrov announced Russia's readiness to supply weapons to Iraq to help halt advances by Islamic State militants.[50]

Moscow faced complications in trying to maintain good relations with both Iraq and Iran, but it tried nonetheless. It lacked diplomatic relations with Iran prior to its 1979 revolution, and even after the revolution, Iran rebuffed Moscow's attempts at gaining a foothold in the country. Indeed, Iran repeatedly condemned the Soviet attempt to "crush the brave resistance"[51] of the Afghan rebels. Iran's ambassador to the Soviet Union made it clear that the Soviets' actions in Afghanistan had "deadlocked their policies in Muslim countries" and had provided Washington with "an excuse to increase its influence in their region."[52] It was recognized in *Pravda* that Iran used the Afghan issue "more often than any other pretext to justify hostile attacks . . . on the USSR's interests."[53]

Moscow's withdrawal from Afghanistan improved bilateral relations. A February 1989 communiqué from Khomeini to Soviet leader Mikhail Gorbachev praised burgeoning relations.[54] In June, significant bilateral agreements were signed in which Moscow agreed to "cooperate with the Iranian side in strengthening its defense capabilities,"[55] which included a major arms sale to Iran.[56] Thereafter, Iran expressed its satisfaction with Moscow on several occasions.[57] By 1991, Moscow was Iran's leading arms supplier after having been virtually closed out of the market, at least since 1982.

The bilateral relations have improved further in the past decade. Political relations had been facilitated by the Treaty on Principles of Cooperation signed on March 12, 2001. Iran has since come close to Russia's position on a number of regional and international issues, such as the desirability of a multipolar world order, strengthening the U.N. role in international affairs, settlement of the Afghan and Iraqi crises, and stability in Central Asia and the Caucasus. Such a convergence of views, even if not powerful, was a response partly to American hegemony and represented a constraint on Washington's leverage.

Certainly Russia and Iran see eye to eye on Syria and coordinated their strategic responses in 2015 in conjunction with the Russian intervention to save President Assad. That cooperation even included Iran's allowing Russia to bomb sites in Syria from Iranian territory, though that arrangement was abruptly discontinued, which reflected just how tenuous it had been in the first place. Whether Russia can solidify any gains with Iran in a more lasting manner depends on numerous factors, including the course of events in Syria and the trajectory of U.S.-Iranian relations, which could improve—or just as easily descend into heightened tensions. Iran has not been interested historically in close relations with Moscow at the risk of losing a more independent course.

Conclusion

To be sure, President Vladimir Putin has made Russia a more serious rival to Washington. Moscow has strongly backed the Assad regime in Syria, which is linked to Iran, and has sought to have better strategic relations with Iran at the expense of the United States, though Iran and Russia have their own serious differences. Moscow has also supported anti-American actors in other areas, such as with regard to backing Iran on the Yemen issue, while Washington has backed Saudi Arabia. Yet such actions, while a possible response to U.S. hegemony, are not as threatening to America's interest and to oil security as was the case during the Cold War years. The Cold War pitted the superpowers in a much more confrontational battle in which regional developments were interpreted through more of a zero-sum global lens and in which rivalry could cause low-level and more open tensions that decreased oil security. During the Cold War, it is hard to imagine Moscow supporting U.S.-led efforts to reverse Iraq's 1990 invasion of Kuwait or to ultimately support global efforts to contain Iran's nuclear aspirations.

While Russian actions in Syria are related to the Persian Gulf because Iran is connected to Syria, such actions have not significantly affected the balance of capabilities in the Gulf. Nor can Russia easily translate its position in Syria, which may be transitory, into real influence with the Arab Gulf states. One might even argue that Russia's intervention in Syria in support of Assad did not undermine American goals insofar as Washington came to believe privately that Assad's regime was less bad than the ascendance of radical jihadis— al-Qaeda and the Islamic State chiefly—who might replace him if he were to fall. In any case, what is more important than Syria's tortuous and somewhat distant dynamics in assessing the international relations of the Gulf is the evolution of Russia's economic position and relations directly in the region, to which we now turn.

8 Russia's Trade and Energy Shift

RUSSIA'S FOREIGN POLICY in the Persian Gulf region has hardly been shorn of strategic objectives, but in its mix of motivations, energy concerns and business potential have grown more important in the post–Cold War period. This change in emphasis has benefited Moscow's standing.

Indeed, oil-rich monarchies offer lucrative markets for Russia's goods and a source of badly needed investment. Although Russia's military position in the Persian Gulf region largely collapsed with the end of the Cold war, it has made gains in the political arena and also in the economic arena in both trade and energy. We sketch these economic gains and assess what they mean in the broader picture of the international relations of the region.

Russian-Gulf State Economic Relations

Improved diplomatic relations between Russia and Gulf states have facilitated unprecedentedly high trade volumes and collaboration in the energy sector, although it is critical to note that such increases have come up from a low level and are dwarfed by those of the United States and China. Such trade gains suggest increasing Russian economic interdependence with regional states and a stronger Russian economic position in the region. Continued development of such interdependence may give Moscow some interest not to challenge too much the American-led security system in the region, which also comprises the very states with which Russia seeks positive relations. Of course, the trajectory of Russia's foreign policy and standing will depend on numerous other factors as well.

The economic dimension of Russia's goals may have some basis in a broader strategy that Medvedev outlined in the 2008 Foreign Policy Concept of the Russian Federation. It stated that with regard to the states in the Gulf region, of strategic importance to Russia's national interests, "priority attention will be paid to developing mutually beneficial economic cooperation, in particular in the energy sector."[1]

In November 2008, Alexander Saltanov, deputy foreign minister, stressed that investment cooperation was "the most promising sphere" in Russia's relations with countries of the Persian Gulf,[2] both in terms of their investment in Russia and vice versa.[3] As Figure 8.1 demonstrates, trade between Russia and the Gulf countries declined in 2008–2009 due to the global financial crisis but has recovered since then. Iran is Russia's main trading partner in the Gulf, sharing a multibillion-dollar trade relationship, and Russia has also developed the Bushehr nuclear power plant with a price tag of $1.2 billion.[4] Moscow was reluctant to stop this cooperation, despite Western pressure that hurt Russian-Iranian trade, fearing that other countries might usurp its role in Iran and that it would lose its edge in winning nuclear power contracts from Third World countries.[5]

During the Cold War and until the 2003 American invasion, Russia's economic ties to Iraq were the strongest in the region (Figure 8.1). Between 1998 and 1999, Russian companies led in the sale of civilian goods to Iraq, amount-

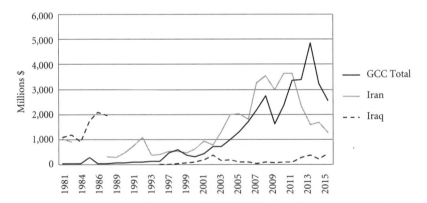

FIGURE 8.1. Total Trade between Russia and the Persian Gulf States, 1981–2015.
SOURCE: Authors' calculations for data in the years 1981–1982 are drawn from *Foreign Trade Statistics Yearbook of the USSR* (Moscow: Ministry of Foreign Trade of the USSR, various years). The rest of data are drawn from United Nations Commodity Trade Statistics Database (New York: United Nations, various years), and United Nations, *International Trade Statistics Yearbook* (New York: United Nations, various years).

ing to $500 million; in 2000 all of Iraq's orders from Russia exceeded $20 billion.[6] In 2001, Russia and Iraq signed contracts worth more than $1.85 billion, and "Iraq secured its position as Russia's leading partner in the Arab World, with a turnover of goods with that country accounting for 60 percent of that with all Arab countries."[7]

Since the 2003 U.S.-led invasion, trade between Russia and Iraq has rapidly deteriorated, although it began to recover in 2011 following the U.S. withdrawal from the country. Trade remains hostage to Iraq's political chaos and instability, and also to far greater global competition that Moscow did not face when it was Iraq's Cold war patron.

Saudi-Russian trade has grown at a high rate, although in absolute terms, it is still quite modest. Economic ties with Saudi Arabia constitute a relatively recent development. Prior to the 1990s, trade between Russia and Saudi Arabia was virtually nonexistent.[8] It was only from the mid-1990s onward that the two countries expanded their economic ties. In just the ten years from 1996 to 2006, total trade turnover between the two countries increased by almost 500 percent, from $160 million in 1996 to $714 million in 2006. Following Putin's visit to the kingdom in 2007, total trade turnout increased even more dramatically, reaching $1.4 billion in 2011 and rising to $1.7 billion by 2013 despite divergent views between Saudi Arabia and Russia on regional developments.

The Russian-Saudi Business Council, established in 2002, regularly serves as a platform to strengthen the contacts between business circles of both countries[9] and generated cooperation in the energy sector, construction industry, and commerce.[10] In March 2011, the council organized the third Russian exhibition, Week of Russian Business in Saudi Arabia, and the business forum, which was attended by over seventy representatives of major Russian companies. During Salman's visit to Russia in June 2015, the two countries signed a $10 billion memorandum of understanding on their public investment funds.[11] The memorandum of understanding was one of six agreements signed during the visit.

Despite Russia's efforts and the Saudis eyeing many investment projects in Russia, no major investments had been actualized by 2016.[12] Saudi Arabia's ambassador to Russia, Ali Hasan Jaafar, reflected the broader view that mutual trade turnover worth several billion dollars "is not commensurate to the potentials of Russia and Saudi Arabia."[13]

The rise in diplomatic visits between Russia and Qatar also translated into increased economic cooperation, though the upward trend was certainly not linear. The mutual relationship had, in the words of the Russian ambassador to Qatar, "one of its most successful years in 2010,"[14] with visits by the Qatari emir, the prime minister, and the foreign minister to Russia and sharp trade and investment increases. In 2013, trade turnover increased to $14.6 million from $8.7 million in 2009.[15] In 2010, the two sides also signed two agreements amounting to $500 million in exploration of polymetallic deposits in Russia's Yamal-Nenets and Sverdlovsk regions, and Qatar declared an intention to invest $500 million in Russian real estate and $10 million to build a shopping center in Astrakhan.[16] The investment has been realized, with Qatar Barwa Real Estate Company and Gazprombank completing the formation of a real estate fund, each contributing $75 million initially in January 2011 in the first collaboration between the two companies.[17] In order to enhance economic, trade, and investment ties, Russia proposed in 2010 to establish the Joint Commission on Trade, Economic and Technical Co-operation and to bolster business ties. The two countries also opened direct flights on the Moscow-Doha route in 2003[18] and continued to develop positive relations,[19] as underscored by mutual cooperation on twelve major projects aimed at elevating natural gas cooperation to a new level.[20]

The Qatari-Russian joint committee for trade, economic, scientific, and technical cooperation held its first meeting in Doha in March 2015, despite a downturn in relations over differences on Syria and Qatar's efforts to supply weapons to Libyan rebels in violation of a U.N. arms embargo. Prior to that, in May 2014, Qatar's sovereign wealth fund, the Qatar Investment Authority, allocated $2 billion to Russia through joint investments with a state-backed private equity fund, the Russian Direct Investment Fund.[21]

The UAE became Russia's largest trade partner in the GCC, with trade volume rising from $200 million in 2001 to more than $2.5 billion in 2013. The two countries also signed a memorandum of understanding to strengthen the legal framework and in 2005 established the Russian-Emirates Business Council.[22] In 2007, Putin's unprecedented visit to the UAE was accompanied by an array of government-business elites[23] and promoted high-level business interaction.[24] In March 2012, the Chamber of Commerce and Industry of Russia hosted a forum to draw investments from Arab countries to Russia. In November 2010, Abu Dhabi's Mubadala Development Co., a state-owned investment fund, announced a $100 million investment in Verno Capital's Russia-focused hedge funds, concluding the first major commitment by a Persian Gulf sovereign-wealth fund into Russia.[25] In September 2010, Russia's state-owned Russian Technologies and Crescent agreed to invest $500 million in a joint investment fund to develop transportation projects in Russia.[26] The fund was set up in April 2012 by Gulftainer, the subsidiary of Crescent and the UAE's second largest ports operator. Gulftainer also signed a $275 million deal in September 2011 to codevelop and operate Russia's Baltic port of Ust-Luga.[27]

In recent years, particularly since 2008, Russian companies also gradually strengthened their position in the UAE market and opened offices there,[28] with more than 350 joint ventures.[29] In the case of the UAE, Russia's efforts to realize trade potential between the two countries have been actualized. For instance, in May 2012, a Russian diplomat to the UAE pointed out that trade between the two countries "has been growing fast and has reached the record amount of nearly $1.5bn in 2011," compared to $1 billion in 2010. Despite divergent positions over Syria and Iran, trade relations continued to increase. Like other countries in the Gulf, the UAE assured Russia in June 2014 that Western sanctions against Russia would not affect economic cooperation between the two countries.[30]

Trade relations with Kuwait also improved, as reflected in the increasing trade level. In 2007, the two sides established the Russian-Kuwaiti Business Council,[31] aimed at developing large investment projects in Russia and Russian companies' participation in infrastructure development in the emirate. In 2009 and 2011, the first deputy chairman of the Central Bank of Russia, A. Ulyukaev, and a delegation headed by the CEO of Vnesheconombank, Vladimir Dmitriev, visited Kuwait,[32] and in September 2011, the two countries held the first meeting of the Sub-Commission on Trade, Economic, Technical, Financial, and Investment Cooperation in Kuwait and agreed to hold regular meetings of the subcommission.[33]

Russian trade with Bahrain spiked in recent years and then declined in 2008–2009 due to the global financial crisis, albeit it has since increased. In May 2007, Russia also set up the Russian-Bahraini Business Council, and both sides signed various agreements on trade, economic, and technical cooperation.[34] In November 2008, a delegation of Bahraini authorities and business circles headed by the minister of finance of Bahrain, Mohammed

Al-Khalifa, visited Moscow, and that same year, Russian Vnesheconombank and the Bahraini Development Bank signed a memorandum of understanding, followed by other bilateral agreements.[35] In October 2014, on his second visit to Russia since 2008, King Hamad Bin Eisa Al Khalifa affirmed Bahrain's eagerness to bolster cooperation with Russia and exchange expertise in the military field, and "commended the pivotal role of Russia as well as its contribution to the efforts of the international community to promote security and stability and consolidated global peace."[36] At a separate meeting in January 2015, Prime Minister Prince Khalifa Bin Salman Al Khalifa described bilateral relations as "strong and steadily becoming more robust," adding that "such a momentum should be reinforced."

In April 2014, the Russian Direct Investment Fund signed a memorandum of understanding with Bahraini sovereign wealth fund Mumtalakat to explore investment opportunities in their countries. During a visit led by Prince Salman bin Hamad Al Khalifa, crown prince, the two countries signed trade agreements including revision in visa policies, direct Manama-Moscow flights, as well as an investment cooperation fund with the aim of encouraging business and trade between the two countries.[37]

Russia has also developed unprecedented business ties with Oman that have helped spawn trade. In the 1990s, the two countries signed agreements on trade and economic and technical cooperation (1994) and on cooperation between chambers of commerce (1994).[38] By December 2010, more than twenty Russian companies worked in the areas of information security, exploration and production of oil and gas, shipbuilding, pipe manufacturing and agricultural machinery in Oman.

The Energy Dynamic

The data show that energy represents a minor part of Russian trade in the statistics cited in the previous section. Thus, a stand-alone analysis of Russia's energy relations is in order because they represent their own important component of Russian interaction.

The share of oil and gas in Russia's GDP has gradually risen from 12.7 percent in 1999 to 16 percent by 2013,[39] accounting for more than 50 percent of federal budget revenues and nearly 70 percent of Russia's exports.[40] Although Russian oil production has reached historic highs, many of its West Siberian oil fields that have accounted for the 50 percent increase in Russian oil production in the past decade have been substantially depleted.[41] Moscow estimates that $600 billion must be invested in the oil industry through 2030 to maintain production in West Siberia and to develop East Siberia and Sakhalin.[42] Lukoil has estimated that $1 trillion would be needed over the next twenty years just to maintain Russian production at the 10 mbd level.[43] Yet attracting investment in Russia's renationalized energy industry has been a challenge, which makes the

Persian Gulf's energy fields enticing because they are easier and cheaper to tap. That is especially true since 2014 due to Western sanctions targeting Russia's energy sector.

Russia also strives to maintain a close partnership with energy-exporting countries such as Qatar to control possible competition within its dominant energy market in Europe. Since energy revenues fill the Kremlin's coffers and help to sustain regime legitimacy, Russia also aims to coordinate on production with other producers and desirable oil price levels.

Bilateral Energy Agreements

Russia has signed numerous bilateral contracts with the Persian Gulf states.[44] In 2007, Russian oil company Lukoil expanded its oil presence in Iran, and Russian Gazprom signed oil and natural gas agreements that would allow it to invest directly in Iranian fields.[45] In 2009, Gazprom Neft, the oil branch of Gazprom, signed a memorandum of understanding with the National Iranian Oil Company to study the development of two Iranian oil fields, Azar and Shangule.[46] Under the memorandum, Gazprom would participate in the development of the North Azadegan oil field, the construction of an oil refinery in northern Iran, and the transportation of crude oil from the Caspian Sea to the Gulf of Oman from Neka to Jask (big port cities in Iran on the Caspian Sea and in the Gulf of Oman). Analysts say Gazprom Neft could earn as much as $3 billion annually from the North Azadegan oil field.[47]

However, in March 2010 Lukoil abandoned the oil project in Iran, with CEO Leonid Fedun indicating that "work on the oil field was impossible until U.S. sanctions were lifted."[48] Moreover in October 2011, Gazprom Neft was forced out by Iran and replaced with a consortium of Iranian companies. Gazprom Neft indicated that besides the tightening of Western sanctions, the company did not like the terms Iran offered. According to Iran, the reason was procrastination over the memorandum of understanding signed in 2009.[49] In February 2012, Fedun stressed that "Russia has stable relations with Iran despite recent hiccups, but now Lukoil doesn't have any contracts with Iran because of sanctions."[50]

However, in February 2013, Iran invited Russian companies to develop a number of its oil and gas fields anew, while also offering to make changes to legislation that would enable Russian companies to gain a stake in Iran's extractions sites.[51] Nonetheless, international sanctions have impeded investments, and the lifting of those sanctions should spur greater global investment.

For their part, Russia and Iraq have elevated interaction in the energy area in the post-Saddam era, including the development of joint projects between Russia's Rosneft and Crescent Petroleum in Iraq and throughout the Middle East. In April 2009, Prime Minister Nouri al-Maliki visited Russia, the first Iraqi leader to visit since 1981. After the meeting, Gazprom Neft won a tender to develop the giant Basra oil field in Iraq,[52] holding a 30 percent stake in the project. The implementation of the project is planned for twenty years, with the possibility of a five-year extension.

In September 2009, Russia's energy minister, Sergei Shmatko, led a Russian delegation to Iraq to discuss longer-term cooperation in electric power and the energy sector. According to Shmatko, the 2009 visit "opened a new page in energy cooperation between the two countries," with the main task being to "create conditions for increased trade and diversifying forms of cooperation."[53] In 2009, Lukoil won a tender to develop Iraq's West Qurna-2 oil field, with a plan to invest $4.5 billion, which positioned Lukoil among the global giants. West Qurna is considered the world's largest underdeveloped oil field, holding 13 billion barrels of crude oil. The aim is to bring production to 1.8 mbd. Lukoil has prepared to mobilize up to 15,000 specialists for Iraq's oil and gas industry.[54]

In April 2012, it started production drilling and construction of an oil processing unit on the field.[55] Lukoil holds 56.25 percent in the project with Norway's Statoil holding 18.75 percent. In March 2012, Statoil decided to transfer its stake to Lukoil, and in March 2015 the first oil production from West Qurna-2 was brought online.

In May 2011, Foreign Minister Sergei Lavrov visited Baghdad and underscored Russian satisfaction with Iraq's energy cooperation,[56] but Moscow has also eyed hydrocarbon riches in Iraq's autonomous region of Kurdistan. This was demonstrated in February 2013 when Gazprom Neft announced the signing of a new production-sharing agreement in Kurdistan, taking an 80 percent share of the major Halabja project. The exploration of the site was planned to start in fall 2013 and was estimated to take seven years.[57] In August 2012 the Iraqi Oil Ministry spokesman, Asym Jihad, warned that "sanctions will be applied against all international companies collaborating with the Kurdish autonomy without the permission of Baghdad, and Russian companies are no exception," further warning that Russia's oil company may lose its share in the Iraq's oil fields.[58] Despite the warnings, Gazprom already completed drilling two wells in Shakal Block, some 100 kilometers west of Halabja, by May 2015.[59]

Russia has also developed energy relations with Saudi Arabia, which both have seen as a priority.[60] In October 2002, at the first session of the Russian-Saudi committee for trading, economic and scientific cooperation, Igor Yusufov, the Russian minister of energy, stated that "Saudi Arabia was Russia's most important partner in the Middle East" and "offered his Saudi interlocutors the sale of Russian technologies in gas and oil extraction."[61] Subsequently, Russia and Saudi Arabia signed an international five-year cooperation agreement in the oil and gas sector, solidifying plans for Saudi and Russian energy companies to cooperate across borders.

Moscow's initial expectation of $46 billion in joint investment projects to develop the Russian economy has not materialized, but in January 2004, Lukoil won a bid for the development of several promising major oil and gas fields in the Rub al Khali.[62] Lukoil was awarded a tender to develop the 11,200-square-mile Zone A natural gas field in the Rub al Khali, signing a forty-year contract with Saudi Arabia to explore and develop the field. Lukoil Overseas holds an 80 percent stake in Lukoil Saudi Arabia, with the remainder held by Saudi Aramco. However, in September 2010, Luksar relinquished 90 percent of its gas exploration position as it has struggled to find gas.[63] In 2009, Russian Stroytransgaz completed two contracts for the construction of the Scheib-Abqaiq, a 900-kilometer-long water pipeline.[64]

In November 2010, Saudi Arabia held talks with Russia over a nuclear agreement on the peaceful development of nuclear energy as the kingdom plans to invest $80 billion to boost capacity as a response to rising demand for electricity, which is expected to triple to 121,000 MW by 2032.[65] The two countries then signed the nuclear power cooperation deal in June 2015.[66] Saudi owner Al Arabiya TV stated that the kingdom planned to build sixteen nuclear reactors, with Russia playing a significant role in operating them. Thus far, Saudi Arabia has signed nuclear agreements only with France, Argentina, South Korea, and, most recently, China.[67] In terms of the energy partnership, Putin expressed that "on the face of it, it seems that we are rivals, but considering the world's growing demand for energy, that is not so."[68] At the same time, during a closed-door meeting in November 2014 between Saudi Arabia and oil officials from Russia, Venezuela, and Mexico, Russia rejected a suggestion that non-OPEC members participate in an oil production cut to prop up prices.[69]

The oil and natural gas sectors are among the most promising directions of cooperation between Russia and the UAE. In 2010, Russia's biggest oil producer, state-controlled Rosneft, established its first Mideast presence when it entered a joint venture with the UAE's Crescent Petroleum to explore for gas in the emirate of Sharjah, marking the companies' first joint project under their broad and longer-run strategic cooperation agreement. The two sides have already invested $35 million in drilling and exploration activities.[70] Gas production was expected to begin in 2013, but in 2015, Rosneft announced its intention to exit joint operations in Sharjah after the gas exploration project proved unsuccessful.[71] Rosneft expressed intent to invest $630 million in the joint venture,[72] though significant future investments would depend in part on Iraqi oil legislation that would protect investment outside the northern Kurdistan region and on Iraqi stability.

Russia and Kuwait also increased cooperation. In April 2009, the Russian company Gazpromgeofizika and the Kuwaiti company Noor Financial Investment signed an agreement to establish two joint ventures to conduct exploration for hydrocarbons.[73] Meanwhile, in December 2008, Gazprom and the National Agency for Oil and Gas of Bahrain signed a letter of intent to jointly explore new opportunities and identify areas of mutually beneficial cooperation in oil and gas, which was expanded in 2009 and 2010,[74] such as with regard to exploration of the Awali field, the only major hydrocarbon field in Bahrain.

Oman, like other Gulf states, has sought to cooperate on atomic energy with Russia.[75] At the constituent session of the Russian-Omani Business Council held in June 2011, Sergey Tishkin, the chairman of the council, said that oil and gas was the priority sector of cooperation with Oman, but that cooperation in other sectors, such as power generation and engineering, to mention just a few, should be developed.[76]

Energy ties between Russia and Qatar have also expanded unprecedentedly. In April 2010, they created a joint Russian-Qatari committee for cooperation in gas and energy. Qatar, the world's largest LNG exporter, is currently one of Russia's most important partners but also a rival in the energy sector. Russia has expressed interest in working with Qatar in the Middle East in general on projects for the exploration and extraction of hydrocarbons, construction, transportation and distribution infrastructure, gas processing, and LNG.

Qatar signed an agreement with Gazprom to create a Russian-Qatari company with a capital of $150 million for the operation of gas fields in Russia, and in November 2010, they also signed a memorandum on cooperation in civil nuclear technologies, followed by plans to work together to provide nuclear materials and nuclear fuel, as well as to arrange training programs for Qatari nuclear sector personnel.[77] Qatar also bought a major stake in British Royal Dutch Shell in May 2012, further infringing on the European resource market.[78]

Russia, the Gulf, and Europe

Interestingly, the prospects of Qatar playing a counterweight to Gazprom's dominance on the European market have led Russia to strive to turn a rival into a partner. Russia understands that greater natural gas flows to Europe would decrease its market there and its political influence. LNG, in particular, is a threat because natural gas can be delivered at long distances at competitive prices. Trying perhaps to preempt rivalry with Gulf producers, Russia has tried to develop, albeit unsuccessfully, a so-called big gas troika, an OPEC-style group composed of Iran, Qatar, and Russia to facilitate coordination in the gas sector. Such a group might also translate into some global and regional influence in Russia's diminished but ongoing rivalry with Washington.

Qatar has emerged as a competitor in the European gas market dominated traditionally by Russia. With the surge of shale gas (a black or dark brown shale containing hydrocarbons that yield petroleum by distillation) in the United States, Qatar, as the biggest LNG producer in the world, was forced to divert its supplies to Europe.[79] This development has coincided with EU efforts to diversify sources of gas and further intensified following Russia's intervention in Ukraine. Consequently in 2010, Gazprom's exports to Europe dropped by 25 percent compared with 2009.[80]

The emergence of shale gas, which has become economically profitable only since around 2008, has transformed the North American energy market and has diminished Russia's energy dominance in Europe.[81] Qatar, the world's largest LNG producer and exporter, currently hosts six LNG plants[82] and is developing greater capacity.[83] As the Russian envoy to Qatar, Vladimir Titorenko, pointed out, the LNG terminals being built in southern Europe create even more competition for Russia's planned South Stream gas pipeline. He emphasized that "Russia wants to avoid spending a lot of money on South Stream and then have to compete with cheaper LNG from Qatar."[84] However, the South Stream project was halted due to the EU's imposed sanctions on Moscow in 2014.[85] Qatar had already penetrated Western Europe, notably the United Kingdom, Italy, France, and Spain, moving closer to Russia's backyard. Its share of EU-28 imports of natural gas rose from less than 1 percent in 2002 to 11 percent in 2011, before dropping under 10 percent by 2014.[86] In April 2010, Poland, which has its own significant shale gas reserves, signed a twenty-year deal to import

1 million metric tons per year of Qatari LNG for its receiving terminal in the port of Świnoujście, which started operation in September 2015.[87] Qatar also initiated talks with Bulgaria, which suffered the most by a cutoff in Russian gas supplies in January 2009. Russia supplies 42 percent of Poland's natural gas consumption and nearly all of Bulgaria's. Qatar also considered investing up to $4 billion in the development of an LNG import terminal at the port of Astakos in Greece but pulled out of the project in fall 2010.[88]

Russia's sudden reluctance to include Qatar as a stakeholder in the Yamal LNG project, as well as Qatar's intensified incursion into the European energy market in 2012, may have been triggered in part by mutual criticism in the context of Qatar's and Saudi Arabia's aggressive support of regime change in Libya and Syria. However, following Gazprom's opening of a representative office in Doha in February 2013, Qatar's energy minister, Muhammad al-Sada, noted that Qatar plans to expand joint investments with OAO Gazprom. Meanwhile, Viktor Zubkov, the chairman of the board of directors of Gazprom, expressed that the office "will contribute to stronger partnership ties and will provide an additional impetus to closer mutually beneficial cooperation with the states in the region."[89] Furthermore, in September 2014, Qatar's energy minister, Mohammed al-Sada, stated that "Qatar doesn't see itself as an alternative to other producers and exporters," noting that "producers complement each other."[90]

Since Iran is a major natural gas producer, Russia could benefit from U.S.-driven economic sanctions against foreign investment in Iran's energy. For instance, Europe's effort to diversify its gas supply away from Russia was originally supposed to be realized in part by feeding Iranian gas into the Nabucco pipeline, the project that directly competes with Russia's push for the South Stream pipeline. Only after relations between the West and Iran dramatically deteriorated did Europe begin the search for alternative sources for Nabucco, such as Azerbaijan, where cooperation with Iran could make sense.[91]

In a search for gas to feed Nabucco, the EU also signed a memorandum of understanding in energy with Iraq in 2010. Furthermore, Iran's vast reserves would inevitably saturate the market, leading to a decrease in Gazprom's and Russia's main source of revenue. However, Iran is forced to buy gas from Turkmenistan to cover its domestic energy needs due to its lack of domestic LNG production. Although the process has been slowed by international sanctions, it aimed to build three gas liquefaction plants: one with China in southern Iran where the North Pars deposit is located and the other two plants, built with Europeans, in the South Pars gas field, which Iran shares with Qatar. All three plants aimed to produce 125 million cubic meters of gas a day by 2015. As a result, as of June 2015, Iran did not have the infrastructure in place to export or import LNG, with LNG projects being years away from completion.[92] In June 2015, Iran announced its plan to revive its LNG projects with the goal of targeting the European market, where the quest for alternative gas sources has intensified amid tensions with Russia.[93]

Russia is dependent on income from energy export to Europe. Thus, mutual cooperation in coordinating energy exports from the Persian Gulf is understandably one of Russia's main commercial interests. In the long term, there may be a competition for energy resources; however, in the short term, the supply is abundant, and producers are competing for markets. For instance, in August 2011, five large Iraqi oil cargoes headed to Europe in what energy experts called an "opening shot in a pricing war with rival Russia."[94] The exports of Iraqi Basra oil were triggered by a release of U.S. oil stocks in June and a strengthening of Russian crude values.[95] As Iraq builds its export facilities and ramps up production, it could compete with Russia for market share, such as in Europe, where Iraqi and Russian crude are of a similar quality. It is no surprise that Putin's visits to oil- and gas-producing countries in the Persian Gulf often focus on coordinating with energy producers.[96] Since the growth in shale gas will likely provide strong competition to traditional pipeline gas, Russia wants to coax Qatar in particular and Iran to manage and coordinate their supply of LNG to ensure price stability.

Energy pipelines and security issues cross borders and regions in that global politics is far less compartmentalized than it was in previous centuries. European affairs are tied to the Middle East in obvious and less clear ways. For instance, Russia started a rapprochement with Turkey in the past decade, which has been driven partly by common energy interests. That includes a potential South Stream pipeline meant to carry Russian gas across the Black Sea through Turkish waters and then to Europe, which would allow Russia in some measure to bypass Ukraine. But Russia and Turkey remain divided on a number of issues, including the crisis in Syria.

Economic Factors and the Broader Picture

If Russia's altered orientation and increased commercial relations continue to develop, it may have added interest in helping to enforce the Iran nuclear deal and contain Iran's missile program. Russia had taken the middle road in its approach to Iran and pursued a purposefully ambiguous policy,[97] an approach that Washington found insufficiently weak. Russia has flip-flopped on selling Iran S-300 air defense systems and a host of other major arms, first banning such sales in line with U.N. Security Council Resolution 1929 of June 9, 2010,[98] and then lifting the ban.[99] Over time, Russia has offered greater cooperation on the Iran nuclear program, which was likely due to American and other international pressure and Russia's own doubts about a nuclear Iran,[100] but it may have been affected by Russia's interest in developing economic links with Arab Gulf states. While Russia has serious economic interests in Iran and probably views its connection to Iran as a potential check on American power, data have shown that its commercial interests with GCC states, as well as Iraq, have been rising, and these states want to contain Iran, notwithstanding the Iran nuclear accord.

Greater Russian-Gulf state cooperation in energy may also help Russia maintain the use of natural gas as a political tool in Europe. LNG is a serious threat to Russia's market and political influence in Europe. Europe imports up to one-third of its gas from Russia and accounts for 65 percent of Gazprom's total exports. But Russia's power in this arena appears to be decreasing. The big energy companies that have signed long-term gas contracts with Russia are winning more flexible pricing arrangements, largely because there is greater competition from LNG, which is transported by ship, and for shale, an unconventional natural gas extracted from sedimentary rocks. The availability of LNG and the discovery of shale resources in Europe have rattled Gazprom's position, especially in Eastern Europe.[101] Gazprom has acknowledged that it was rapidly losing leadership in the European market, that demand for Russian pipeline gas dropped due to the unprecedented increase in LNG supply, and that it needed to take various actions such as price adjustments and market diversification to try to remedy this situation.[102] While Gazprom, the world's biggest gas producer, has supplied about a quarter of Europe's gas needs, it has lost market share to Norway and Qatar, in part as LNG shipments to Europe rose significantly.[103]

As we have suggested, Russia has responded in part with greater cooperation with natural gas exporters. At the 2011 Gas Exporting Countries Forum, it won the support of the world's twelve largest natural gas exporters on developing projects for the production and sale of the fuel in order to raise prices, marking a new stage in the history of the ten-year-old organization. On the forum's sidelines, Russia, Qatar, and Algeria have agreed to cooperate on the European natural gas market.[104] This step is the primary reason for the EU's concerns over any meetings of these countries' leaders.[105] If Russia can continue to build energy relations with Qatar and Iran, despite sanctions against the latter and political problems with both countries, it may counter the LNG threat. In this sense, it can use its growing economic relations in the Middle East to advance broader global goals, which are not in the interest of the United States and Europe. Some might consider such action to be a form of soft balancing against the United States.

Finally, Arab states have been investing more in Russian oil and gas exploration and production, and vice versa. Such investment is important for a reason not often discussed or understood. The authoritative IEA radically changed its forecast on oil production in 2008. Until then, it largely dismissed notions that oil supplies might peak or reach a point where global oil production no longer increases and then decreases thereafter. By contrast, in November 2008, the agency provided a somewhat alarming forecast that oil will likely peak around 2020. It then changed its forecast because the previous 2007 report was based on best-of-knowledge assumptions about what global oil fields could produce. The 2008 report, by contrast, was based on actual studies of the production rates of the world's largest oil fields. To be sure, the North American energy boom has decreased peak oil concerns and rightly so, but it has not eliminated the problem.

One major factor driving the possible peak oil problem is underinvestment by major oil companies and countries in oil discovery and production. Underinvestment is caused by a variety of factors, but greater Russian-Arab Gulf state interaction may help ameliorate this problem if it continues to develop over the longer run and if Russia maintains positive relations with the West. In this sense, if such cooperation continues, it may increase investment in energy that helps buy some more time in the case that peak oil does become a serious future problem in world politics.

Conclusion

Russia's foreign policy toward and capabilities in the Persian Gulf have changed dramatically since the fall of the Soviet Union. Russia has been making an uneasy and fitful transition from heated rivalry during the Cold War to a somewhat different approach toward the region. Commercial interests are gaining in importance; if that continues to develop, it may contribute to Russia's interest in greater regional stability.

Moscow's rising commercial interests, however, hardly imply an absence of rivalry. Russia and China, for that matter, are enmeshed in relationships with

Washington that are marked by important elements of both cooperation and serious rivalry. They sometimes seek to curb U.S. influence in the region, partly to meet their regional goals and partly to check America at the global level. The real question is not whether they are rivals with Washington, but to what extent their rivalry is tempered by other factors. These factors differ in the case of China and Russia, but they include potentially more developed interdependence, vested interests in stability for commercial purposes, and the challenges of managing strategic and economic rivalry in a region where they lack strong allies. Of course, the nature of such rivalries will also be affected by Washington. That will be true no matter who sits in the Oval Office, though different presidents have pushed relations more toward cooperation or rivalry.

III THE UNITED STATES, CHANGING DYNAMICS, AND OIL SECURITY

9 How America, China, and Russia Have Changed

GREAT ATTENTION has focused on whether America remains a hegemon at the global level in world affairs, but we have taken a different turn by focusing in this book on the international relations of a region. We have explored global power politics and dynamics in the Persian Gulf while also treating the global and regional levels as linked. To what extent and how has American capability changed over time in the Persian Gulf relative to that of China and Russia? What do we find when we more formally compare China, Russia, and the United States over time?

First, it is worth repeating that the indicators that we used to examine America, China, and Russia had a dual purpose: they provided insight into the changing role and interaction of the great powers and their changing capabilities. It is the latter goal that is most closely related to the bigger question of American standing in the world. In addition, exploring the capabilities of great powers is different at the global and regional levels. Measures such as GDP illuminate great power capabilities at the global level but tell us little about their capabilities in regions. That is why we created different metrics for examining the capabilities and standing of external powers in the Persian Gulf.

The United States has become and remains predominant across all of the indicators that we examined. This is true even though China and, and to a far smaller degree Russia, have expanded, sometimes profoundly, their diplomatic contacts and economic ties to regional states. We now present the accumulated evidence and explore what this data comparison means in the bigger picture of oil security, American hegemony and its challenges, and great power rivalry.

The Diplomatic Dimension

The diplomatic position of states represents the most qualitative of the factors that we explored, but something can certainly be learned in studying changes in diplomatic visits, treaties and accords, and official and unofficial statements, even if all of that needs to be considered in context. A few points are worth restating in this conclusion.

Most notably, America's diplomatic position has improved over time, although its relations with Saudi Arabia experienced serious strains. In the post-2003 period, the United States also established diplomatic relations with Iraq, which it had lacked since the 1991 Gulf War.

For its part, Russia's overall strategic position in the broader Middle East weakened substantially following the collapse of the Soviet Union and the loss of Iraq as a main ally. However, the fall of the empire did not altogether undermine Russia's role in the region, and with respect to the GCC states, it in fact proved beneficial politically and economically.

In the Cold War, Russia and even China suffered due to their ideological differences with GCC states. Russia was also hurt by its menacing military reputation and the need of GCC states to side with Washington. But evidence clearly shows that in the post–Cold War period, Russia, and particularly China, have expanded, in some cases dramatically, their diplomatic contacts to all the regional states. That has particularly accelerated in the 2000s, driven largely by commercial matters, including trade, energy investments, and arms sales.

The Security Dimension

America has become and remains peerless in its military position in the region, which is one of the most distinguishing features of modern Middle East politics. The United States evolved from a period in the 1940s when its ability and will to affect Persian Gulf security was minimal, to a period where it is now the primary external protector of oil supplies.

The rise of American regional capabilities is quite distinct. In 1979, at the time of the Iranian revolution, Washington was not strategically prepared to protect Persian Gulf oil supplies militarily. It lacked access to regional facilities and could not project force there. In response to the Iranian revolution, Afghanistan intervention, and the Iran-Iraq War, America developed the military alliances, base structure, and rapid deployment capabilities necessary to guard against and manage serious oil supply threats and disruptions, even as its presence in the region also stokes controversy and generates problems that need to be considered. For its part, Saudi Arabia established a state-of-the-art Combined Air Operation Center at Saudi Prince Sultan Air Base. These capabilities proved critical to the liberation of Kuwait following the Iraqi invasion, enabling the largest U.S. movement of U.S. forces since World War II. In response to the evolving threat, American capability increased dramatically during the 1990s and then further in the 2000s.

In sharp contrast to the American regional role, China's and Russia's increased political ties and economic interdependence with regional states have not spurred security ties. China has not concluded any security agreements with regional powers, and its overall arms sales to the region dropped significantly in the 1990s and diminished further in the 2000s, although limited arms sales to Iran have continued since the 1990s. Interestingly, economic and energy cooperation, rather than security and politics, have overwhelmingly dominated the agenda of diplomatic visits between China and the regional states since the 1990s. Despite China's unprecedented diplomatic and economic ties with the GCC countries, it's unclear that this has yielded Beijing much influence in the region, given divergent policies toward Iran and Syria where the Arab Gulf states and China are at great odds.

While China and Russia have been driven by energy and commercial interests, security ties represent the cornerstone of U.S.-GCC relations, including in the post–Cold War period and of U.S.-Iraqi relations in the post-Saddam period. Since the 1991 Gulf War, the GCC states have gained much-desired American security guarantees, albeit U.S. forces left Saudi Arabia in 2003 and moved to Qatar instead. Throughout the 1990s and first decade of the 2000s, they have subsidized facilities expansion and modernization in support of the U.S. presence and the U.S.-led wars in Afghanistan and Iraq. Despite the outcome and cost of the U.S. invasion of Iraq in 2003 and the embarrassing fact that Iraq had no weapons of mass destruction, the Iraqi debacle has not diminished U.S. regional capabilities.

U.S.-GCC relations took a quantum leap forward in 2012 when the UAE became home to the new Integrated Air Missile Defense Center, which serves as a key training facility for U.S.-GCC cooperation on missile defense. Since 2005 in particular, the United States has embarked on myriad new collaborative initiatives and cooperation in nontraditional security areas such as counterterrorism, critical infrastructure protection, and cyberdomain.

While America's military capabilities, security relations, and arms sales to the region expanded exponentially from the 1980s through the post–Cold War era, Russia's position reversed after the Cold War and Beijing's remained minor at best. Their security relations have been largely limited to arms sales to Iran and, to some extent, cooperation on its nuclear program, although that was curtailed by sanctions. Indeed, although Russia has historically used arms sales and transfers to build influence in the Middle East, its ability to do so significantly decreased in the post–Cold War period. The 1991 Gulf War and the ensuing embargo against Iraq shut down its most lucrative regional market, resulting in a drop in sales from $4.1 billion across 1988 to 1991 to near zero. Russian arms exports to the region remained concentrated on Iran through the mid- to late 1990s, and Iran remained the only major buyer of Russian arms.

While in the 1990s and even more so since 2000, energy cooperation became the fulcrum of Sino-Gulf relations, arms sales were central during the 1980s. China entered the Gulf arms market during the Iran-Iraq War, with arms sales to both parties totaling over $12 billion. Arms sales provided the PRC with leverage and served as a source of hard currency to modernize China's own military program. Like Russia, China's arms sales dropped significantly after peaking at the end of the 1980s due to the dominance of Western suppliers, and Iran remained the chief buyer of China's arms. By 2001, China's arms agreements with the region fell to around 2.2 percent, dropping to 1 percent from 2008 to 2011, which is the lowest since China's penetration of the market in the 1980s (see Figure 9.1).

Since the end of the Cold War and particularly since 2006, Moscow and Beijing have sought to penetrate the lucrative GCC arms markets but achieved success only with the UAE, despite improved relations with Saudi Arabia. Consider a telling statistic: during the 2000s, Riyadh bought only $800 million worth arms from China, while spending $50 billion on American arms between 2004 and 2011 alone.[1]

As Figure 9.2 shows, U.S. arms sales to the GCC states rose substantially over time and dwarfed those of China and Russia. They grew more than eightfold between 2004–2007 and 2008–2011 alone, and the demise of Saddam Hussein's regime also gave Washington access to what had been Russia's market. Such sales indicate but do not establish that security relations are positive, and they can yield the outside actor influence in the region. America's sales have also been aimed at helping Arab states check Iran.

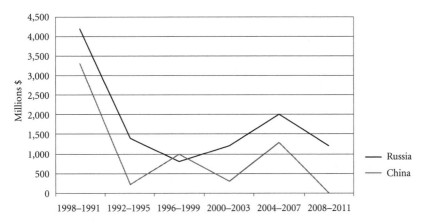

FIGURE 9.1. China and Russia: Arms Trade with the Gulf States, 1988–2011.
SOURCE: Compiled by the authors from Richard Grimmett, "Conventional Arms Transfers to Developing Countries" (Washington, DC: Congressional Research Service, various years).

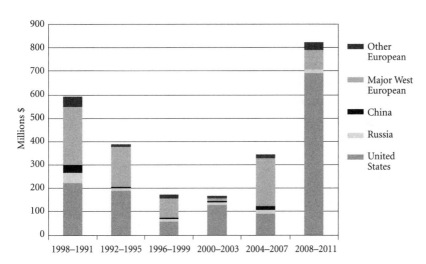

FIGURE 9.2. External Arms Sales to the Persian Gulf States, 1988–2011.
SOURCE: Compiled by the authors from Richard Grimmett, "Conventional Arms Transfers to Developing Countries" (Washington, DC: Congressional Research Service, various years).

Economic-Energy Capabilities

While America remains the dominant external economic power and the value of its trade has increased, Beijing has significantly expanded trade and energy cooperation with regional states in the post–Cold War period, and particularly since 1990. Prior to 1990, China's trade, investment, and energy cooperation was very limited. However, as Figure 9.3 shows, it has skyrocketed since then, driven chiefly by hydrocarbon trade and investments. Russia has also made some strides, but they are minor compared to those of China and, of course, the United States.

As Figure 9.4 demonstrates, the PRC, like the United States, has expanded trade relations with Iraq unprecedentedly. That is remarkable given the extraordinary costs to America of the invasion of Iraq, on which Beijing clearly capitalized. Meanwhile, Russian-Iraqi trade has outright flatlined, a remarkable change given that the two states were allies in the 1970s and 1980s. That turnaround is one of the most significant in the international relations of the region.

China has clearly exploited the vacuum left by American and, later, EU economic sanctions against Iran, as has Russia to a far smaller degree. During the 1990s, the EU, and especially Germany, Italy, and France, were Iran's biggest trading partners, but those relations were clipped by international sanctions. Beijing was happy to fill the void to the extent possible. In 2003, China was Iran's sixth biggest trading partner, but Beijing gradually overtook the EU as Iran's largest oil customer and trading partner in 2007 and most years thereafter. The rise in the PRC's trade also tells us something about its politics: it preferred to score economic gains than to cooperate fully with the international community on Iran.

Russia's trade remains minuscule compared to that of China and America (see Figures 9.3–9.5), partly because it is not a major energy importer. But it has seen unprecedentedly high trade volumes and collaboration with the Gulf states as reflected in Figure 9.6 which we reprise here for the reader's benefit. If this trend continues, it could have important effects.

While China–Gulf state trade appears to be approaching American trade levels, the composition of trade reveals a rather different trend. The PRC's exports consist largely of low-tech, low-value goods that are easy to substitute, whereas American exports are dominated by high-tech, high-value products. That makes the United States much more valuable on the economic level. In contrast to China and Russia, the United States also continues to be the main source of and destination for GCC investment, which furthers economic interdependence.

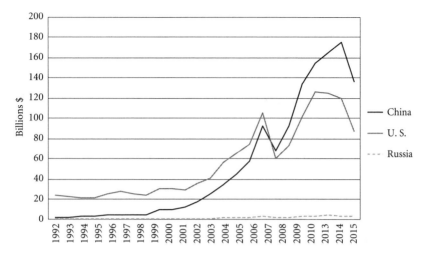

FIGURE 9.3. Total Chinese, American, and Russian Trade with the GCC States, 1992–2015.

SOURCE: Compiled by the authors from UN Comtrade database.

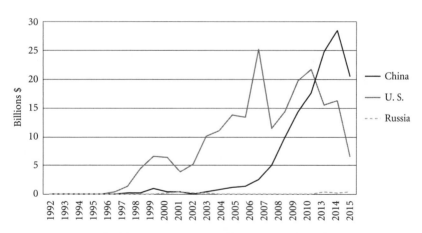

FIGURE 9.4. Total Chinese, American, and Russian Trade with Iraq, 1992–2015.

SOURCE: Compiled by the authors from UN Comtrade database.

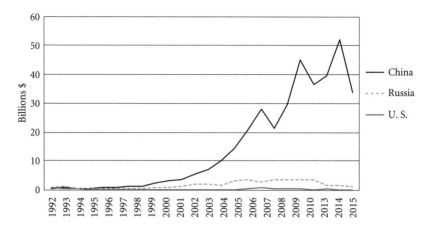

FIGURE 9.5. Total Chinese, American, and Russian Trade with Iran, 1992–2015.
SOURCE: Compiled by the authors from UN Comtrade database.

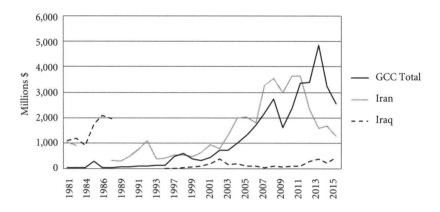

FIGURE 9.6. Total Trade between Russia and the Persian Gulf States 1981–2015.
SOURCE: Authors' calculations for data in the years 1981–1982 are drawn from *Foreign Trade Statistics Yearbook of the USSR* (Moscow: Ministry of Foreign Trade of the USSR, various years). The rest of data are drawn from United Nations, Commodity Trade Statistics Database (New York: United Nations, various years), and United Nations, *International Trade Statistics Yearbook* (New York: United Nations, various years).

Nonetheless, the United States has been losing trading share to China. For example, in 2000, U.S. exports to Saudi Arabia represented nearly 20 percent of total Saudi imports; by 2007, it was only 13.5 percent. In contrast, China's total market share of the Saudi market more than doubled from 4.1 percent to 9.6 percent in the same period.

China and Russia have significantly expanded their energy cooperation with all Gulf states, especially with Iraq and Iran. In fact, just between 2009 and 2013, Chinese national oil companies accounted for more than 50 percent of Iraqi oil output. In Iran, they gained traction in the energy sector following the withdrawal of Asian and European energy companies, making Iran largely dependent on Chinese investment, technology, and equipment.

The Regional Balance of Power

The evidence we have marshaled underscores the rise of American hegemony. But can America be considered a hegemon given the perceived ascendance of Iran in the region, especially since the 2003 war that eliminated Saddam Hussein?

The 2003 U.S.-led Iraq invasion felled Iraq's Saddam Hussein, weakened Iraq as a state, and yielded Iran's influence. That has left Iran stronger in the region not so much because its own capabilities have grown substantially but rather because Iraq could not play balancer against Iran nearly as well, if at all, in the foreseeable future. As a result, the U.S. invasion of Iraq allowed Iran, which was already stronger than U.N.-sanctioned Iraq, to expand unchecked by Iraq and, in fact, to gain some influence over Iraq as well.

However, the story is not so simple. Examining the distribution of capabilities in the region over time suggests a different tale. Even among the relatively weaker states of the Persian Gulf, Iran on paper is not that much stronger than Saudi Arabia if we use GDP as an indicator. As Table 9.1 shows, Saudi Arabia and Iran have been roughly matched in terms of GDP from 1979 to 2014, albeit the Saudis have been stronger than Iran since 1990.

Iran's economy has been in shambles since the Iranian Revolution, through the Iran-Iraq War, and into the period of international sanctions against it. This will change due to the Iran nuclear accord, but Iran has a long way to go toward fixing its economic morass. Its economy has relied overwhelmingly on oil export revenues—around 80 to 90 percent of total export earnings and 40 to 50 percent of the government budget. And Tehran spends around $25 billion per year, or roughly 15 percent of the country's GDP, on heating oil and energy subsidies. Iran's budgetary pressures have worsened over time and certainly

TABLE 9.1. Relative Economic Capability of Iran, Iraq, and Saudi Arabia

	Iran GDP	Iraq GDP	Saudi Arabia GDP
1979	84.7	38.6	97.3
1980	93.9	54.0	147.6
1981	92.8	31.8e	165.9
1982	99.7	34.6e	153.0
1983	157.6	30.6	119.9
1984	158.9	27.0e	105.4
1985	174.5	21.9	93.7
1986	268.0	17.7	77.4
1987	369.0e	39.0e	71.1
1988	447.3	46.09e	75.3
1989	53.06	35.0e	83.0
1990	59.5	15.0e	87.9
1991	68.2	15.0e	109.1
1992	54.2	17.0e	121.1
1993	57.8e	17.0e	125.5e
1997	106.4	0	170.9
2000	96.4	0	194.8
2005	202.9	0	328.2
2010	419.1	138.5	526.8
2014	402.7	232.2	777.9

NOTE: GDP is based on information from governments, and thus is not fully accurate, particularly given huge fluctuations in exchange rates.

e: Indicates estimates rather than actual figures provided by governments.

SOURCES: *The Military Balance* (London: International Institute for Strategic Studies, various editions); *Brassey's* (all editions from 1984–1985 through 1994–1995). In addition, interviews with International Monetary Fund (IMF) officials, and the *International Financial Statistics Yearbook* (Washington, DC: IMF, various editions, esp. 1981–1982 through 1984–1985). These figures are educated conjecture (indeed, figures from *The Military Balance*, which are based on *International Financial Statistics Yearbook* (IFSY) data, differed significantly after 1985 from IFSY figures based on this author's calculations), and reflect data revisions.

Between 1997 and 2014 were extracted from IMF Data, World Economic Outlook Database, 2014.

have been magnified by U.S.-led economic sanctions. It is no wonder that the Iranian regime engaged in negotiations over its nuclear program. Under public pressure, President Hassan Rouhani campaigned on doing so and on breaking Iran's international isolation, which was damaging its economy. Yet even with the gradual lifting of economic sanctions, Iran will still need high oil prices to satisfy its people with subsidies and manage its autocratic state.[2] Tehran will need much higher oil revenues just to meet the increased needs of a growing population. Although studies project that Iran's rate of population growth will continue to slow, after having risen at a high rate in past decades, it is still expected to rise and stabilize above 100 million by 2050, from around 77.5 million today.[3]

While the economic balance in the region may be more evenly matched than some might guess, Iran remains far stronger than Saudi Arabia at the military level, as Table 9.2 demonstrates. However, Saudi Arabia has become much stronger over the past few decades. Riyadh has gained in absolute and relative terms in virtually every military category.

To be sure, assessing military capability based on numbers alone is usually misleading. Saudi Arabia has better aircraft than Iran, which boosts its position in more sophisticated measures of military capability that move beyond straight number comparisons.[4] Some observers even consider the Saudi air force to be on par with or better than Iran's, notwithstanding Saudi Arabia's lack of combat experience. In fact, by some combined measures, Saudi Arabia is ranked as the third best military in the Middle East, with Iran coming in fifth.[5] While that is doubtful, it does underscore the premium that some studies put quality of weapons over quantity and underscores the improvement in the Saudi military in the past several decades.

In 2015, one complex index that uses fifty factors to determine a nation's power ranked Iran at twenty-third and Saudi Arabia at twenty-eighth.[6] In brief, Iran and Saudi Arabia are not incomparable in strength, contrary to what one might gather from media coverage or from past views of their capabilities.

The nuclear agreement with Iran, if it lasts, will likely affect these balance-of-power dynamics. It will strengthen the Iranian economy, though it may well impede Iran's path to nuclear weapons as well. At the same time, Washington and other actors may bolster the GCC states against Iran, which may strengthen them as well.

Beyond examining the regional balance of power, we should also factor into our analyses that the United States and Saudi Arabia, in effect, are in a strategic

TABLE 9.2. The Regional Military Balance

Country	Men (1,000s)[a]				
	Total	Army	Tanks	Artillery	Combat Aircraft
1979					
Iran	240	150	1,735	1,000	447
Iraq	243	200	2,750	1,240	339
Saudi Arabia	44	35	350	-	178
1989					
Iran	604	550	500–600	875	60–165
Iraq	1,000	955	5,500	2,800	500–800
Saudi Arabia	56	32	550	400–500	179
1994					
Iran	513	345	1,295	2,320	294[b]
Iraq	382	350	2,200	1,650	325
Saudi Arabia	104	70	1,085[c]	700	292[d]
1999					
Iran	545	350	1,410	2,460	307
Iraq	429	375	2,700	1,950	353
Saudi Arabia	162	70	1,055	538	432
2003					
Iran	513	-	1,565	2395	283
Iraq	424	-	2,200	2050	316
Saudi Arabia	230	124	-	260	-
2014					
Iran	523	475	1,663	2322	334
Iraq	271	193	336	196	3
Saudi Arabia	374	310	252	274	153

[a] Includes Revolutionary Guards forces and Popular Army forces.
[b] Probably less than 50 percent of U.S. aircraft types are serviceable.
[c] This includes 315 M1A2 tanks under delivery in summer 1995.
[d] Excludes 72 F-15s and 48 Tornados on order at the time.

SOURCES: Adapted by the authors from off-the-record interviews and from U.S. Department of Defense, *Conduct of the Persian War: Final Report to Congress* (Washington, DC: Government Printing Office, April 1992), 154, 157; International Institute for Strategic Studies, The Military Balance (London: International Institute for Strategic Studies, various editions); Center for Strategic and International Studies, *The Military Balance in the Middle East* (Washington, DC: Center for Strategic and International Studies, various editions).

alliance, even if it is marked by tense political relations. While Riyadh has the U.S. strategic alliance to count on against worst-case scenarios and some allies in the region, Iran has very few allies at the global or regional level. China and Russia want to do business with Iran, but they are hardly strategic allies. In addition, Syria is more of a burden than a serious ally and the Assad regime may not even survive. U.S.-Saudi strategic relations, for instance, allow both countries to draw on the strengths of the other to protect security in the region. Iran has far more adversaries in the region than allies.

With rudimentary Saudi support, such as continued access to its military facilities in the event of some security crisis, America's military capability in the region and the capabilities that it can bring to the region in a relatively short time are far superior to those of Iran. This is true not only of the high-performance aircraft, but also in terms of war-fighting capability. Indeed, it is quite telling that Iran fought Iraq to a stalemate in the eight-year Iran–Iraq War but that U.S.-led forces, mostly American, routed Iraq's military in a matter of weeks in 1991 and in 2003. Iran had difficulty protecting its homeland, much less projecting its force.

Let's also consider another indicator of American capability: the protection of the critical choke point for global oil security, the Strait of Hormuz. Estimates vary as to Iran's abilities to shut down the Strait of Hormuz. It has some developed capabilities such as mine laying and missile warfare. However, the American military believes that Tehran could do so for only a short period of time,[7] and few scholars believe that Iran could maintain such a closure for more than several weeks.[8] That expected outcome in favor of the United States strongly reflects its rise in capability over the past decades. America could not have exercised that type of security role in the 1970s or even in the early 1980s, though it started to demonstrate such capabilities and 1986 and 1987 with the reflagging of Kuwaiti tankers.

Whether the Iran nuclear accord meets the test of time, the rise of American capability helps contain Iran in a way that was not possible in the past. That is important because Iraq had been the natural balancer against Iran until the United States eliminated the Saddam Hussein regime and because Iran, even with the nuclear accord in place, remains a possibly threatening regional actor.

Conclusion

In great power and regional competition, the United States has emerged as the de facto hegemon in the Persian Gulf, even though China and, to a far lesser extent, Russia have made major strides politically and economically. Over the past several decades, America has developed major diplomatic ties to regional states, peerless military capabilities, deep but sporadically troubled security ties, a more powerful economic position, and meaningful trade interactions. That does not mean that it has translated such capability into power or that hegemony has not come with great costs. Those are different questions that we explore next, but the rise of such capabilities is directly linked to global oil security, as we explore in the next chapter.

10 The Rise and Not Fall of Oil Security

T HE CHANGES in the position of the United States, China, and Russia in the Persian Gulf are important in their own right, but they also
have implications for global oil security. A defining feature of our age is that oil
has become increasingly tied to Middle East realities, which have affected U.S.
national and global security.[1] Failure to understand oil and its effects leaves us
with blind spots about security in general. Students and scholars of U.S. national and global security need to understand better how oil affects security and
fits into security studies. This is because oil cross-cuts key security issues ranging from war, power, and national interests that are posited in more traditional
definitions of security, to broader definitions that include political, economic,
societal, human, and environmental factors.[2] Indeed, no other commodity and
few other factors of any kind cross-cut such a wide range of security issues.

We have explored oil security thus far and now focus on it more intensively. In
large part, oil security is about reliable oil supplies or supplies that are not easily
subject to such things as severe oil supply disruptions and the exploitation of oil
supplies for foreign policy goals. This includes, of course, the free flow of oil, most
prominently from the Middle East, but also from actors such as Russia, which has
periodically cut off its oil and natural gas exports to try to influence European
politics. This aspect of oil security is sometimes referred to as geopolitics.

Another aspect of oil security that is important but not salient here has to
do with the negative effects of using oil, such as pollution and military conflicts. Oil has been a central driver of global growth as a relatively cheap energy

source and has played a critical role in fostering globalization. But the negative effects of using oil are sometimes ignored, overlooked, or misunderstood when we try to comprehend the costs of its widespread use.

We have focused on the reliable and uninterrupted oil supply to the global economy at reasonable prices.[3] Defined this way, global oil security is affected by two critical dimensions in the Persian Gulf: the free flow of oil from the Gulf region and adequate investment into oil exploration and development. Few other goals are more important for the global economy than ensuring the free flow of oil and, to a lesser extent, LNG from the Persian Gulf. In fact, past American and global recessions have been preceded by or accelerated by an increase in oil prices, often the result of Persian Gulf instability, including the 1973 oil embargo, the 1979 Iranian Revolution, and the 1980 outbreak of the Iran-Iran War, among others. To be sure, the security of the Persian Gulf oil and a need for oil investment in the region is poised to become even more important in the future. This is because world dependence on oil and LNG is projected to increase in the decades ahead, with the Persian Gulf serving as the principal source of supply to meet rising demand over the next two decades. In addition to holding the largest oil reserves, two regional states, Saudi Arabia and Kuwait, hold 80 percent of the world's spare capacity that can be used in times of disruptions to calm jittery global oil markets and stabilize oil prices.

Given the Persian Gulf's strategic importance, it is interesting to explore how changes in American, Chinese, and Russian regional capabilities have affected oil security. We do not examine oil security and threats to it in their entirety. However, we do argue that America's rising capabilities have been positive for oil security, all things being equal. Since the 1980s, the rise in its regional military, political, and economic assets has enabled the United States to protect the free flow of oil from the region against a range of threats. This in turn has helped calm international markets, while providing conditions necessary for adequate investment into oil exploration and development.

U.S military capabilities for Gulf contingencies were minimal when the shah of Iran fell in 1979. In contrast, they increased substantially in the 1980s and even more dramatically in the 1990s and since the start of the 2000s. Indeed, whereas in 1979 America was unable to protect regional security, its ability to project force improved significantly between the 1980s and 2014 in response to evolving regional threats. In the 1980s, the United States developed RDF; improved airlift, sealift, and prepositioning capabilities; convinced Saudi Arabia to build massive military infrastructure for deployment of U.S. forces;

and gained access to key regional military facilities. These capabilities proved critical in addressing the Iraqi threat in 1990–1991. In the aftermath of the 1991 Gulf War and the 9/11 attacks, U.S. ability to project forces to the region and sustain them while in the region increased even more dramatically.

In fact, there has been no major oil crisis in the region since the rise of American capabilities in the 1980s. To be sure, oil prices spiked in the wake of the 1990 Iraqi invasion of Kuwait and the 2003 Iraqi War; however, prices declined when the United States demonstrated resolve to use its regional capabilities, particularly its naval forward presence, to respond to the regional crises, thus alleviating traders' concerns over oil availability.[4] Although oil prices spiked dramatically in 2008, this price shock was largely unrelated to geopolitical issues in the Persian Gulf.[5]

While the rise of U.S. capabilities represents a major shift in regional security, the rise of China's political and economic capabilities and, to a lesser extent, those of Russia has produced mixed results. They have led to some rivalry with Washington, which is not positive. However, the rise of Chinese and Russian economic and political capabilities in the region in the post–Cold War era and particularly in the past decade has not been accompanied by the establishment of a military presence in the region or commensurate security relations with the regional states. Consequently, they do not pose a serious security challenge to the U.S. regional position, although continued growth in their economic and political position in the region could complicate U.S. foreign policy, as we briefly demonstrate on the case of Iran. On the positive side, the rise of China's and Russia's economic interdependence with the regional states has benefited global oil security by bringing more oil and gas on the global energy market through mutual investments and, second, increasing their stake in regional stability.

Basic Threats to Oil Security in the Persian Gulf

The next sections of this chapter explore various threats to oil security: military threats, extremism in Saudi Arabia, and the use of oil as a weapon of political coercion. We also examine the role of the United States in helping to mitigate these threats.

Regional Military Threats

Three military threats to oil security have been most prominent: efforts to shut down the Strait of Hormuz, engage in interstate aggression, and use or threaten to use WMD.

Much of the world's oil travels through the Strait of Hormuz, which consists of 2-mile-wide channels for inbound and outbound Gulf tanker traffic, as well as a 2-mile-wide buffer zone. The EIA classifies the Strait of Hormuz as "by far the world's most important chokepoint [for oil trade]."[6] Closure of the strait would require the use of alternative routes (if available), such as the Abqaiq-Yanbu natural gas liquids line across Saudi Arabia to the Red Sea. But that would impose higher transportation costs and greater lag times for delivery. Around 40 percent of the world's oil exports pass through the strait daily, a number that the U.S. Department of Energy projects to climb to 60 percent by 2030.[7]

Iran has posed the key threat to the Strait of Hormuz. Its ability to interdict or shut down oil traffic is enhanced by antiship missiles, mine warfare, amphibious assets, and submarines. Such assets are probably not enough to challenge American military forces seriously and in a sustained manner, but they do certainly offer the ability to conduct forms of unconventional warfare. Such capabilities are enhanced by virtue of Iran's long coastline dominating the strait and by its position on the Greater and Lesser Tunbs and Abu Musa, islands near the strait that it seized in 1992.

Prior to the U.S.-led reflagging of Kuwaiti tankers in 1986–1987, Iran harassed tankers to prosecute the war against Iraq, which it launched in September 1980. Later, in November 1994, it began increasing troop strength and deploying antiaircraft missiles on the Gulf islands near the strait in ways that Washington viewed as threatening oil traffic. It also tripled the number of missiles deployed on its Gulf coast and began fitting Chinese-built cruise missiles on its naval boats in 1995–1996. Since 2006, it has further developed various antiship missile capabilities, antiship mines, and surface ship capabilities. It has also engaged in regular major military exercises in the Strait of Hormuz in an escalating set of military moves following the U.N. Security Council's approval of economic sanctions against it on December 23, 2006. These have included military demonstrations in summer 2012 aimed at showing that it could hit hundreds of short- and long-range targets with missiles, including Israel's missile defense shield radar sites, and major naval exercises in late 2012 aimed at demonstrating its naval warfare abilities in the region. Indeed, as U.S.-led economic sanctions against Tehran tightened in 2012, Iran repeatedly threatened to block the strait.[8] Such brinkmanship continued through 2015, when Iranian forces came close to American ships on at least two occasions, prompting some to believe that they sought some type of limited confrontation.

To be sure, Tehran must recognize that disrupting Gulf shipping would produce countermeasures and would also diminish its own oil exports. Yet Iranian officials have stated repeatedly that while Iran, the world's fourth largest exporter, supports the stable flow of oil, it reserves the option to shut the strait down if it is threatened. The Iran nuclear accord decreases the chances of such a showdown with Washington, but it is too early to tell if the accord will stick and if it will remove other friction points in relations with Washington and the GCC states. Moreover, the accord deals with Iran's nuclear aspirations but does not address its broader foreign policy goals and behavior.

The United States has remained committed to playing a vital role in protecting the Strait of Hormuz and has developed the capability and willingness to deter, contain, and address threats to oil and regional stability. The United States has also significantly bolstered its sea- and land-based defenses in the Persian Gulf to deter and counter any efforts to close the Strait of Hormuz.[9]

The American capability to deter or deal with these and other threats to oil security helps reassure volatile global oil markets, thus decreasing the potential for market instabilities. This in turn helps to stabilize insurance rates for shipping through the Persian Gulf. The global economy depends on Gulf oil at reasonable prices. If prices rise significantly, the global economy as a whole is impaired. Without a demonstrable U.S. ability to protect the strait, such rates would likely increase significantly,[10] and oil markets would experience a higher risk premium in the price of a barrel of oil. Such effects have been clearly demonstrated in other contexts, such as in the Gulf of Guinea, where growing piracy attacks and insufficient international naval presence to address this threat have led to a sharp increase in shipping and insurance costs, deterring investors from investing in oil projects along Africa's West Coast.[11]

The United States has played, and will likely continue to play, a vital role in protecting the Strait of Hormuz, especially if the nuclear accord with Iran falters due to its cheating or to a change in administration in Washington or Iran. The Pentagon has asserted that while Iran can block the Strait of Hormuz for a while, such upgrades including significant enhancements in mine-sweeping capability and naval force realignments, allow the United States to reopen it without great difficulty.[12]

The United States can use its predominant military capability to protect Gulf shipping, as it did during the mission to reflag Kuwaiti tankers that were being attacked by Iran to punish Kuwait for supporting Iraq during the Iran-Iraq War. By the end of 1987, U.S. forces stopped frequent Iranian attacks on Gulf shipping and escorted twenty-three convoys without attack from either Iraq or Iran.[13] Iran's naval forces were effectively neutralized by American naval capabilities. Iran's capabilities have improved immensely since 1987, but the United States can now use a plethora of precision-guided weapons, antisubmarine helicopters, attack submarines, the immense enhanced defense capabilities of carrier battle groups, and weapon systems that remain classified to protect the Strait of Hormuz and deter or punish Iranian actions.

Washington has also protected oil security in another way: exerting political pressure on outside states in order to decrease the flow of arms to Iran. That has been a difficult task but one marked by some successes. For instance, by the late 1980s, China agreed not to sell more Silkworm missiles to Iran after repeated U.S. complaints on how such sales make it harder to protect Gulf shipping and after receiving assurances from the United States that it would lift the freeze that had been placed on technology sales to China in 1987 in response to such sales to Iran.[14] By August 2002, Beijing announced and signed into effect long-awaited regulations to restrict company sales of missile-related items or any dual-use technology that could be used to launch such weapons,[15] and it has appeared to try to abide by this agreement, though it claims that it cannot control all of its businesses.

Iran represents the chief threat to global shipping, but it is not impossible that Iraq may once again become a military threat to Kuwait. Democratizing states can be more violent than democracies or autocracies.[16] An autocratic or dictatorial Iraq could also threaten Kuwait if its regime was buoyed by continuing public views that Kuwait is part of Iraq, if faced with domestic ills from which it wanted to divert attention, and if it had conflicts with Kuwait over oil production.

Furthermore, although it is unclear how much influence Iran has in Iraq, it has increased significantly since the 2003 invasion of Iraq. A serious Iranian bid for regional hegemony, especially in the relative absence of influence by Iranian moderates at the domestic level, could also generate the types of broader instabilities in the region that usually spook oil markets.

In addition to threats against the Strait of Hormuz and regarding Iraq, WMD represent an indirect threat to oil security. Iraq nearly developed nuclear capability prior to the 1991 Gulf War, and Iran may be able to produce nuclear weapons in the future despite the nuclear accord. It had repeatedly asserted that its program is for peaceful purposes, a point accepted by a majority of Iranians[17] yet doubted around the world.

However, let's say Iran obtains a nuclear weapon in the future. Even a small nuclear weapon could destroy major oil facilities, and threats of radiological, chemical, and biological weapons attacks cannot be discounted. Even if Iran or other states in the region never use WMD, they could enable brinkmanship or coercion because others would be aware of their existence. This could facilitate efforts by Iran to coerce other OPEC states such as Saudi Arabia into lowering oil production to raise the price of oil or into launching an embargo for various political ends. Nuclear weapons could also make it harder for the United States to deploy regional forces, for the obvious reason that leaders would be less willing to take the risk of massive casualties, and, of course, it could trigger a nuclear arms race in the region.[18]

The shifting regional distribution of capability has also shifted in Iran's favor. Iran and Iraq were roughly equal in military capability in 1980; Iraq gained the upper hand by 1990, but the U.S.-led invasion of Iraq in 2003 and subsequent occupation left Iran much stronger compared to its historic balancer, Iraq. Riyadh has known full well at least since the 1991 Gulf War that the United States is the only state that can leverage military, economic, and political strength to protect the regime against a major ground and air threat, as well as an WMD threat in the region.

Despite the embarrassing fact that Saddam's Iraq had no WMD and the disastrous outcome of the 2003 invasion of Iraq, the United States has played a central role against the proliferation of WMD, especially since September 11.[19] It did spearhead repeated U.N. action to constrain Iran's nuclear program and global economic sanctions. Iranian officials openly noted the negative impact of American-led sanctions on their economy, which was under much stress and facing significant cutbacks in oil exports from around 2.5 mbd to 1.5 mbd.[20]

America's regional and global influence has been critical to generating pressure on Iran and others to negotiate. For instance, China repeatedly stressed that the dispute over Iran's program should be resolved within the IAEA framework through negotiation.[21] But Beijing was reluctant to challenge the United States, partly because it is a dominant global economic and military leader, as well as a regional hegemon, that can influence China's energy security. Thus, it encouraged Iran to accept the Iran nuclear deal.

The United States has other avenues as well for dealing with the WMD threat. The Cooperative Defense Initiative has been a central CENTCOM activity that seeks to strengthen deterrence by reducing the vulnerability of the GCC states to "WMD coercion and to the effects of WMD use."[22] It enhances interoperability, active defenses, and medical countermeasures to protect soldiers and civilians against WMD.[23] GCC states have also sketched plans for a nuclear program that might counter Iran's,[24] and such an option, while inchoate, would depend fundamentally on American technology, support, and backup.[25]

As a last-resort measure, Washington also has the intelligence assets and the capability to try to destroy Iran's WMD facilities and maintain a vigilant watch on any of Iran's efforts to rebuild them, in conjunction with its allies. Predominant U.S. capabilities may also enhance international bargaining leverage with Iran, provided that Iran does not assume that a U.S.-led attack is inescapable no matter what Iran does. Arguably, such capabilities gave Iran more reason to accept UN offers of economic support in exchange for forgoing its nuclear enrichment program and more reason not to cheat on the accord or to develop nuclear weapons down the road.

There is one highly unlikely, but not impossible, future scenario: should the Iran accord fail and the crisis end in conflict, Iran could retaliate by attacking Saudi oil facilities—something that Washington has considered. In such a case, the substantial U.S.-backed military and political infrastructure may well diminish Iran's ability to disrupt the oil flow from Saudi Arabia.[26] Thus, one of the most feared scenarios for oil security could be tempered, barring any major surprises.

Terrorism

In addition to more conventional threats, terrorists can threaten oil security in several ways. Terrorist acts could produce significant spikes in oil prices by disrupting oil supplies, but more probably by their psychological impact on markets. Traders would have to ask if more attacks of this nature were coming.

Terrorists could do damage in various ways. Based on a database of global terrorist attacks, global oil facilities have not been the primary target of terrorists, accounting for only 262 of 5,000 incidents across the period from 1922 to 1999.[27] Nor has al-Qaeda focused on them in particular. However, its attacks on them have increased since September 11 and could become a serious threat.

Terrorists could hit sensitive points in Saudi Arabia's eight most significant oil fields, both onshore and offshore, and cause major problems in supply that could last months. Oil pipelines could also be hit along the broader Saudi oil system or from within Saudi oil facilities to outside markets. The Abqaiq extra light crude complex with a capacity of 7 mbd is the "mother of all processing facilities" and a grand target, because a moderate to severe attack could create a loss of oil equal to that of the 1973 embargo. Terrorists could also hijack ships and use them to attack ports and facilities[28] or hit large oil reservoirs such as Kuwait's Burgan Field, which was crippled by Iraq's invasion in 1990.[29]

In fact, it is very likely that al-Qaeda has targeted a range of oil facilities. Loading terminals such as at Ras Tanura, which transfers 5 million barrels of oil each day, have been targeted by al-Qaeda.[30] The Saudis claimed in April 2007 that they foiled a major terrorist effort to attack their oil facilities.

Terrorism aimed at regional monarchs, if successful, could also hurt oil security by weakening their position and slowly creating an atmosphere conducive to their overthrow. Increased domestic terrorism could dispose them to appease their anti-American domestic critics and decrease cooperation with Washington in the hope that they could placate at least part of the political spectrum that might sympathize with the terrorists. In fact, the Saudis moved in that direction after the September 11 terrorist attacks while seeking to preserve their relations with the United States. Meanwhile, after a lengthy national debate, the United States substantially diminished its military profile in Saudi Arabia and started to build sophisticated military facilities in Qatar, where it moved its CENTCOM headquarters in 2003.

American hegemony may well contribute to terrorism, but it also enables the United States to deal with terrorism. Along with foreign governments and major oil companies, Washington has taken many steps on this front[31] and has worked closely with Saudi Arabia in the intelligence arena despite the bilateral tensions caused by September 11.[32] Since 9/11, it has substantially increased antiterrorism financing, training, and support to all Gulf states.[33] In particular, the United States has supported Saudi efforts to create a 35,000-person force to protect critical Saudi oil infrastructure; the force was launched with 5,000 members in 2007 and will be critical in dealing with terrorist threats against the world's largest facilities.[34]

Extremists in Saudi Arabia

While terrorism could affect oil security, a much larger threat is the fall of the Saudi regime to Islamist radicals.[35] It is impossible to know exactly what such a radicalized regime would do, but based on the views of such radicals, it is possible that they would limit or cut U.S. relations, deny the United States worst-case-scenario access to Saudi strategic facilities, oppose Mideast peace efforts, eschew antiterrorist measures at the domestic and international level, and decrease oil production to increase oil prices and oil revenues and defy Washington. The combined effect of these actions would be to hurt oil security and raise prices, even if the new regime did not resort to oil embargoes and sought to provide a stable flow of oil to the global economy.

Interaction between the House of Saud and the United States antagonizes the regime's detractors, as it did with al-Qaeda prior to the September 11 attacks. Extremists dislike the royal family for many reasons, not the least of which are claims of corruption and illegitimate rule, but cozy relations with America certainly are a contributory factor. Yet while the United States is a lightning rod with extremists, we must also consider that it helps protect the regime. Would-be coup plotters, outside actors who might aid them, or extremists who simply want to undermine the House of Saud know that America is probably committed to the regime. One can surmise that such knowledge raises the potential costs of subversion and decreases prospects for success in the minds of some extremists. While the Carter Doctrine committed Washington to protect the Gulf from external threats, the Reagan Doctrine, which shaped subsequent U.S. policy, committed it to prevent the internal overthrow of the Saudi regime.[36] Moreover, U.S.-Saudi cooperation puts significant technological, intelligence, and financial tools at the kingdom's disposal, as do American oil companies in Saudi Arabia. The United States has played a critical role in organizing, equipping, training, and coordinating the Saudi Arabian National Guard, the regime's internal security force. The two states have not trumpeted this connection, but Washington is crucial to Saudi internal security.

On the whole, the United States could not prevent an unlikely grassroots revolution in Saudi Arabia such as the one that toppled Hosni Mubarak in Egypt, but it could try to help deter and perhaps reverse some types of serious subversion from within or by external actors like Iran. Washington may also complicate efforts by regional states to use real or potential military threats to undermine the Saudi regime, and it may also allow for military intervention in the event that the Saudi regime tumbles and Saudi oil fields fall to extremists. It is hard to imagine any other state playing this role, and even for Washington, it would be quite a risky and perhaps questionable gambit under some conditions, albeit one that the United States has considered openly, as recently as November 2005.[37]

The Oil Weapon

Global attention has focused increasingly on the question of oil dependence, especially in the post–September 11 period and in light of the U.S.-led war in Iraq. Irrespective of the fate of the Saudi regime, other Arab states or Iran could be motivated independently, multilaterally, or through OPEC or the Arab League to use the oil weapon. Many Saudis, despite close U.S. ties, still believe, as political scientist Gregory Gause puts it, that their "country's finest hour was when it defied the United States with the 1973 Arab oil embargo."[38]

Some evidence suggests that the United States has played an important direct and indirect role in preventing the use of the oil weapon. Despite the U.S.-led war in Iraq and despite the tensions in U.S.-Saudi relations created by September 11, it is fair to say that Saudi dependence on the United States against worst-case scenarios and its other strategic and economic benefits from U.S.-Saudi relations place some limits at least on how far Riyadh can satisfy Iran or on how far Saudi price hawks who seek greater oil production cuts can rail against Saudi moderates.

Washington not only protects Saudi Arabia; it also provides it with arms, spare parts, and technical training and support that lie at the heart of its defense. In fact, it has poured tens of billions of dollars into building the regional and Saudi military infrastructure. Such dependence hardly enables the United States to dictate terms to Riyadh, but as in the case of Kuwait, it likely increases U.S. influence. Indeed, a committed Arab oil policy has not manifested itself since the 1970s. This is in part because the Saudis have usually resisted OPEC oil production cuts, with some major exceptions.[39]

While the U.S.-Saudi connection has probably decreased prospects of an Arab oil embargo, it may also affect oil production decisions. Saudi Arabia needs oil revenue to maintain political stability, which has sometimes pushed it to support cuts or fail to support increases, as was the case glaringly in 2007 and 2008, but it also has feared that such cuts could spike oil prices high enough to cause inflation in the West and a backlash against Arab states.[40] Historically, the Saudis have sought to prevent price spikes. For instance, they increased oil production to address market jitters in the week preceding Iraq's invasion of Kuwait,[41] and U.S. oil companies provided Saudi Aramco with the technical assistance and equipment to increase oil output quickly to make up for the 5 mbd lost due to the invasion.

Direct and indirect American pressure may well have been applied to influence Saudi and, in turn, OPEC policy. In spring 2000, for instance, Energy Secretary Bill Richardson exerted pressure during quota negotiations to convince OPEC officials that oil production cuts would hurt the United States and other global economies. Richardson described such "quiet diplomacy" as effective pressure on OPEC to boost production.[42] Subsequent events seemed to support Richardson's contention that U.S. diplomacy was related to an immediate OPEC production increase of 1.8 mbd.[43] OPEC ministers had some difficulty arriving at a final agreement, in part because Iran was offended by what it saw as U.S. "intrusion" into its deliberations, although it subsequently signed on.[44] Iran's Foreign Ministry spokesman, Hamid Reza Asefi, asserted that the "use of political and military levers and forcing other countries to secure one's own economic interests are among hegemonic methods which do not go with any logic."[45] That would not be an unfamiliar refrain, as OPEC continued to consider its strategy. On July 18, 2000, for instance, Iran's oil minister, Bijan Zanganeh, stated that the Clinton administration was "trying to force the OPEC into increasing its production" for its own narrow, national interests,[46] the type of comment that Iran would repeat many more times. At the same time, the Saudis were trying to talk prices down, promising an extra 500,000 mbd if prices did not fall, a pledge made necessary by the failure of previous OPEC production increases to lower prices.[47]

Later in September 2000, Saudi Arabia, under some pressure from the United States, which feared that higher oil prices could trigger a global recession, also took the lead role in convincing OPEC to raise production.[48] That was against objections from Iran, which disliked Riyadh's unilateral decision to increase its production by 500,000 mbd.[49] In January 2001 when OPEC decreased oil production and ignited fears of rising prices, Crown Prince Abdullah assured Richardson that the Saudis were eager to stabilize oil markets and would increase production when necessary to ensure world economic growth.[50]

In the week preceding Iraq's invasion of Kuwait in 1991 and also in 2003 on the eve of the U.S.-led invasion of Iraq, Saudi Arabia persuaded OPEC to increase production to calm the global oil market. Some evidence also suggests that the Saudis may have primed oil prices ahead of the 2004 U.S. elections when Americans were bemoaning high prices.[51]

The period 2007–2008, however, underscores the limits of U.S. influence. From February 2007 through summer 2008, oil prices skyrocketed from $50 to over $140 per barrel. The Saudis did little until summer 2008 to stem this rise, and even then, their actions were not significant despite public pressure from President Bush. While this period raises serious questions about American influence with Saudi Arabia and about Saudi ability to meet ever growing oil demand in the world, three decades of behavior suggests that the Saudis are likely to be more cooperative in oil production because of their U.S. connection than other OPEC states. That became evident regarding the Iran nuclear crisis, when the Saudis repeatedly asserted that they would supply the markets with enough oil to make up for any of Iran's lost export should the United States attack it.

Saddam Hussein's demise also made the United States less critical to the Saudis as a protector of their security. This is because the biggest threat to Saudi Arabia, in terms of a potential military invasion by ground forces, always came from Iraq, not Iran. Of course, Iran poses the more serious ideological threat to the Saudis because it assails the Saudi monarchical form of government as illegitimate and because it is Sunni led, whereas Iran's government is clerical and Iran is predominantly Shiite. Iran has sought, partly based on this ideology, to overthrow the Saudi government indirectly by supporting the Shia against the leadership and trying to delegitimize its rule.

Still, with Saddam gone and with the Iraqi military threat removed for the foreseeable future, Riyadh needs the United States less than it did before. Given this shifting geopolitical calculus, the Saudis may well feel less of a need to support Washington's economic interests by increasing their oil production in order to try to lower global prices and a lot more concerned with their domestic problems. In sum, the lower the ground threat is from Iraq—and today there is little or none—the less leverage the United States is likely to have regarding Saudi oil policy.

All of this does not mean that the Saudis have stopped counting on the United States on a wide range of security and economic areas. Furthermore, it does not mean that Washington is without influence. The United States will remain the guarantor of regional security for some time to come. Nonetheless, a near-term reduction of U.S. influence in relation to the Saudis, who have pressing needs of their own that outweigh any concerns over U.S. displeasure, does appear to have taken place in recent years despite Iran's nuclear aspirations.

Meanwhile, just as the geopolitics of energy has shifted in the Persian Gulf, it has done so globally as well. With oil demand booming in Asia and elsewhere and with the rising economic and military power of China, oil exporters like the Saudis have options that they lacked in the past when it comes to customers and allies. Despite the fact that the world oil market is roughly global, the Chinese are more than willing to pay a high price for oil, as well as to invest in oil projects in places like Iran and Sudan where the United States is reluctant to tread.[52]

We have noted that the Saudis decided not to play the role of swing producer in 2014–2015, which contributed to a massive drop in oil prices. However, while that hurt American oil producers, the U.S. government itself was not against the steep drop in prices, which may well have helped the American and global economy.

China, Russia, and Oil Security

While the rise of U.S. military capabilities in the region has benefited global oil security by ensuring the free flow of oil from the region and calming the international markets, what about the changing position of China and Russia? That has also been salutary on the whole, though to a much lesser extent than the rise of the American role. The following sections turn to China and Russia.

Economic Dynamics and Security

China's economic interdependence with the Persian Gulf states has benefited global oil security. China's rise in the region may give it some leverage to check the United States and compete with it economically. But it also gives China a vested interest in regional stability. China wants oil to flow freely at the cheapest cost possible.

The dynamic regarding Russia is quite different. Moscow wants higher oil prices and does not mind some level of instability in the Persian Gulf. That would improve its budgetary picture by pushing oil prices higher and giving Russia's leaders more power. But Russia has far less capability now than during the Cold War to foment serious trouble in the Persian Gulf region, even if it can affect events outside the region in Syria, nor does it have the links to Iraq that used to give it some leverage. In the main, it can be uncooperative, such as with regard to Iran's nuclear program or in supporting Syria's dictator. Moscow also has faced some limitations because it would prefer positive relations with Washington, even as it challenges some of its interests. It can go only so far in undermining those relations, while in pursuit of regional goals.

In essence, then, China does not want trouble in the region, and Russia doesn't really have the ability to generate it in any serious way, which is sharply different from dynamics in the 1970s and 1980s.

China's Strategic Dependence and America's Unique Role

China needs the United States due to the rise of the U.S. military capabilities in the Persian Gulf. Washington has been and will continue to be critical to protecting the free flow of oil to the global market because no other power or combination of states appears willing or capable to assume the Gulf policing task.

Even if China wanted to play a larger role and the United States and regional actors were willing to cooperate in this scenario, that would be quite difficult. Although China has continued to debate how to secure oil sea-lanes and its increasing dependence on regional oil may eventually give rise to security relations with regional states, Beijing is decades away from having the military, logistical, and communications technology to protect the 7,000 miles of oil supply lanes. In fact, a number of Chinese scholars have been proponents of free riding on American policing role in the Gulf; however, others would prefer China to become less dependent on the U.S. policing role in the Gulf.[53]

While the evolution of European states' relations with the regional states is outside our scope, America's NATO allies lack the capability and will to assume the U.S. security role in the region. In fact, with a few exceptions, they lack the power projection capabilities to contribute meaningfully to the defense of the Persian Gulf against regional threats that could disrupt the energy flow, albeit Britain and France do maintain modest military capabilities in the region. To be sure, European states' capability to protect the Gulf oil supplies is poised to diminish even further. In 2013, only three of NATO's Europe countries spent the NATO goal of 2 percent or more of GDP on defense.[54] Current and planned defense cuts in the United Kingdom, France, Germany, Italy, and Spain will in particular affect NATO Europe's ability to deploy and sustain power over long distances.[55] This was demonstrated by Ivo Daalder, then-U.S. ambassador to NATO, and James Stavridis, former NATO's Supreme Allied Commander Europe, who warned in 2012, "If defense spending continues to decline, NATO may not be able to replicate its success in Libya [let alone in the Gulf] in another decade."[56] Similarly, NATO's secretary general, Anders Fogh Rasmussen, cautioned in 2011 that "if European defense spending cuts continue, Europe's ability to be a stabilizing force even in its neighborhood will rapidly disappear."[57]

Finally, while GCC countries have demonstrated an increased willingness to operate on the international scene and shoulder a greater share in protecting their own security and oil sea-lanes, they continue to be heavily dependent on U.S. leadership and military capabilities in the region. Also, while the GCC countries have made substantial progress in modernizing and building their capabilities since the 1990s through massive purchases of U.S. defense articles and U.S.-provided training, they are still developing faculties to maintain equipment, logistically support forces, and provide command, control, and intelligence fusion. Despite expanded diplomatic, security, and economic relations between the United States and GCC members in the post–Cold War era and the past decade in particular, the Gulf states' interests are not always aligned with those of the United States when it comes to regional security issues. Finally, if the GCC states pooled their burgeoning capabilities together, especially in the realm of regional missile defense, they would represent a menacing force to mitigate the regional threats and thereby diminish the need for U.S. dominant security role in the region. However, despite numerous attempts to upgrade the GCC alliance into an effective security and collective defense union over years and particularly since the U.S. withdrawal from Iraq and the Arab Spring uprisings in 2011, diverging interests, lack of trust among several GCC members, and the preference of some GCC states to continue to tie their security to the United States makes an effective security union that could diminish the need for the U.S. military presence in the region unlikely in the foreseeable future.

China, Russia, and Global Investment

China and Russia have become more economically interdependent with the Persian Gulf states, and that has benefited global oil security by bringing more oil and gas on the global market through mutual investments. Arab states have been investing more in Russian oil and gas exploration and production, and vice versa. Such investment is important for a reason not often discussed or understood. The authoritative IEA radically changed its forecast on oil production in 2008. Until then, it largely dismissed notions that oil supplies might peak or reach a point where global oil production no longer increases and then decreases thereafter. By contrast, in November 2008, the agency provided a somewhat alarming forecast that oil will likely peak around 2020. The IEA changed its forecast because the previous 2007 report was based on best-of-knowledge assumptions about what global oil fields could produce. The 2008 report, by contrast, was based on actual studies of the production rates of the world's largest oil fields. One major factor driving the possible peak oil problem is underinvestment by major oil companies and countries in oil discovery and production. In other words, the long-term primary risk to energy supply is not likely to be geological availability or terrorism but simply a lack of investment. Estimates are that an average of $615 billion per year in upstream oil and gas investment will be necessary between 2012 and 2035.[58] A great amount will go solely to the maintenance of the current level of production just to offset decline rates. For instance, Russian Lukoil has estimated that $1 trillion would be needed over the next twenty years just to maintain Russian production at the 10 mbd level.[59] Yet attracting investment in Russia's renationalized energy industry has been a challenge, which makes the Persian Gulf's energy fields enticing because they are easier and cheaper to tap.

Underinvestment is caused by a variety of factors, but greater Russian-Arab Gulf state interaction may help ameliorate this problem if it continues to develop over the longer run and if Russia maintains positive relations with the West. In this sense, if such cooperation continues, it may increase investment in energy that helps buy some more time in the case peak oil does become a serious, future problem in world politics.

Investment by post–Saddam Hussein Iraq, the West, Russia, and particularly China has been critical to Iraq's ability to develop its oil potential. Due to its vast oil reserves, second to Saudi Arabia, Iraq plays a vital role in the international oil market and will have a major impact on oil supply and pricing trends in the coming decades. It may account for substantial oil supply growth over the next two decades if it stabilizes. As a consequence of Iraq's isolation over the past two decades, Iraqi's oil sector eroded dramatically. Starved for investments after more than a decade of sanctions followed by a decade-long war, Iraq opened its upstream to foreign companies in 2009 to recover its production and increase revenue. While before the invasion, Iraq's oil industry was largely walled off from world markets by international sanctions against Saddam Hussein's government, in 2012, Iraq overtook Iran as the second-largest OPEC oil producer. Since 2012, Iraq has been producing oil at the highest rate since Saddam Hussein seized power in 1979.[60] By October 2013, less than two years after President Barack Obama officially declared the end of the war in Iraq, Chinese NOCs had been operating three fields in southern Iraq and producing more than 50 percent of Iraqi oil output: 1.4 mbd. In fact, Chinese state-owned companies invested more than $2 billion a year into recovery of Iraq's oil sector.[61]

China's expanded role in the Iraqi oil industry has been largely facilitated by its willingness to accept poor oil terms offered by the Iraqi Oil Ministry, which offers foreign operators as little as a couple of dollars per barrel produced, making it difficult for foreign companies to make a profit. Since Chinese national oil companies are not accountable to shareholders as in the case of Western IOCs, the Chinese NOCs accept the strict terms of Iraq's oil contracts even at the cost of generating minimal profit. For instance, although in 2008 CNPC was able to recover its contract to develop the al-Ahdab field signed under Saddam Hussein in 1997, the company had to change the terms of contract from the initial production-sharing agreement into a less profitable and riskier technical service contract.[62]

The remaining contract that China has secured since Iraq opened its sector to investment has been subject to technical service contracts. Securing access to energy supplies for its expanding economy relegates profit seeking to a secondary role. Illustratively, CNPC, along with BP, agreed to develop the Rumaila field under tough bidding terms, for a remuneration fee of only $2 per barrel. Similarly, CNPC-Total-Petronas consortium accepted a remuneration fee of only $1.40 per barrel, and CNOOC-TPAO agreed to develop the Maysan fields for a fee of $2.30 per barrel.[63] Abdul Mahdi al-Meedi, an Iraqi oil ministry official, praised the role of Chinese companies in the Iraqi oil sector, noting that we "don't have any problems with them [Chinese companies]. They are very cooperative. There's a big difference, the Chinese companies are state companies, while Exxon or BP or Shell are different."[64] While the Chinese state-backed oil companies are able to develop fields at lower costs, other companies, including ExxonMobil, have moved to secure separate deals with Iraq's semiautonomous Kurdish region or withdraw altogether. As noted by Lin Bogiang, director of the China Center for Energy Economics Research at Xiamen University, "It's not that China likes going to Iraq, [but] not that many places are left."[65] Given China's increasing role in the Iraqi oil sector, nearly a third of the future oil production in Iraq is projected to come from fields that are either directly owned or co-led by Chinese companies.

Conclusion

On the surface, it appears that oil security is periodically in great jeopardy. Media headlines reinforce such concerns and illuminate all of the chaos and instability in the Middle East. In contrast, as we have argued, America's rising capabilities have been positive for oil security partly by helping to protect the free flow of oil at reasonable prices. China and Russia have certainly tried to rival the United States in the Persian Gulf, but that rivalry has been minor in the security arena, even if Moscow has sought greater influence in the broader Middle East. China's growing need for oil also has tempered its propensity to challenge Washington by increasing its stake in regional stability, and Russia's regional ambitions and capabilities have remained tame compared to the Cold War period. These long-term changes in the international relations of the Persian Gulf tell a much more revealing story of its dynamics and those of oil security than short-term analyses.

11 The Travails of Hegemony: A Classic Problem

I T IS A SIGN of profound change in world history that we no longer speak of the many great powers that traversed the terrain of the Middle East. It has been said that upon realizing the imminence of death after the eruption of Mount Vesuvius, a resident of Pompeii had the presence of mind to write on a wall that "nothing can endure forever."[1] Change is an immutable factor of the human condition and the central subject of this book, which has canvassed the trajectory of the key outside states in the Gulf region over decades. Within this panoramic context, America's rising capabilities in the Gulf have helped to protect oil security, but American hegemony also faces many challenges and costs.

Scholars are divided on whether America is a hegemon, but many have debated the desirability, feasibility, and effects of U.S. hegemony. In contrast to hegemonic stability theory, which assumes that regional or global stability is served best when one state has preponderant capabilities over the others, most scholars view hegemony as a major problem. Theorists of neorealism and many other balance-of-power theorists view (or would view based on their theoretical positions) American hegemony as creating the potential for serious and destabilizing counterbalances.[2] For their part, some scholars see soft balancing in motion against American hegemony, which falls short of traditional balancing but is still aimed at checking U.S. capability.[3] Meanwhile, the liberal camp overwhelmingly sees myriad problems with hegemony and American hegemony. Liberal institutionalists see institutions, and not hegemony, as the best path to international stability, and constructivists find hegemony to be counterproductive,[4] or see balance of power in world politics in dramatically different ways, such as in terms of the balance of ideas rather than the balance of capabilities.[5] The minority argue that hegemony is the most stable distribution of capability[6] and downplay the general problems of maintaining hegemony and the potential that it will trigger balancing against the United States,[7] with the possible exception of Chinese and Russian counterbalancing.[8]

Our views fall in between these schools of thought: we see American hegemony in the Persian Gulf as positive for oil security and as yielding America some global political influence as well, but as hardly unproblematic. In this chapter, we begin by examining the high strategic costs of hegemony in the turbulent Persian Gulf and proceed to explore the other costs of involvement in the region. Such analysis is more than academic. The externalities of using oil have not been properly priced into what we pay at the pump, and that hampers our ability to produce a sensible national energy plan and decrease oil consumption. Many scholars and analysts who focus on energy have made this argument,[9] but it remains underappreciated and not factored into how we think about the costs of oil use.

Strategic Costs and Free Riders

The United States has spent heavily on protecting oil security, but in particular has borne disproportionate costs in protecting the Persian Gulf. Energy economist Roger Stern, for instance, applies the geographic distribution of aircraft carriers as an indicator and finds that the cost of keeping Middle Eastern crude flowing has been more than $225 billion a year over the past three decades.[10] Previous work finds a much lower but still significant price tag. The average estimation of various independent studies for the post-1990 period, not including the Iraq War of 2003 and occupation, is around $40 billion to $50 billion per year.[11] That comparison underscores the heavy burden that the United States has assumed for regional defense, a burden that was passed to it in the early 1970s when Great Britain withdrew from the Persian Gulf and increased as a result of the Iran-Iraq War (1980–1988), Iraq's invasion of Kuwait (August 1990), the September 11 attacks (2001), the rise of Iranian nuclear aspirations, and the ill-planned invasion of Iraq and subsequent war (2003–).

The comparatively massive American expenditures on the Persian Gulf, not to mention the more important factor of disproportionate American casualties in regional conflicts, might be less notable if U.S. dependence on imported oil were higher than that of most other states. However, it is far lower and has been decreasing due to the oil boom in the United States.

Some influential decision makers already believe that the United States should not bear the significant costs of protecting global oil. This sentiment even existed at the first U.S. National Security Council meeting on August 2, 1990, following Iraq's invasion of Kuwait[12] and throughout the 1990–1991 crisis. Arab Gulf states were fully aware that for a variety of reasons, the U.S. public and Congress were reluctant to move toward war against Iraq. President George H. W. Bush feared in September 1990 that key members of Congress might even support a "compromise" on Kuwait,[13] which could fall short of his demand that Iraq withdraw unconditionally and that Kuwait's royal family be restored to power.

September 11 elevated the question of the proper U.S. role in the Gulf to a national debate. Many observers started to wonder why the United States was protecting oil-rich, nondemocratic Saudi Arabia whose citizens committed this atrocity and sacrificing lives and treasure in the region. Of course, the Iraq War and occupation raised concerns over the high costs of interventionism to a new level. Such concerns are not without reason, even if part of the American burden is a function of deliberate U.S. foreign policy choices.

The onerous nature of American strategic costs raises the question of free-riding on hegemony, which is partly endogenous to hegemony. Hegemonic stability theory assumes that the hegemon provides for stability largely by provisioning impure public goods. For our purposes, the public good in question is the protection of the free flow of oil at reasonable prices to the global economy. However, some versions of hegemonic stability theory also underscore that free-riding can become too burdensome and push the hegemon to retrench. One can posit that the greater the level of free-riding, the more likely is that outcome. At a higher level, free-riding may decrease the hegemon's capability over the longer run by stressing its assets, but it will more likely affect willingness to play a hegemonic role. This is chiefly because the absence of support from others will make it more costly to protect oil security than would otherwise be the case.

America's fiscal health has made the question of free-riding even more salient. It is possible that if the United States fails to deal with its national debt problem and if free-riding is not addressed through greater multilateralism, Washington and the American public may increasingly question the American role in the Persian Gulf. Under some presidential administrations, that may begin to alter the U.S. role in the Persian Gulf. Certainly the story of hegemons, imperial states, and other great powers in history counsels not to ignore such outcomes.

Hegemony and Terror

Hegemony and terrorism are linked, even though terrorism is a response to numerous factors, many of which are more important than hegemony.[14] Hegemony is not a foreign policy, but it allows for greater intervention than would otherwise be the case.

There is no justification for terrorism, but it is important to understand its many causes. U.S. hegemony has contributed to a negative narrative about America and oil. Through its distorted lens, al-Qaeda saw America's role in evicting Iraqi forces from Kuwait in 1991 as an affront to Muslims, even though the United States was protecting Saudis and liberating Kuwaiti Muslims. Osama bin Laden and his cohorts identified the presence of non-Muslim infidels in Arabia as the main grievance against the United States and the Saudi leadership prior to the 9/11 attacks.[15] Through bin Laden's grossly distorted view of Islam and America,[16] the September 11 attacks were part of a twisted plan aimed in part at evicting the United States from the Gulf.[17] Since at least 1992, bin Laden had singled out the United States for attack, suggesting a direct connection to the 1991 Gulf War.[18] In his August 1996 Declaration of Jihad against the Americans Occupying the Land of the Two Holy Places, he asserted, in fact, that to "push the enemy—the greatest *kufr* [infidel]—out of the country is a prime duty."[19] After describing a variety of perceived aggressions against the Muslim world by the Zionist-Crusader alliance, the declaration referred to the occupation of the two holy places, Mecca and Medina, as the most serious transgression of all.[20] He asserted in an interview in 1998 that the Muslim world and Islam were under siege, noting that others "rob us of our wealth and of our resources and of our oil. Our religion is under attack."[21] In particular, he repeatedly claimed that Americans stole Arab oil,[22] failing to understand the distinction between protecting and appropriating oil. Trying to put a figure on this perceived thievery, bin Laden asserted that America had stolen oil revenues over the past twenty-five years that were worth $4.05 billion, entitling each of the world's 1.2 billion Muslims in the world to claim $30 million each in compensation from America.[23]

Al-Qaeda has certainly been diminished by various developments in recent years, including the death of bin Laden.[24] However, fighting al-Qaeda in Afghanistan, Iraq, and elsewhere has been very costly. Some analysts even put the cost of the Iraq and Afghanistan wars at $3 trillion.[25] Al-Qaeda, which has sought to bankrupt the United States because it realizes that it cannot defeat it militarily,[26] has also diverted American attention from other critical issues and put it at odds with other countries in the world.

Broader Views of the United States

Insofar as hegemony is perceived in the region as too muscular and as reflecting American dominion over Muslims, such views also complicate America's relations with Middle Eastern countries, negatively affect its reputation among Muslims, bolster Islamic radicals, and hurt its global image.[27] These effects in turn hurt its soft power, a concept that we elaborate on in the final chapter.

An accurate view of the United States is central to a range of factors that are important to U.S. interests worldwide and to American and global energy security. They include cooperation in the production of energy, the protection of energy supplies, the avoidance of conflict in or near the region, and the decrease of radical terrorism that emanates from the Middle East. Misconceptions of oil-stealing America or correct perceptions of an America seeking to be dominant make such cooperation harder to achieve, with attendant and serious costs. Such blowback costs must be added to the ledger when evaluating the cost of hegemony and of a barrel of oil.

Balancing and Checking the United States

Predominant actors often face some pushback in world politics. Balance-of-power theory predicts that the strongest actor will be counterbalanced.[28] This will occur through hard balancing—in other words, efforts to balance by making alliances against it or developing military capabilities to challenge it. The predominant actor can also be checked by soft balancing. Short of hard balancing, actors can soft-balance against the hegemon through international institutions and by doing such things as failing to cooperate with it.

The United States has faced all of these countermeasures across the past several decades, and they represent a significant challenge and cost of hegemony. If America had less capability and power in the region, it would probably face fewer countermeasures by others. At the same time, we argue that hard balancing has declined over time, and that while soft balancing and other measures to check Washington have increased,[29] they are limited by a number of factors.

The Regional Factor: Caught between Iraq and Iran

Whatever the nature of American relations with Iran, Iran sees the Persian Gulf as its backyard. It wants U.S. capability trimmed in the region and would like to supplant American hegemony with its own dominion. That is one reason that it reacts against American hegemony in numerous ways. Iran has developed greater influence with Shiites in the broader Middle East. It also has far greater influence in Iraq than it did when Saddam Hussein was in power. Those are major gains in its effort to establish influence in the Middle East writ large[30] and to check Washington and its allies.

The Iranian Revolution clearly made Iran a far greater threat to the region because Iran's ambitions would now be wedded to revolutionary fervor. In 1979, Iran's Ayatollah Ruhollah Khomeini sought to export Iran's revolution across the oil-rich Gulf. His agenda was anti-American at the global level and antimonarchy at the regional level. Khomeini sought to overthrow politically the oil-rich Arab monarchs whom he considered to be illegitimate and corrupt lackeys of the United States. The notion of theocracies replacing monarchies was not a fantasy. Iran nearly beat Iraq in the Iran-Iraq War that raged from 1980 to 1988. Had Iran won, such a picture of regional theocracy may have had some chance of emerging.

Overall, then, one can argue that Iran's threat was significant even before the rise of American capability in the region. This suggests that while American capability may well threaten Iran, Tehran's ambitions in the region have to do with much more than just reacting to Washington. Unfettered by the American-led role, Iran's appetite could also be whetted, as many Gulf Arab leaders fear.

While Iran will likely continue to check Washington, Iraq is another story. Despite its domestic chaos, Iraq seeks to stabilize rather than threaten oil supplies in the region. Saddam Hussein's Iraq was a veritable powerhouse in 1979, bent on regional domination at America's cost. The oil-rich Arab monarchs were scrambling to mollify Iraq, even while they feared it to be the only real land threat to their states. Post-Saddam Iraq could try to threaten the region again in the future. However, it is far less aggressive now than it was under Saddam Hussein, and it sometimes cooperates with Washington.

Checking America: The China and Russia Factor

So far we have argued that the rise of China in the Gulf and changes in Russia's position have benefited oil security. At the same time, however, hegemony has contributed to counterchallenges by Russia and China, which have been concerned about American hegemony in the region and much prefer a multipolar world. The United States faced far more balancing pressures from the Soviet Union during the Cold War than it faces from Russia or China now, but these pressures are part of the complex mix of action among these states.

In 1979, the superpowers were locked in dangerous global rivalry. Moscow had some potential to balance during the Cold War chiefly through its alliance with Iraq struck in 1972. That alliance unraveled with the end of the Cold War, as underscored when Russia grudgingly cooperated with United States against Iraq in the 1990–1991 Gulf crisis. For its part, China lacks the military capability and alliances to hard-balance against the United States in the region. Beijing's dependence on Washington complicates its ability to try to balance America.

While China is unlikely to be able to be a strategic threat in the region for the foreseeable future, it cannot be dismissed either. This is because it has established political and economic relations in the region and because Washington as a hegemon faces challenges that could weaken it or decrease its will to play a big role in the region. Moreover, while neither Russia nor China can seriously hard-balance against America, even if the China is trying to develop some military influence related to the Gulf and an arms sale relationship in the region, it does soft-balance and take other measures against Washington, which have to do, for instance, with not cooperating on its initiatives.

While Beijing faces limits on how it can balance, there is reason to believe that at least one strain of its foreign policy is aggressive. Since September 2005 when Chinese president Hu Jintao introduced the idea of a "harmonious world" as a concept that China would pursue, Beijing has invoked this notion many times.[31] But while this concept suggests that China is peace-loving and seeks a "win-win world," the PRC's actions have also clashed with this concept. This may explain why China's global venture to enhance its soft power as a peaceful approach to national strength has run aground and why questions repeatedly arise about its supposed beneficence.

Balancing as well as actions that fall short of balancing but aim to check America generate costs for America. First, the rise of China's political and economic capabilities has allowed for some rivalry with Washington. While Russia's security profile in the region was diminishing, the PRC's economic profile was rising substantially. The global level changed with the end of the Cold War, and China's global rise was being reflected in the Middle East as well. Insofar as the economic pie is limited, the PRC's economic gains, such as in gaining lucrative oil contracts in Iraq, bolstered its position at the expense of American energy companies.

China's global strategy aims to achieve a stronger position in global trade and that certainly is a challenge to American dominance. In July 2014, China launched the New Development Bank, which also included Brazil, Russia, India, and South Africa. It has aimed to lend at least $50 billion in development funding to emerging markets. That was followed in June 2015 when China spearheaded the Asia Infrastructure Investment Bank by forming a group of more than fifty nations to invest at least $100 billion to build new infrastructure projects across Asia.

The Persian Gulf may well be part of such grand planning for trade domination, even if China is driven chiefly by energy in the region. China's growing set of interlinked trading relationships in the Persian Gulf may become part of its own pivot to the Gulf region. This aligns well with Beijing's attempts to revive the Silk Road by creating a new strategy for transporting energy between Asia and the Middle East that depends on political and economic tools of foreign policy, with some concern for strategic influence.[32]

Second, some of this rivalry and soft balancing plays itself out in the United Nations. The case of the American invasion of Iraq is an example. China and Russia opposed it and, along with France, which sometimes also aims to check Washington, not only prevented Washington from receiving the U.N.'s imprimatur but lobbied against America's efforts to obtain even a simple majority vote on the Security Council. Such efforts at the United Nations also undermined America's case to the world community.

Third, China and Russia can check Washington through their foreign policy toward regional states. Iran is a prime example. For example, as we have already shown, the PRC enjoyed rising trade with Iran while that of America stayed flat due to international sanctions. That strongly suggests that China preferred to score economic gains than to cooperate fully with the international community on Iran, until noncooperation became too obvious and costly to its relations with Washington. Although it is hard to parse out to what extent this action was driven by mercenary goals as opposed to checking Washington, Beijing clearly was not so concerned about American interests and pressures to quickly curtail its interaction with Iran, as did most other industrialized states around the world. The effect of its action was to undermine U.S.-led efforts, regardless of the exact motivation, until it had no choice but to somewhat change course around 2010.

Fourth, regional and global checks on America are related. If Beijing and Moscow do more to check Washington at one level, that could reinforce the other level. For example, Russia and China are increasingly linked in terms of energy at the global level.[33] Exhibit A is the Eastern Siberia Pacific Ocean (ESPO) pipeline.[34] It reflects Russia's interest in diversifying its energy market in the face of U.S.-led economic sanctions and China's need for massive energy from multiple sources. ESPO stands out as the first large-scale accomplishment in Russia's intentions to create an energy export market in Asia. Prior to the completion of ESPO, China's oil imports from Russia came by rail; ESPO grants Russia easier and cheaper access to the Asian oil market. The Oxford Institute for Energy Studies cautions that by 2030, one-third of China's gas could come from Russia,[35] nearly matching what the EU imports from Russia and creating mutual dependence between China and Russia. While these countries have faced serious disagreements historically and checkered relations, energy could potentially bring them closer in the Gulf and globally, and through synergies between the regional and global level. A bolder energy relationship with Russia might even slow the increase in China's need for Middle East oil, even if that continues to grow significantly.

The Limits on Checking the United States in General

American hegemony has faced balancing and other pressures from Russia, China, and Iran. However, for a variety of reasons, those pressures have been circumscribed and in some ways have diminished over time. These reasons need to be understood to put the American experience in context.

First, at the regional level, Iran is the only state that could balance against the United States. It is not a major global power, and it lacks allies in the region, with the partial exception of Syria, whose regime may fall to internal insurrection. Quite the contrary, Sunni states in the Arab world are balancing against Iran such as with respect to the Saudi bombing of Shiite rebels in Yemen in 2015 that Iran supports. In fact, leaked documents show that Saudi Arabia is focused on combating the influence of Shiite Iran, as well as Iran's proxies in the Middle East.[36]

Second, regarding the global level, international relations scholar G. John Ikenberry and his colleagues have argued that the United States has not faced balancing in the post–Cold War period.[37] Some argue that the American lead over other states may be so large that they may not be able or willing to take the risks of trying to challenge the hegemon. That may be true of China and

Russia in the Persian Gulf, where they are far behind American capabilities, and are also distant geographically. As some scholars note, states are more likely to focus on others that are in close proximity.[38] The American role in the Gulf is not proximate to the other great powers in world politics.

Third, oil security is a special case in the sense that so many actors depend on it. China must consider that counterbalancing can hurt its own national security, partly because it free-rides on America's security role in the Persian Gulf.[39] As our data have shown, the PRC has scored major economic gains in a region that America protects at high cost. That is not to say that other countries are not free riding. Western Europe and Japan are also benefiting, as are all other countries that import oil, but they are not trying to rival America for global hegemony.

Statements by Chinese officials strongly suggest that Beijing values the U.S. role in the Persian Gulf so long as the United States does not flex its military muscles too much.[40] In fact, Beijing has at times appeared concerned about America's decreasing its role in the region, a concern that has been widely bandied about in the press and in capitals of the world.[41] The more specific idea within this type of thinking is that America's oil boom will allow it to diminish seriously its role in the Persian Gulf. As one energy analyst points out, many in China think that "U.S. self-sufficiency in energy, should it come to pass, would weaken U.S. interest in the Persian Gulf, leading to a military withdrawal from the region. This could in turn compromise China's energy security."[42]

Some Chinese thinkers have argued that Beijing's aim of ensuring oil supply lanes can be achieved best by free riding on American protection, but others want a more active approach.[43] China's problem is that it lacks capabilities to protect its oil supply. America has played that role in the Persian Gulf through either proxy powers like Iran and Saudi Arabia in the 1970s or its own military power, combined with local support from the Arab Gulf states, beginning in the 1980s. China dislikes such dependence on the United States, but it is decades away from having the military, logistical, and communications technology to cover the 7,000 miles of sea-lanes that lie between Shanghai and the Strait of Hormuz—if it can ever develop such capabilities. For the foreseeable future, China cannot escape reliance on the American security blanket in the Persian Gulf, and all military operations of magnitude in the region depend on U.S. rapid deployment capabilities.

China's strategy has been to score as many political and economic gains as it can in the Gulf, especially with Iran, without crossing any serious American red lines. For example, China slowed its energy investment in Iran from late

2010 up to late 2013 when American pressure on Beijing mounted to abide by economic sanctions against Iran. Such red lines are sketched not only by the president but also by Congress, which has been more inclined than the executive to punish Beijing, on such issues as Iran.

There is another dimension of China's energy interest: its energy companies want greater access to the U.S. energy sector, including resources in the United States and partnerships with U.S. companies overseas. China does not want its Iran account to provoke unilateral U.S. sanctions to punish Chinese firms with operations in the United States. Congress supports such action, but the Obama administration preferred to pressure China directly, which appears to have worked since 2010. Future U.S. administrations may be more punitive, but that remains to be seen.

Fourth, while Russia and China engage in various types of balancing and rivalry with America, their global relations are more interdependent than in the past, regardless of conflicts over issues like Ukraine or the South China Sea. They sometimes seek to curb U.S. influence in the Gulf region, partly to meet their regional goals and partly to check it at the global level. But that is also tempered by vested interests in stability for commercial purposes. That is especially true in China's case, not only in the Persian Gulf but globally, and also for Russia. Such hedging consists of pursuing strategies of engagement and interdependence, while also engaging in balancing behavior. Some scholars might refer to this dual strategy as strategic hedging.[44]

The case of Iran exemplifies how China and Russia seek to check Washington, but can only go so far in doing so. This results in a mix of challenges, amid some cooperation.

Heretofore, Russia took the middle road in its approach to Iran and pursued a purposefully ambiguous policy,[45] an approach that Washington has found weak. Russia has cooperated with Washington and its allies, changing course in 2009 on some arms sales[46] and on Iran's nuclear program. But it still dragged its feet on tougher sanctions against Iran in early 2012, calling them provocative,[47] and it took Iran's view on negotiations concerning Iran's nuclear program.[48] Still, it roughly joined Washington to pressure Iran into a negotiated settlement. Obama even asserted that Putin was instrumental in securing the accord on Iran's nuclear program, noting that "we would have not achieved this agreement had it not been for Russia's willingness to stick with us."[49]

For its part, China's expanded relations with Iran have made it more difficult to contain Iran. As Iran's largest oil customer, China has been central to the

U.S.-led strategy of reducing Iran's revenue from oil sales. Like Russia, China initially stressed that it would abide only by sanctions required by U.N. Security Council resolutions[50] while hoping to solve the issue through negotiations.[51] Over time, Beijing became more reluctant to challenge the United States as sanctions continued to tighten. In fact, China encouraged Iran to accept an offer from the five permanent members of the U.N. Security Council plus Germany on its nuclear programs. Following the negotiations in mid-2012, China agreed, albeit reluctantly, to cut Iranian oil imports by about 21 percent from an average of about 550,000 bpd in 2011 to about 435,000 bpd in 2012.[52] That earned China an exemption from U.S. financial sanctions,[53] as similar action had for myriad other states.

Overall, Russia and China have had serious economic interests in Iran and view their connection to Iran as a potential check on American power. But for China, America is far more important economically and in other ways than Iran is.[54] Moreover, our data have shown that the PRC's commercial interests with GCC states, as well as with Iraq, have risen, and that is also true of Russia, albeit to a far lesser extent, and the GCC states want to check Iran. Nor would Moscow and Beijing want to see a nuclear Iran under most circumstances.

In sum, Russia and China offered just enough support against Iran to please the other regional actors without disrupting their link to Teheran, but that balancing act may be harder to achieve if global tensions with Iran rise. That is especially true given that Moscow and Beijing have serious misgivings about Iran's nuclear aspirations,[55] as well as other differences with it.[56]

Transforming Hegemony into Influence: No Easy Matter

As many scholars have noted and historical cases reveal, neither primacy nor hegemony in various issue areas in world politics necessarily means influence.[57] The challenge of turning capability into influence is age-old and has occupied the attention of thinkers and writers for just as long.[58] A giant literature now explores the question of America's superpower status and the challenges it faces in maintaining its position.[59]

The experience of foreign powers in the Middle East offers textbook cases of the inability to turn superior capability into outcomes. For instance, Iraq's instability in the post-2003 invasion period resulted not because the United States lacked predominant capability but for other reasons.

Hegemony cannot easily translate into influence for a plethora of reasons including opposition that arises at all levels—tribal, group, national, and international. But a more recent development has added a further complication to the mix. The Arab Spring has generated instability within states that hegemonic capability cannot easily influence because such predominant capability is not easily usable inside states.

The Rise of Domestic Instability

Hegemony cannot address all threats equally. The rise of American capability has been positive for stability at the interstate level. But it has not done much to stem domestic instability in the region and has probably stoked it. While the threats to regional security at the interstate level have decreased, they have increased at the domestic level.

Iraq represents a clear example of this dynamic. Saddam Hussein is gone, and Iraq does not pose an interstate threat to the smaller Arab countries, but the Islamic State represents an internal threat rather than a cross-border military threat of any significance to them. The United States could possibly destroy the Islamic State if it committed massive ground forces, but that is very hard to do and would not ensure success either, given that the Islamic State might transform into an insurgency group. Such groups use the terrain to their advantage, hide among civilians, and can resort to urban warfare if need be. Their asymmetric threat requires a response from the United States that extends beyond its major military assets and approaches in general. Of course, it helps when the United States can bring its intelligence assets and aircraft into campaigns against the Islamic State, but it could probably do so without being a hegemon.

In February 2014, two of the nation's chief intelligence officials confirmed to Congress that al-Qaeda was no longer "on the run," as leaders, including Presidents George W. Bush and Barack Obama, had been saying for years. Director of National Intelligence James Clapper and Lieutenant General Michael Flynn, director of the Defense Intelligence Agency, instead underscored what President Obama in more recent times acknowledged: al-Qaeda's core leadership was attenuated, but the threat has evolved as al-Qaeda affiliates and other extremists have taken root in different parts of the world from Afghanistan to Pakistan, from Syria to Yemen and into Africa. The status of these affiliates in relation to the original core organization is not fully clear, but they often appear to act like franchises of al-Qaeda, with varying levels of allegiance to, direction from, and inspiration by the core al-Qaeda group.

Of course, America's capabilities did not ultimately stabilize Iraq, nor could they prevent it from being torn apart. Iraq could conceivably splinter over time in either a de facto or de jure sense. From the sixteenth century to approximately 1920, present-day Iraq was under Ottoman rule. It consisted of three disparate provinces: Mosul in the north, Baghdad in the heartland, and Basra in the south. By 1920, control over Iraq had devolved to the British. When Iraq achieved independence in October 1932, Mosul, Baghdad, and Basra united into one state.[60] Saddam kept Iraq unified with brute force and sheer terror, but the United States cannot play a unifying role in perpetuity.

Even if Iraq does not split, the country could face a continuing sectarian war and sporadic attacks on Iraq's government and civil structures, oil pipelines, and oil production facilities. Iraq could break down into areas of warlord or tribal conflicts that crisscross the religious divide between Shias and Sunnis, with outside powers seeking to consolidate their power in Iraq. Iran, for instance, would like to gain even more influence over Iraq's southern Shias, though it is vital to note that the Shias of Iraq and Iran are quite different, making such a goal difficult to achieve.[61]

The GCC states are not impervious to serious instabilities against which Washington might play some role, but with great difficulty. Indeed, when the Arab Spring started to catch fire at the regional level, concerns existed around the world that Saudi Arabia might also face serious instability. Unlike in Tunisia, Egypt, or even Libya, trouble in the kingdom created the specter of much higher oil prices, which could send the American economy into a double-dip recession and tip the rest of the world that way as well.

Eyes were focused on even minor events in Saudi Arabia, such as a proposed rally in the eastern al-Hasa oil province that never materialized after gripping the attention of oil markets and global purveyors. And Riyadh was not without its problems. On October 4, a brief, ominous release came from the state-controlled Saudi Press Agency in Riyadh acknowledging violent clashes in the eastern city of Qatif between restive Shiites and Saudi security forces and intimated that Iran was to blame for the riots.

While Saudi Arabia has been more stable than many have expected over the past five decades, it faces challenges from chronic unemployment (and underemployment), political unrest, extremist groups like al-Qaeda (not to mention Wahhabi radicals and other antiregime elements within the kingdom), and the reverberations from the Arab Spring.[62] The House of Saud has had to expand its expenditures—military, security, and domestic handouts—in order to maintain its welfare state and help ensure stability. The late King Abdullah spent $130 billion on social benefits, housing, and jobs in efforts to quell dissent, especially from the Shia minority.[63] As political scientist Michael Ross has pointed out, oil-rich regimes were more effective at deterring attempts to unseat them during the Arab Spring, and that had to do with oil.[64] Saudi Arabia played an unprecedented role as an interventionist state throughout the Arab Spring, working hard to manage events across the region.[65]

The rise of the Islamic State has concerned Saudi officials, partly because it garners support among a minor but potentially dangerous segment of Saudis. In November 2014, an attack attributed to the Islamic State killed eight people and wounded thirteen others in the Eastern Province Shiite village of Dalwa. The Saudi government has cracked down on the Islamic State. In April 2015, "more than 90 Saudi and foreign suspects were arrested in connection with alleged IS plots that drew new attention to the potential for IS-related terror attacks in the kingdom."[66] There have also been attacks on security forces in Riyadh, which led to an increase of arrests of those suspected of being party to plotting terrorist attacks.

In the worst-case scenario, America could not easily use its predominant capability to save the Saudi regime from serious instability. Washington cooperates with Saudi security forces, but it is unclear how effective that cooperation would be in a serious threat scenario.

Hegemony and the Will to Act

Hegemony also cannot easily translate into influence in the region because it does not equal the will to act. It is important to distinguish between America's willingness to continue to protect oil security and its capabilities for doing so. Willingness is affected by such factors as the proclivity of national leaders to support America's defense mission in the Persian Gulf in the face of a major national debt and other costs associated with such a presence, as well as public support for such a role. Capabilities refer to the military assets and preparedness that such a role requires. While willingness and capabilities are related insofar as willingness may well motivate defense expenditure and preparedness, they are also distinct in that America's willingness to protect oil security can decrease even if it remains militarily capable or its willingness may remain strong even if its military capabilities wane.

For example, the United States has the capabilities, access to regional sites, and political support to crush the Islamic State. But depending on the president and administration in office, it may not have the will to act in doing so. After the failure of the Iraq invasion in 2003, the Obama administration was tentative about large-scale involvement in the Middle East. It became much more reluctant to use American power than had been the case under the George W. Bush administration. Capability becomes less fungible when it is not matched with will to act. That is not to say that a ground war in the Middle East against the Islamic State would make sense. Rather, Washington has not wanted to use predominant American capability in a major ground war against the Islamic State. That may change with future administrations, but the difficulty of the Iraq and Afghanistan wars after September 11 may well serve as a cautionary signal.

Conclusion

Hegemony has benefits and costs, and it's important to understand both sides of the equation to gain perspective. Maintaining hegemony has been financially costly to the United States in direct military costs and the indirect costs of confronting terrorists who have a distorted view of Islam and America. Hegemony also contributes to countermeasures which are costly, even though hard balancing has decreased and such countermeasures face their limits. Furthermore, hegemony does not equal influence in world politics—perhaps a classic phenomenon as we look back at the fate of hegemons in history. The strongest don't always get their way, and they sometimes struggle in ways that they could not anticipate and may not even fully understand after the fact.

12 Conclusion

THE GREAT POWERS of the nineteenth century—Britain, France, Russia, Austro-Hungary, Prussia, and the Ottoman Empire—did more to define and control the regions that they colonized than the modern protagonists of our story about the Persian Gulf. But these modern great powers are hardly distant actors. They certainly do affect local politics, political economy, and security in meaningful ways, while engaged in their own odd combinations of cooperation and rivalry in regions and at the global level.

Globalization began in previous centuries, gained its roots in the nineteenth century,[1] and expanded in the past several decades. The rise of globalization contributed to a condition where the international and regional levels intertwine and interact more significantly than ever before. We have sought to offer a guide about one stream within the complex mosaic of Persian Gulf affairs: the international dimension.

America has shuddered through intense turbulence in the Persian Gulf but has emerged as hegemonic, challenged though it is. The trajectory of the United States in the Middle East compared to that of China and Russia is critical to regional and world politics, and yet it is remarkably understudied over longer time periods. We have sought to fill this gap.

As noted in Chapter 1, we decided for good reason to explore a relatively long period of time, from the 1970s through 2015. We have aimed in part to offer insight into broader trends and larger questions of world affairs that may outlast the time and scope of our work. While the story of great powers is just one part of the more complex tale of the Persian Gulf, it is a story with broader meaning as well. This conclusion sketches some of the broader themes.

Hegemony and Oil Security

We sometimes ask if the world has become multipolar at the global level.[2] That is a question of special interest to Americans who are concerned periodically about decline. This may be because Americans are especially concerned with who is number one. Witness the myriad competitions over best restaurants, musicians, frog jumpers, best- and worst-dressed stars, and even hotdog eating. It's no surprise that Americans would also focus some attention on the relative station of the United States in world politics. The stakes here are big. Exaggerated views of American weakness can create a self-fulfilling prophecy at home, encourage global troublemakers, and produce world economic and strategic instability. Meanwhile, excessive views of American strength can encourage dangerous adventurism, unilateralism when multilateralism would work better, and less compromise when deal making is in order.

Whether or not the world as a whole has gone multipolar, our analysis strongly suggests that the United States has become a hegemon in the Persian Gulf over time or a state with preponderant strength. That development is important to the entire world economy, because even amid regional chaos at the domestic level in the Middle East, oil security has been strengthened by changes in the position and role of America, China, and Russia. Washington has become better able to protect oil security, and China has become more dependent on oil, making it more reliant on America's security blanket and on its regional allies for energy cooperation and supply.

China's rise in the Persian Gulf mirrors its broader rise in world politics at the global level, with one major exception: Beijing is developing a major military capability at the global level, but less so for the Persian Gulf. This is the only region in the world where China will depend on the U.S. military for the foreseeable future, which underscores the importance of examining regions individually in addition to global-level indicators of great power dynamics.

China has also become more economically interdependent with the region and needful of regional stability to protect its economic gains, not to mention its energy pipeline. Although its increasing economic penetration of the region has helped it obtain energy through bilateral contracts, its overall energy needs have skyrocketed over the past several decades, making America's regional role even more vital.

The PRC has rivaled the United States but primarily in the economic arena. While its economic gains in the Gulf take away from America's part of the pie, these gains also give it less reason to undermine the United States. The economist Albert Hirschman theorized that the state that benefits more economically from a relationship loses political influence because it has more to lose if the relationship falters, yielding power to the less needy side.[3] That provides some insight into the complex features of Sino-American interaction in the Gulf arena. China's economic gains give it a vested interest in the stability of the region and the American-favored status quo. That yields Washington some influence and probably helps check Beijing's tendency to want to rival America in and outside the region.

For its part, Russia has become less able to hard-balance against the United States with the end of the Cold War and the loss of Iraq as a major regional ally, and also more economically interdependent with the GCC states than it was during the Cold War. Therefore, even if Russia benefits from some types of regional instability that raise oil prices and even if it wants to check Washington aggressively in and outside the region, it has less capability and probably some less interest to do so in the Persian Gulf.

These positive developments for oil security far outweigh the tendency of China and Russia to want to balance Washington. They also outweigh the threat that Russia and, far more significant, China may use their improved economic foothold in the region against America in the future.

Great Power Conflict or Cooperation at the Global Level?

Regional and global dynamics are different, but they are also linked in world politics today by virtue of such features as global markets and trade, power, communications, alliances, and compressed political space. What does our analysis mean for global conflict outside the Middle East?

In Asia, unlike in the Persian Gulf so far, China has been trying to challenge American predominance and push back U.S. military influence, partly because it seeks access and energy resources and faces America's key ally, Japan. China is building a modern naval force to protect what it sees as its maritime rights and interests, including in the South China Sea, while also taking measures to challenge America's presence in these areas.

In a series of meetings and lectures among China's leaders that eventually were turned into a documentary series for hundreds of millions of viewers, much thought was given to the question of the rise and fall of great powers in history and how China can rise without having military conflicts with the dominant actors.[4] While most scholars believe that the PRC is a rising power of great magnitude, some see it as a peaceful transition;[5] others predict a serious Sino-American conflict.[6] In particular, thinkers such as Christopher Coker believe that the United States and China are on a major collision course.[7] What does our analysis suggest about such possible conflicts?

The likelihood of conflict between the United States and China, be it a military skirmish or some type of political or economic crisis, will depend on many things.[8] One of those things would be how dependent or interdependent the countries are on each other in a variety of issues. As we have shown, Beijing's dependence on America's security role in the Gulf has become more profound over time, as has its economic interests there. While such factors could conceivably make China more aggressive,[9] we believe that on the whole, they militate against Sino-American conflict at the global level, although that will be decided by myriad factors, some of which are far more important than the dynamics of the Persian Gulf.

Despite the conflict-ridden nature of the Persian Gulf, it may be one region in which the United States and China can cooperate with spinoff benefits for their global relations. Energy is one area in which the two countries have similar interests, all the way from developing electric vehicles and fighting climate change to preserving the free flow of oil to the global economy at reasonable prices.

For its part, Russia is different from China in many ways, and that needs to be emphasized. Moscow prefers higher oil prices given the importance of oil and natural gas to its bottom line, and can benefit from and sometimes stoke instability in the Gulf. Russia also does not need Washington for the protection of Gulf energy because it has its own supplies. Moreover, Russia has far less trade with Persian Gulf countries than does China. These factors make Russia more eager than China to check Washington in the region, even if its ability to do so, as well as its interest, has decreased. These factors also make Moscow more likely to balance America at the global level as well and to challenge its global security interests, as the Ukraine intervention underscored.

One other scenario is interesting to consider. Despite their different cultures and ideologies and their serious historical rivalries, China and Russia have grown closer, and both clearly want to check America in general at the global level. This has led some thinkers to argue that they may attempt to pose a far more dangerous challenge to America's world order.[10] Our analyses suggest that China's increasing dependence on the Persian Gulf will be one factor that makes such a coordinated threat less likely, even though prospects for such a tectonic shift in world politics will depend on many factors, some which are surely unknown at this time.

Chaos and Hegemony?

A cursory glance at the Middle East suggests that American standing in the region is in trouble, and a hearty digestion of media coverage of the region might even induce alarm about the position of the United States. After all, its interests are challenged every day by terror groups, rogue states, and the sheer rigors of nation building and politics. So how can we square these realities with the dynamic of hegemony?

Hegemony is about predominant capability, and that does not preclude regional chaos. An actor can be the strongest in a chaotic region. While chaotic elements are vital to understand and add to the challenges of hegemony, they do not mean that the region is not hegemonic.

In any case, chaos is relative and requires diachronic study to comprehend well. Examining developments over time, one of our themes, gives some perspective. For example, exploring the security situation over time shows more clearly that while Iraq is in chaos, it is not a bigger threat to regional security than in previous decades. The threat has just changed. In the 1970s and 1980s, Iraq and the Soviet Union were allies against the United States and sought to overturn the regional status quo. By the 1990s, the Soviet Union was gone and Iraq's capabilities were trimmed, and after 2003, Saddam's threat to the smaller Gulf states was eliminated but Iraq fell into greater domestic chaos.

Yet Iraq has rebounded in energy production. Expectations were initially dashed that Iraq would become an oil powerhouse after the American invasion. The real story was far more complicated. Domestic instability and attacks by insurgents dropped Iraq's production from around 2.5 mbd under sanctioned Iraq to about 1.5 mbd. That was down from 3.5 mbd prior to the Iranian Revolution. However, since 2012, Iraq's oil output has been at the highest level since 1979.[11] That is despite the chaos in Iraq engendered by the Islamic State, sectarian strife, the dubious rule of law, the absence of an effective Iraqi military force, and weak nation-building efforts.

The Decline of the Hegemon?

It is worth repeating in this conclusion that maintaining hegemony and achieving oil security is very costly and freighted with serious challenges. Our story is about both the rise of hegemony and its many travails. We should not conflate hegemony with influence. Hegemony can generate influence, but that depends on numerous factors that are time and case specific. Even so, it is important to put this in historical context. For example, as we argued in Chapter 11, hard balancing by Russia decreased over time, and China, Russia, and Iran have faced limits in the extent of the countermeasures that they could take against America.

Nonetheless, some might still argue that hegemony is untenable and that America's position in the Persian Gulf will decline. That may or may not be so, but one distinction is worth suggesting for future consideration. While the United States has become and remains hegemonic, that is not to say that it is imperial. Historians have studied empire for some time, from Thucydides to Gibbon's *Decline and Fall of the Roman Empire* through the seminal and acclaimed work of Braudel, who investigated the clash of empires and cultures in the Mediterranean in the sixteenth century.[12]

In more recent times, historians of various stripes have addressed questions of empire,[13] which can inform current debates.[14] Some thinkers assert that the United States is an empire like those of the past, even in the Persian Gulf,[15] but we argue against this view. Historiography reveals the limitations of commonly cited arguments that the United States is an empire simply because it is powerful or that it is anti-imperial simply because it disavows conquest.[16] However, unlike empires of the past, it does not seek to aggrandize territory in the Gulf.[17] That is a crucial distinction. In fact, America has never regulated the economic, political, and security dimensions of the Persian Gulf to the extent characteristic of the British hegemonic era.[18] Even in the security arena where U.S. capability is greatest, it has usually intervened only when an actor has seriously threatened regional security.

Although America is not imperial in the historical sense, it does face some of the serious challenges, sketched in Chapter 11, that empires have faced and have contributed to their decline.[19] In this sense, studying empires provides some insight into the American experience, if we understand how it differs from empires as well.

History teaches that hegemony cannot last forever. But how would U.S. hegemony decline in the Gulf? It is less likely that this will occur due to threats from China or Russia than from several other scenarios. They include instability in Saudi Arabia, greater Iranian influence over Iraq and in the region, U.S. foreign policy blunders, pressures for America to retrench due to budgetary pressures and domestic opposition to foreign involvement, and black swan events that we simply can't predict.

Why Does the United States Bear the Burden?

Hegemony is about the distribution of capabilities and, thus, to argue that the United States has become hegemonic is to say that it is much stronger than other actors, including China and Russia. But maintaining hegemony is a costly enterprise. If America expends enormous treasure on the Persian Gulf and faces serious blowback for its regional involvement, why is it so heavily involved?

It is necessary to ask if the benefits of American hegemony in the Persian Gulf really outweigh the costs and if there are different arrangements for providing regional security in the future. These are questions that students, scholars, and practitioners of world affairs should debate with more vigor.[20] Whatever one believes, it seems certainly true that if the world becomes less dependent on oil, the benefits of the American role in the Persian Gulf will decrease. But the opposite is also true. If the world struggles to decrease its dependence on oil, the American role in the region will remain much more important.

Having said that, the benefits of hegemony for purposes of summation are fourfold. First, while oil markets can help manage oil price spikes, U.S. military capability in the Gulf remains vital for the foreseeable future in an over-the-horizon posture. This is partly because such capability helps oil markets perform this task in the first place. Quantitative studies show that the U.S. response to regional crises has decreased oil prices,[21] and that finding is certainly supported by historical cases. To reiterate, none of the major oil crises and price shocks in the past forty years have occurred when American capability has been predominant in the Gulf. They have occurred when it was weak and undeveloped. The 1973 oil crisis, the 1979 Iranian Revolution, the Iran-Iraq War, and the Iraqi invasion of Kuwait crises occurred before either the rise of American capability in the 1980s or the demonstration of such capability in 1991.[22] The 2008 price spike was largely unrelated to geopolitical problems in the Gulf. Nothing had occurred in the region that could drive oil prices that high in contrast to key major events in the past—revolution, embargoes, and wars. In addition, U.S. military capability sometimes combines with oil sector responses to keep oil price spikes in check. For example, oil prices dropped after the U.S.-led attack on Iraq's forces in 1991 due to the U.S.-IEA joint release of international oil stocks and the realization that U.S.-led military forces had launched a successful set of attacks on Iraqi targets, with no planes shot down.[23]

Second, the United States is less dependent on Gulf oil than are many other industrialized states, but if oil prices that are set on global markets rise significantly, the global economy as a whole will be affected, which would have an impact on America's economy in a globalized world. It would not matter if one country receives most of its oil from the Gulf or from Canada and Venezuela. Even if the United States received no oil from the Persian Gulf, any serious disruptions of oil from that region would raise the price of oil (and derivatives like gasoline) for all Americans. And an American withdrawal would make it harder to prevent or contain such disruptions, because Washington has played the role of regional gendarme since the British relinquished that role in 1971.[24]

Third, for the foreseeable future, Iran's influence will rise further if America's capability weakens. This is not only because Washington has helped contain Iran, but also because the Arab Gulf states have always had to weigh to what extent they should genuflect toward Iran within the context of generally positive relations with Washington. If America weakens, the Arab Gulf states may eventually move more in Iran's direction on a range of issues. That could threaten oil security by giving Iran more influence over regional politics and oil decisions within and outside OPEC. Even if the United States used little oil, it would still want to contain nuclear proliferation, deal with rogue states, confront terrorist groups such as al-Qaeda and the Islamic State that may emerge or operate from the region and obtain funds from oil-related sources in the region, and help to protect Israel.

Fourth, hegemony in the region probably yields Washington leverage and global power. For example, consider China. As we have noted, China free-rides on America's security role in the Persian Gulf.[25] The PRC has made major economic gains in a region that America protects at high cost, and it benefits greatly from the protection of oil at reasonable prices. Chinese officials appear to believe that the U.S. regional role benefits Beijing so long as the United States does not use force too easily.[26] Thus, it stands to reason that Washington may leverage such a role in its broader relations with China. For example, all other things equal, Beijing will be less likely to counterbalance Washington in the region and elsewhere when it depends on its security role in the Persian Gulf.[27]

Beyond these benefits, there are three other reasons that American leaders have been consistently willing to risk such high stakes on preserving U.S. hegemony in this conflict-prone region. First, there are no serious alternatives to the United States for protecting oil security in the foreseeable future. Some observers might argue that other actors or institutions could protect the free flow of oil as well[28] and that the United States is a troublesome superpower whose role should be replaced by other actors. The problem with this counterargument is not that America's regional role and position are desirable or that U.S. foreign policy has always made sense in the Persian Gulf. Hegemony means far less if combined with questionable foreign policy actions, and sometimes U.S. foreign policy has made sense, and sometimes not. In some ways, U.S. actions have contributed to anti-Americanism and regional instability over the past two decades at least.[29]

States and institutions can and should help the United States bolster oil security and can even play a vital role in dealing with any particular threat, but none are equipped or disposed to address the range of threats to oil security. As was made clear in the 1990–1991 Persian Gulf crisis, doing so requires major military facilities and access in the region, a significant force projection capability, and overwhelming military capability as a last resort. That is extraordinarily hard to achieve and has taken America decades to develop.[30]

The second reason that American leaders have sought to preserve U.S. hegemony has to do with inertia. Some policies gain momentum and consensus backing over time, and that is not simple to change. Leaders are busy and have to decide where they want to spend their time and energy. If they spend time, energy, and political capital on changing American foreign policy in critical regions, they can't spend that time on their domestic agenda or on other foreign policy issues. Moreover, if they diminish the American commitment to the Persian Gulf and a crisis occurs there that raises oil prices and causes a recession, their political futures could be over. They will be held far more accountable for this failure than for spending great treasure to maintain the American position in the region.

The third reason is more speculative. It has to do with the so-called military-industrial complex. As this argument goes, this complex has a strong interest in maintaining the strength of the United States in regions around the world, and the Persian Gulf is especially important. Maintaining this position helps burnish the stature of the military and also increases its ability to maintain or increase defense spending. By contrast, a diminishing American role in the Persian Gulf would almost certainly bring calls for less military spending.

The Global Debate on American Power

At the broadest level, we suggest that the debate on whether America remains a global hegemon relative to China in particular should account for what happens in regions. It is useful to look at global indicators of capability like gross domestic product, but such indicators cannot inform us about how great powers express themselves differently in regions of the world. Macrolevel indicators need to be informed by microlevel indicators and study. The two together, when combined with the work of area specialists, can provide a much fuller picture of the extent to which America remains a hegemon or the world has shifted to multipolarity. Studying regions can also give us a better qualitative picture of the challenges that great powers face and what that means for global standing, cooperation, and rivalry.

To be sure, analyses of global power dynamics don't ignore regions. For example, thinkers explore events in the South China Sea to discern what they mean about the PRC's global power, and Russia's intervention in Ukraine is examined to understand Moscow's standing in Europe. But we refer to a different level of analysis—one that is longitudinal, comparative, and systematic. How have the position, standing, and role of these countries changed over time? Such analysis requires area specialists who focus almost solely on regions, international relations scholars who are globally oriented, and those like us who fall in between.

Enormous Change Amid Continuity

In essence, we have offered a portrait of change in world affairs, and with some sense of history, we see that much has changed in sharp contrast to the pithy French notion that the more things change, the more they stay the same. Some say that Russia seeks its former glories, but that ambition, if it exists, is belied by the weight of history. There was a time when Russia was a great global power in the true sense of the word. Russia's expansion in the seventeenth and eighteenth centuries was quite significant and raised alarm bells in London and Paris. In 1790, the agent of Catherine the Great in Paris, Baron Grimm, told the empress that two nations, Russia from the eastern side and America, would eventually dominate the world,[31] a notion that Alexis de Tocqueville also made famous. These predictions would prove correct until the ravages of history took their toll on the Soviet Union, underscoring that nothing stays the same. In fact, so much has changed from the 1830s, when the British figured that Russia sought to influence, if not invade, India, their crown jewel; to 1979, when the Soviets were perceived as threatening the Persian Gulf and encircling the Persian Gulf; to the current period, where the biggest Russian threat pales by comparison, even if the Russian czars were never as large a threat as the British thought.

While the nineteenth-century great powers had to negotiate the recognition of territorial sovereignty so as to avoid conflicts, that is not a concern of the modern great powers in the Persian Gulf. Even during the Cold War, America was not challenged in that sense. In the past, regions were arenas for great power rivalry, but in the modern era, regions have gained more independence, and although the rivalries continue, they are tame compared to what they were in previous centuries and during the Cold War.

The Soft Power Dimension over Time

While we have tended to focus on material bases of power, it is also interesting to ask how the United States, Russia, and China have compared in terms of soft power in the Gulf region. International relations scholar Joseph Nye defined the term *soft power* in 1990 as the ability of one state to change the behavior of others through the means of attraction and persuasion rather than coercion or payment.[32] He argued that soft power rests on the ability to shape the preferences of others or change their view because they admire and share your values, emulate your example, and appreciate your foreign policies.[33] Soft power is about the attractiveness of such culture and policies.[34]

By contrast, hard power usually refers to economic or military capabilities and approaches of a coercive nature that are aimed at getting others to change their position. This can be accomplished by inducements and threats. Soft power is in most instances a less-threatening tool of foreign policy than hard power because it is indirect and passive. For instance, it does not cause direct and sudden military or economic damage as may hard power, nor need it typically challenge the national pride and honor of other states. Soft power may be less risky, but as Nye points out, it can be hard to use.[35] While that is a problem with any type of power, hard power is more direct and its outcomes are easier to observe, although it is often inappropriate as a tool. Of course, states don't pursue either hard or soft power in their grand schemes or even in single cases of foreign policy. Smart power, a concept that emerged from the soft power debate, combines both hard and soft power to achieve foreign policy outcomes.[36] However, for purposes of analysis, we can separate out soft and hard power.

We have not focused on soft power partly because it is extremely hard to study regarding the international relations of the Persian Gulf, especially going back decades where data are unavailable. Instead, our data-driven approach allows for more reliable comparisons of the capabilities of the United States, China, and Russia over time. In fact, comparing soft power at the global level is complex and not often done, even though it is easier to accomplish than exploring the complexities of great powers in regions.

We can offer some general ideas on the subject of the soft power of outside states in the Gulf. We can start by examining the attractiveness of the political and economic culture of outside states to regional actors. The United States does not have much soft power in this regard. The regional autocrats do not subscribe to democratic ideas. Such ideas would undermine their power, except with respect to Iraq, where democratic approaches have taken root. Nor do Arab states appreciate U.S. exceptionalism or the view that its culture and policies are superior.[37] They resent being counseled on the importance of democracy, which they tend to see as both questioning their culture and threatening their power. And anti-Americanism, an indicator of the lack of soft power, also decreases the appetite of regional actors for democratization.[38] In fact, one study based on extensive polling finds that anti-Americanism even translates into lessened soft power for Saudi Arabia and Turkey, which are viewed roughly as allied with the United States, and greater soft power for Iran, which is viewed as anti-American.[39]

Russia and China, however, have even less cultural soft power than the United States, which must concern the Chinese because they increasingly seeks global soft power.[40] Chinese media organizations are even supported with an approximate annual budget of $10 billion and are expanding their global presence, behind President Xi's exhortations that the PRC's media "tell China's story well."[41]

Yet just because Gulf states do not like democracy does not mean that they are attracted to China's form of governance or that of Russia. They have always been wary of Soviet communism, and the Gulf states, including Iran, have seen communism as atheistic, secular, and unworthy. Moreover, the Arab Gulf countries are much more involved in U.S. society and educational institutions. For example, America is by far the most popular destination for Saudi students, often capturing more than half of all Saudi students studying abroad—numbers that dwarf those of Russia and China, even given that China's numbers have gone up over time.[42] It is fair to say that the United States is much more attractive in this regard, which is an aspect of its soft power.

But what about the attractiveness of the foreign policy of the outside states? The United States and Gulf Arab states differ on regional issues such as how to deal with Iran, Syria, and the Palestinian issue, although due to a shared fear of Iran the GCC, states have moved closer to Israel in the past few years.

The divergence in policy views between the United States and Saudi Arabia has fluctuated over time. Despite some serious differences in policy, U.S.-Saudi security cooperation has largely remained positive. While America lost soft power with Saudi Arabia and some of the Gulf states on the issue of Iran, it gained with Iraq. That is not because relations with Iraq became smooth, but because they improved after the fall of Saddam Hussein despite Iran's growing influence in Iraq.

The end of the Cold war made Russia's foreign policy more attractive to regional states. They had doubted Russia's intentions for decades, which is one reason that Moscow rarely made serious inroads at Washington's expense. Even Ayatollah Khomeini, who loathed the United States and what it represented, repeated the mantra that Iran would lean "neither East nor West," effectively shutting off Moscow's attempts to capitalize on America's loss in the wake of the Iranian Revolution. Views of Russian foreign policy, while improved, remained highly problematic due to Russia's dogged support of President Assad of Syria and, indirectly, Iran. Such support also put Moscow on the side of Shiites against the interests of Sunni-led regimes in the Gulf. In fact, the GCC's greatest security concerns have to do with this Shiite arc of influence, which animates their foreign policies from Syria to Yemen.

Meanwhile, at the core, the GCC states still ultimately depend on the United States for their security, and U.S.-GCC state security cooperation has strengthened over time. Numerous security policies converge around the fundamental goal of mutual security. That creates a driving attraction or core element of soft power in the most important arena of security. Even as tensions have arisen in U.S.-GCC relations, these core security concerns have been sustained. On the cost side, Washington's security involvement and presence in the region have also generated anti-Americanism, which hurts its soft power and, in its worst incarnation, becomes a motivation for terrorists and extremists to strike out violently. That is a cost of hegemony.

For its part, China is chiefly opportunistic and materialistic in its interests in the region. It wants increasing amounts of secure oil at reasonable prices. It has not really gotten involved in the region's issues and largely does not share or pursue fundamental policy goals with regional states. At the same time, China has made some important gains in soft power partly because it has become less ideological as a communist-run state and more of a trading state that shares economic interests with regional actors. As we have shown extensively, Beijing has developed economic policies and rising trade with the region that make it more economically attractive than it has been in the past. That is certainly important and could translate into broader soft power gains in the future. However, such arrangements may reflect economic convenience and business as much as soft power attraction to culture or policy. It is no surprise that in global rankings of soft power, China is usually ranked around twentieth in the world compared to the near-top standing of the United States,[43] and even as low as thirtieth, partly due to the unattractiveness of its ideology and government.[44]

In brief, then, regional states are not especially attracted to the political systems of any of the outside powers nor do their foreign policy interests clearly align with any of them. The exception is that the regional countries except for Iran share fundamental security interests and policy goals with Washington regarding their own security from outside threat. That is a major factor. Moreover, the regional states are more attracted to Washington's type of capitalism. In this sense, Washington clearly gets the advantage in overall soft power in the region, even if China has made gains over time. That should be added to the ledger of comparative power of the outside states.

However, it is important to understand that soft power is not part of what defines a hegemon. Hegemony is typically defined in terms of preponderant capabilities, although some scholars would expand that definition. Such a definition may well include soft power, making it important to discuss it here but also to note that this is not the concept of hegemony that we have chosen for this book.

We end with two qualifications. The question of soft power is hard to describe generally because each Gulf country has had its own perceptions of the attractiveness of outside powers. Iran, for instance, has more shared policy goals with Russia, even if their relations have been strained, than with Arab countries. That Russia favors Syria and Iran against Arab state interests limits its soft power potential. It is also important to distinguish between public soft power and elite soft power. The leaderships of the Arab Gulf countries are more likely to view the United States positively than their people do. Thus, surveys that show that anti-Americanism is strong in the region do not indicate lower soft power in the leadership.

Conclusion

The sweeping saga of hegemony and challenge is classic in history. All hegemons gain important benefits from hegemony but eventually meet serious challenges that they must try to surmount. Were that not the case, we would still be dealing with the Romans and Mongols and countless other former great powers. Some of the challenges that hegemons face come from other actors that are uncomfortable with the hegemon's predominant strength and would like to see it balanced against or weakened otherwise, but many of the challenges are more directly inherent in hegemony itself and in the sheer difficulty of translating superior capability into influence. That difficulty is profoundly important in explaining why great powers eventually get eclipsed in the course of history.

We have told the story of the rise of hegemony and of these challenges, and of great powers whose fortunes have undergone extraordinary change in one of the most fascinating regions of the world. The story is both age-old and new in its trappings.

The United States has risen from its vulnerable position in the aftermath of the Iranian Revolution and the Soviet invasion of Afghanistan to become a hegemon in the Persian Gulf. That development is quite weighty. Indeed, it has practical significance for policymakers around the world who have to understand, plan, and react to the dynamics of the oil-rich Persian Gulf; to scholars who are interested in the region and in the broader issues of power, change, and stability; and to international relations theorists who are debating American decline, the rise of China, and the question of hegemony in world politics.

The fate of the United States in this region, as well as that of China and Russia, may well shape important aspects of world politics well into this century, ranging from transnational terrorism to regional war to the trajectory of the oil-dependent global economy. Meanwhile, the international relations of the Persian Gulf will continue to intersect meaningfully with great power rivalry and cooperation in the Middle East and elsewhere in a world that has become increasingly globalized.

Notes

Chapter 1

1. Many observers see China's rise as largely peaceful. For example, see Charles L. Glaser, "Will China's Rise Lead to War? Why Realism Does Not Mean Pessimism," *Foreign Affairs* 90, no. 2 (2011): 80–91, and G. John Ikenberry, "The Rise of China and the Future of the West: Can the Liberal System Survive?" *Foreign Affairs* 87, no. 1 (2008): 23–37. For a more pessimistic view, see John J. Mearsheimer, "Can China Rise Peacefully?" *National Interest*, October 25, 2014.

2. Joseph Dunford, chair of the Joint Chiefs of Staff, sees Russia as the "greatest threat" to U.S. national security. Cited in Karoun Demirjian, "Russia or ISIS? Who Is America's No. 1 Enemy?" *Washington Post*, August 4, 2015, http://www.washingtonpost.com/news/powerpost/wp/2015/08/04/russia-or-isis-who-is-americas-no-1-enemy/.

3. Amitav Acharya, *The End of the American World Order* (New York: Polity Books, 2014), 4. Also see Randall L. Schweller, *Maxwell's Demons and the Golden Apple: Global Discord in the New Millennium* (Baltimore: Johns Hopkins University Press, 2014).

4. See Joseph S. Nye Jr., *Is the American Century Over?* (New York: Polity Press, 2015); Joseph S. Nye Jr., "The Twenty-First Century Will Not Be a 'Post-American' World," *International Studies Quarterly* 56, no. 1 (March 2012): 215–217; and Carla Norloff, *America's Global Advantage: US Hegemony and International Cooperation* (Cambridge: Cambridge University Press, 2010).

5. See Nuno Monteiro, *Theory of Unipolar Politics* (Cambridge: Cambridge University Press, 2014), and Ian Bremmer, *Superpower: Three Choices for America's Role in the World* (New York: Portfolio/Penguin, 2015).

6. Glaser, for his part, shows how dependence on oil fits into traditional definitions of security by exploring its link to interstate competition and war involving the United States. See Charles L. Glaser, "How Oil Influences U.S. National Security," *International Security* 38, no. 2 (Fall 2013): 112–146; Also see Meghan O'Sullivan, "The Entanglement of Energy, Grand Strategy, and International Security," in Andreas Goldthau, ed., *The Handbook of Global Energy Policy* (Hoboken, NJ: Wiley-Blackwell, 2013), 30–47.

7. For an excellent discussion and set of graphs on what shapes oil prices, see U.S. Energy Information Administration, "What Drives Crude Oil Prices?" March 11, 2014, http://www.eia.gov/finance/markets/reports_presentations/eia_what_drives_crude_oil_prices.pdf.

8. See, for instance, Jakub J. Grygiel and A. Wess Mitchell, *The Unquiet Frontier: Rising Rivals, Vulnerable Allies, and the Crisis of American Power* (Princeton: Princeton University Press, 2016).

9. See Bobo Lo, *Russia: The New World Disorder* (Washington, DC: Brookings Institution Press and Chatham House 2015).

10. On that potential, see Christopher M. Davidson, *After the Sheikhs: The Coming Collapse of the Gulf Monarchies* (New York: Oxford University Press, 2013).

11. Soft balancing aims to check the strongest actor but by use of international institutions and other nonmilitary means. See T. V. Paul, "Soft Balancing in the Age of U.S. Primacy," *International Security* 30 (Summer 2005): 46–71.

12. For an earlier argument on why that is so, see Steve A. Yetiv, *Crude Awakenings: Global Oil Security and American Foreign Policy* (Ithaca, NY: Cornell University Press, 2004).

13. For example, see Jan H. Kalicki and David L. Goldwyn, eds., *Energy and Security: Strategies for a World in Transition* (Baltimore: Johns Hopkins University Press, 2014), and Glaser, "How Oil Influences U.S. National Security."

14. For good exceptions, see Robert Vitalis, *America's Kingdom: Mythmaking on the Saudi Oil Frontier* (Stanford: Stanford University Press, 2006), and F. Gregory Gause III, *The International Relations of the Persian Gulf* (Cambridge: Cambridge University Press, 2009).

15. U.S. Energy Information Administration, *Annual Energy Outlook 2013: with Projections to 2040* (Washington, DC: U.S. Department of Energy, April 2013), http://www.eia.gov/forecasts/aeo/pdf/0383(2013).pdf.

16. On how oil has revolutionized our world, see Brian C. Black, "Oil for Living: Petroleum and American Conspicuous Consumption," *Journal of American History* 99 (June 2012): 40–50; Daniel Yergin, *The Quest: Energy, Security, and the Remaking of the Modern World* (New York: Penguin, 2011); Michael T. Klare, *The Race for What's Left: The Global Scramble for the World's Last Resources* (New York: Picador, 2012); and John S. Duffield, *Over a Barrel: The Costs of U.S. Foreign Oil Dependence* (Stanford: Stanford University Press, 2008).

17. For a comprehensive account of how oil contributes to international conflict, see Glaser, "How Oil Influences U.S. National Security, and Jeff D. Colgan, *Petro-Aggression: When Oil Causes War* (Cambridge: Cambridge University Press, 2013).

18. For more evidence, see U.S. Environmental Protection Agency, "Overview of Climate Change Science," accessed June 12, 2015, https://www.epa.gov/climate-change-science/overview-climate-change-science.

19. See BP, "BP Statistical Review of World Energy," 2013.

20. Fareed Zakaria, *The Post-American World* (New York: Norton, 2008); Christopher Layne, "This Time Is Real: The End of Unipolarity and the Pax Americana," *International Security Quarterly* 56, no. 1 (March 2012): 203–215.

21. National Intelligence Council, *Global Trends 2025: A Transformed World* (Washington, DC: U.S. Government Printing Office, November 2008). See also Arvind Subramanian, "The Inevitable Superpower: Why China's Rise Is a Sure Thing," *Foreign Affairs* 90, no. 5 (September/October 2011): 66–78; G. John Ikenberry, "The Rise of China and the Future of the West," *Foreign Affairs* 87, no. 1 (January/February 2008): 23–37; and Joseph S. Nye Jr., *Bound to Lead: The Changing Nature of American Power* (New York: Basic Books, 1990).

22. Michael Beckley, "China's Century: Why America's Edge Will Endure," *International Security* 36, no. 3 (Winter 2011/2012): 41–78. Nye, "The Twenty-First Century Will Not Be a 'Post-American' World."

23. Robert Keohane and Joseph S. Nye Jr., *Power and Interdependence* (New York: Pearson, 2012).

24. For a partial exception, see Steve A. Yetiv and Chunlong Lu, "China, Global Energy, and the Middle East," *Middle East Journal* 61 (Spring 2007): 199–218.

25. For example, see F. Gregory Gause III, *The International Relations of the Persian Gulf* (Cambridge: Cambridge University Press, 2009); Louise Fawcett, *International Relations of the*

Middle East (Oxford: Oxford University Press, 2013); and Geoffrey Kemp, *The East Moves West: India, China and Asia's Growing Presence in the Middle East* (Washington, DC: Brookings Institution Press, 2010).

26. Christopher Davidson, *The Persian Gulf and Pacific Asia: From Indifference to Interdependence* (New York: Columbia University Press, 2010); Mark N. Katz, "Russian-Iranian Relations in the Ahmadinejad Era," *Middle East Journal* 62, no. 2 (Spring 2008): 202–216; Carol R. Saivetz, "Moscow's Iranian Policies: Opportunities and Dangers," Middle East Brief, Brandeis University, January 2007; John Calabrese, *China's changing relations with the Middle East* (New York: Pinter, 1991).

27. Yale H. Ferguson and Richard W. Mansbach, "Polities Past and Present," *Millennium* 37 (2008): 366.

28. Nye, "The Twenty-First Century Will Not Be a 'Post-American' World."

29. Beckley, "China's Century?"

30. On definitions of *power*, see Joseph S. Nye Jr., *The Future of Power* (New York: Public Affairs Press, 2011).

31. For an example of such a definition, see Joshua S. Goldstein, *International Relations* (New York: Pearson-Longman, 2005), 83.

32. Robert O. Keohane, *After Hegemony* (Princeton: Princeton University Press, 1984), 32–35, and Robert Gilpin, *War and Change in World Politics* (Cambridge: Cambridge University Press, 1981), 29.

33. For elaboration, see Christopher Layne, "The Unipolar Illusion Revisited: The Coming End of the United States' Unipolar Moment," *International Security* 31 (Fall 2006): 11–12.

34. See, for instance, John A. Agnew, *Hegemony: The New Shape of Global Power* (Philadelphia: Temple University Press, 2005).

Chapter 2

1. See J. M. Cook, *The Persians* (London: Orion, 1983).

2. Cited in Daniel Yergin, *The Prize* (New York: Simon & Schuster), 393.

3. David S. Painter, "Oil in the American Century," *Journal of American History* 99, no. 1 (June 2012), 24–25.

4. According to the U.S. Department of Energy, Energy Information Administration, Petroleum & Other Liquids database, accessed January 5, 2014.

5. For a concise development of this argument, see Painter, "Oil in the American Century," 24–39.

6. On the origins of these oil relations, see Yergin, *The Prize*.

7. On the evolution of these relations, see Josh Pollack, "Saudi Arabia And the United States, 1931–2002," *MERIA* 6 (September 2002), esp. 78–79.

8. On these origins, see Robert Vitalis, *America's Kingdom: Mythmaking on the Saudi Oil Frontier* (Stanford: Stanford University Press, 2006).

9. On this oil and security relationship, see Parker T. Hart, *Saudi Arabia and the United States: Birth of a Security Relationship* (Bloomington: Indiana University Press, 1998), and Anthony Cave Brown, *Oil, God, and Gold: The Story of Aramco and the Saudi Kings* (Boston: Houghton Mifflin, 1999). On ARAMCO in particular, see Irvine H. Anderson, *Aramco, the United States, and Saudi Arabia* (Princeton: Princeton University Press, 1981).

10. On the seven sisters and the global oil industry, see Yergin, *The Prize*.

11. These percentages are rough but reliable estimations. Data obtained from "OGJ 200/100," *Oil and Gas Journal*, 2011; *BP Statistical Review of World Energy*, June 2012. Data cover NOCs' and IOCs' control over gas and oil reserves for years 2010/ 2011.

12. Vlado Vivoda, "Resource Nationalism, Bargaining and International oil companies: Challenges and Change in the New Millennium," Centre for International Risk, 2009.

13. Yergin, *The Prize*, 633–634.

14. Steve A. Yetiv, *Myths of the Oil Boom: American National Security in a Global Energy Market* (New York: Oxford University Press, 2015).

15. For a classic work on this period, see E. V. Gulick, *Europe's Classical Balance of Power* (New York: Norton, 1955).

16. Evgeny Sergeev, *The Great Game, 1856–1907: Russo-British Relations in Central and East Asia* (Baltimore: Johns Hopkins University Press, 2013).

17. See, for example, U.S. Congress, U.S. Senate, Committee on Energy and Natural Resources Access to Oil, *The United States Relationship with Saudi Arabia and Iran*, Publication 95–7 (Washington, DC: GPO, December 1977).

18. Yergin, *The Prize*, 382.

19. Howard M. Sachar, *Europe Leaves the Middle East, 1936–1954* (New York: Knopf, 1972), 315, 176.

20. Ickes letter to Franklin Roosevelt, December 1, 1941, cited in Gerald D. Nash, "Energy Crises in Historical Perspective," *Natural Resources Journal* 21 (1981): 349.

21. On the development of OPEC, see Jahangir Amuzegar, *Managing the Oil Wealth: OPEC's Windfalls and Pitfalls* (London: I. B. Taurus, 2001), chap. 3.

22. Fiona Venn, *The Oil Crisis* (London: Longman, 2002); Richard H. K. Vietor, *Energy Policy in America since 1945* (Cambridge: Cambridge University Press, 1984).

23. Daniel Yergin, *The Quest: Energy, Security, and the Remaking of the Modern World* (New York: Penguin, 2011).

24. Shibley Telhami and Fiona Hill, "America's Vital Stakes in Saudi Arabia," *Foreign Affairs* 81 (November/ December 2002): 170.

25. Cited in Michael A. Palmer, *Guardians of the Gulf* (New York: Free Press, 1992), 56.

26. See Yergin, *The Prize*.

27. Perhaps the best analysis of this effort is in Mostafa Elm, *Oil, Power and Principle: Iran's Oil Nationalization and Its Aftermath* (Syracuse, NY: Syracuse University Press, 1992).

28. Yitzhak Shichor, *The Middle East in China's Foreign Policy, 1949–1977* (Cambridge: Cambridge University Press, 1979), chap, 1.

29. For a good history on China's regional approach, see Lillian Craig Harris, *China Considers the Middle East* (London: I. B. Tauris, 1993).

30. By 1965, opposition to the British role in the Gulf spread well outside the Labour Party and included a number of influential Tories. Jacob Abadi, *Britain's Withdrawal from the Middle East, 1947–1971: The Economic and Strategic Imperatives* (Princeton, NJ: Kingston Press, 1982), 39, 203.

31. Michael A. Palmer, *Guardians of the Gulf* (New York: Free Press, 1992), 101–102.

32. See David Lesch, *1979: The Year That Shaped the Modern Middle East* (Boulder, CO: Westview Press, 2001).

33. See, for instance, "Transcript of President's Speech on Soviet Military Intervention in Afghanistan," *New York Times*, January 5, 1980; Steve Yetiv, *America and the Persian Gulf: The Third Party Dimension in World Politics* (Westport, CT: Praeger, 1995). See also Richard W. Cottam, "Revolutionary Iran and the War with Iraq," *Current History* 80 (January 1981): esp. 5–9.

34. See, for instance, the statement by former Under Secretary of State for Security Assistance Matthew Nimitz, "U.S. Security Framework," *Current Policy* 221 (September 1980): 1–4.

35. Quoted in Halliday, *Soviet Policy in the Arc of Crisis* (Washington, DC: Institute for Policy Studies, 1981), 9.

36. Jimmy Carter, interview by Bill Monroe, Carl T. Rowan, David Broder, and Judy Woodruff, *Meet the Press*, NBC, January 20, 1980.

37. "Transcript of President's State of the Union Address to Joint Session of Congress," *New York Times*, January 24, 1980, A12.

38. Carter, interview on *Meet the Press*, January 20, 1980.

39. Jimmy Carter, *Keeping Faith: Memoirs of a President* (Tuscaloosa: University of Arkansas, 1995), 472. Based on documents from the Carter Presidential Library, one scholar argues that Carter exaggerated the threat of the Soviet invasion of Afghanistan and grossly overreacted. Kaufman, *Presidency of James Earl Carter, Jr.* (Lawrence: University Press of Kansas, 1993).

40. Carter, *Keeping Faith.*

41. Jimmy Carter, "The State of the Union Address Delivered before a Joint Session of the Congress," January 23, 1980.

42. Ronald Reagan, *Public Papers of the President of the United States* (Washington, DC: Government Printing Office, 1981), 873, 952.

43. On the evolution of the three doctrines under Nixon, Carter, and Reagan, see Palmer, *Guardians*, particularly chaps. 5 and 6.

44. White House, *National Security Strategy of the United States*, January 1987, 17, https://catalog.hathitrust.org/Record/011411732.

45. For extensive evidence on this paragraph, see Yetiv, *Explaining Foreign Policy.*

46. See Richard N. Haass, *War of Necessity, War of Choice: A Memoir of Two Iraq Wars* (New York: Simon & Schuster, 2010).

47. Haass, *War of Necessity.*

48. On the substantial failure in planning, see David Mitchell and Tansa Massoud, "Anatomy of Failure: Bush's Decision-Making Process and the Iraq War," *Foreign Policy Analysis* 5, no. 3 (July 2009): 265–286.

49. For useful accounts of this period, see Gordon and Trainor, *The Endgame* (New York: Pantheon Books, 2012).

50. Cited in Pillar, *Intelligence and U.S. Foreign Policy*, 59.

51. Feith, *War and Decision* (New York, NY: Harper, 2008), 275.

52. President George W. Bush, *"President's Address to the Nation,"* Office of the Press Secretary, January 10, 2007, https://georgewbush-whitehouse.archives.gov/news/releases/2007/01/2007 0110-7.html.

53. Lori Plotkin Boghardt, "Saudi Funding of ISIS," Washington Institute for Near East Policy, June 23, 2014, http://www.washingtoninstitute.org/policy-analysis/view/saudi-funding-of-isis#.U6 ijnu5c9Ww.twitter.

54. Michael Morell, *The Great War of Our Time* (New York: Hachette Book Group, 2015), 305–307.

55. Lori Plotkin Boghardt, *Saudi Funding of ISIS*, The (Washington, DC: Washington Institute for Near East Policy, June 23, 2014).

56. "Statement of General Lloyd J. Austin III before the House Armed Services Committee on the Posture of U.S. Central Command," March 5, 2014, http://docs.house.gov/meetings/AS/AS00 /20140305/101826/HHRG-113-AS00-Wstate-AustinIIIUSAL-20140305.pdf

57. Michael R. Gordon and Eric Schmitt, "Iran Still Aids Terrorism and Bolsters Syria's President, State Department Finds," *New York Times*, June 19, 2015, http://www.nytimes.com /2015/06/20/world/middleeast/state-department-terrorism-report-iran-syria.html?&hp&action= click&pgtype=Homepage&module=first-column-region&region=top-news&WT.nav=top-news.

58. The IEA's annual *Medium-Term Oil Market Report* forecasts that North American supply

will grow by 3.9 mbd from 2012 to 2018, or nearly two-thirds of total forecast non-OPEC supply growth of 6 mbd.

59. Kjell Aleklett, "An Analysis of World Energy Outlook 2012 as Preparation for an Interview with Science," Association for the Study of Peak Oil and Gasoline, November 29, 2012, http://peak oil.com/geology/kjell-aleklett-an-analysis-of-world-energy-outlook-2012-as-preparation-for-an -interview-with-science.

60. Ibid. According to BP, non-OPEC supply of oil is projected to increase thanks to unconventional production, albeit modestly, mostly offsetting continued declines in a number of mature fields. The United States and Brazil will continue to dominate production; together they will account for 68 percent of total output in 2030.

61. U.S. Energy Information Administration, Petroleum and Other Liquids Database: Crude Oil Projections, March 14, 2014, http://www.eia.gov/dnav/pet/pet_crd_crpdn_adc_mbblpd_a.htm.

62. Aleklett, "An Analysis of World Energy Outlook."

63. See Yetiv, *Myths of the Oil Boom*.

64. U.S. Energy Information Administration, *Annual Energy Outlook 2013 with Projections to 2040* (Washington, DC: U.S. Department of Energy, April 2013).

65. See Guy C. K Leung, "China's Energy Security: Perception and Reality," *Energy Policy* 39, no. 3 (2011): 1330–1337.

Chapter 3

1. See, for instance, Rachel Bronson, *Thicker Than Oil: America's Uneasy Partnership with Saudi Arabia* (New York: Oxford University Press, 2006). F. Gregory Gause III, *International Relations of the Persian Gulf* (New York: Cambridge University Press, 2010).

2. See "Texts of Letters Exchanged by Ibn Saud and Roosevelt," *New York Times*, October 19, 1945, 4.

3. For details on Saddam's foreign policy actions prior to his invasion of Kuwait, see Lawrence Freedman and Efraim Karsh, *The Gulf Conflict 1990–1991: Diplomacy and War in the New World Order* (Princeton: Princeton University Press, 1993), 45–50. Iran, and Iranian commentators, also often refer to the United States as a hegemon. For example, see *Tehran SALAM* in Foreign Broadcast Information Service: Near East and South Asia, April 25, 1995, 50.

4. Saudi Arabia contributed over $36 billion of a total $60 billion. Rachel Bronson, *Thicker Than Oil: America's Uneasy Partnership with Saudi Arabia* (New York: Oxford University Press, 2006), 206. See also Youssef M. Ibrahim, "Gulf War's Cost to Arabs Estimated at $620 Billion," *New York Times*, September 8, 1992.

5. For a detailed discussion of Desert Storm's effect on bilateral relations, see Steve A. Yetiv, *America and the Persian Gulf: The Third Party Dimension in World Politics* (Westport, CT: Praeger, 1995), 105–107.

6. For a detailed discussion of Desert Storm's effect on the bilateral relations, see ibid, 105–107.

7. See, for instance, Martin Indyk, "The Clinton Administration's Approach to the Middle East" (speech to the Soref Symposium, Washington Institute for Near East Policy, Washington, DC, May 18, 1993).

8. Quoted in John M. Goshko, "Christopher Reassures Gulf States on Iraq," *Washington Post*, April 28, 1994, A21.

9. For instance, Saudi disappointment over the Camp David Accords spurred Saudi leaders to intimate that diplomatic relations with the Soviets, a major political gain for Moscow, were possible. See Jacob Goldberg in Yaacov Ro'i, ed., *The U.S.S.R. and the Muslim World* (London: Allen

and Unwin, 1984), 264–268. Igor Belayev, the Soviet author of this controversial article, further confirmed this point in a personal correspondence with Steve Yetiv.

10. "House of Saud," *PBS Frontline*, February 8, 2005.

11. See, for instance, National Commission on Terrorist Attacks upon the United States, *The 9/11 Commission Report* (Pittsburgh: U.S. Independent Agencies and Commissions, 2011), 373–375.

12. Bronson's interview in *Thicker Than Oil*, 238.

13. Michael R. Gordon, "Saudis Warn against Attack on Iraq by the United States," *New York Times*, March 17, 2002.

14. On opinion polls of the Arab world in 2002–2003, see Abdel Mahdi Abdallah, "Causes of Anti-Americanism in the Arab World: A Socio-Political Perspective," *Middle East Review of International Affairs* 7 (December 2003): 70–71.

15. Kevin Matthews, "U.S.-Arab Relations Broken after Iraq War, Scholar Reports," UCLA International Institute, October 25, 2005, http://www.international.ucla.edu/africa/article/32236.

16. Eric Schmitt, "U.S. to Withdraw All Combat Forces from Saudi Arabia," *New York Times*, April 29, 2003, http://www.nytimes.com/2003/04/29/international/worldspecial/29CND-RUMS.html.

17. Ibid.

18. Gause, *International Relations of the Persian Gulf*, 147.

19. National Commission on Terrorist Attacks upon the United States, *9/11 Commission Report*, July 22, 2004.

20. U.S. Department of State, "Joint Statement by President Bush and Saudi Crown Prince Abdullah," April 25, 2005, https://2001-2009.state.gov/p/nea/rls/rm/45327.htm.

21. Ibid.

22. For the official press statement and the full text of the U.S.-Saudi Strategic Dialogue, see U.S. Department of State, "U.S.-Saudi Strategic Dialogue," press statement, May 16, 2006, https://2001-2009.state.gov/r/pa/prs/ps/2006/66463.htm.

23. U.S. Department of State, Office of the Spokesman, "Media Note: U.S.-Saudi Arabia Memorandum of Understanding on Nuclear Energy Cooperation," May 16, 2008.

24. "Taking Down Walls in Saudi-US Relations—Ambassador James Smith," Saudi-US Relations Information Service, November 19, 2009.

25. "Prince Saud Address to the Council on Foreign Relations," September 20, 2005, http://www.mofa.gov.sa/sites/mofaen/aboutMinistry/Minister/OfficialSpeeches/Pages/NewsArticleID39973.aspx.

26. "US Embassy Cables: Saudi King's Advice for Barack Obama," *Guardian*, November 28, 2010, http://www.theguardian.com/world/us-embassy-cables-documents/198178.

27. Ibid.

28. Ibid.

29. Scott Wilson, "King Abdullah Greets Obama in Saudi Arabia," *Washington Post*, June 4, 2009, 20014, http://www.washingtonpost.com/wp-dyn/content/article/2009/06/03/AR2009060300943.html.

30. U.S. Department of State, "Remarks with Saudi Arabian Foreign Minister Prince Saud Al-Faisal," Remarks by Hillary Rodham Clinton, July 31, 2009, http://reliefweb.int/report/occupied-palestinian-territory/opt-remarks-saudi-arabian-foreign-minister-prince-saud-al.

31. "President Obama and King Abdullah Meet at the White House," White House, June 29, 2010, https://www.youtube.com/watch?v=HJNRW3TKULA.

32. Bruce Riedel, "Obama Mending Fences in Riyadh," Brookings Institution, March 19, 2014, https://www.brookings.edu/opinions/obama-mending-fences-in-riyadh/.

33. "Saudis Told Obama Not to Humiliate Mubarak," *Times*, February 10, 2011, http://www.thetimes.co.uk/tto/news/world/middleeast/article2905628.ece.

34. Robert F. Worth, "Saudi Arabia Rejects U.N. Security Council Seat in Protest Move," *New York Times*, October 18, 2013, http://www.nytimes.com/2013/10/19/world/middleeast/saudi-arabia-rejects-security-council-seat.html?pagewanted=all&_r=0.

35. Ibid.

36. U.S. Department of State, "Remarks with Saudi Arabian Foreign Minister Saud al-Faisal," meeting with John Kerry in Riyadh, Saudi Arabia, November 4, 2013, https://geneva.usmission.gov/2013/11/05/secretary-of-state-john-kerry-remarks-with-saudi-arabian-foreign-minister-saud-al-faisal/.

37. Ibid.

38. Helene Cooper, "Saudi Arabia Says King Won't Attend Meetings in U.S.," *New York Times*, May 11, 2015, http://www.nytimes.com/2015/05/11/world/middleeast/saudi-arabia-king-wont-attend-camp-david-meeting.html.

39. "Joint Statement on the Meeting between President Barack Obama and King Salman bin Abd alAziz Al Saud," White House, September 4, 2015, https://www.whitehouse.gov/the-press-office/2015/09/04/joint-statement-meeting-between-president-barack-obama-and-king-salman.

40. Ibid.

41. Helene Cooper and Gardiner Harris, "An Arms Deal Is Aimed at Saudis' Iran Worries," *New York Times*, September 3, 2015, http://www.nytimes.com/2015/09/04/us/politics/iran-deal-will-top-agenda-when-saudi-king-visits-white-house.html.

42. Peter Baker, "Obama and Saudi King Sidestep Dispute over Iran Nuclear Deal," *New York Times*, September 4, 2015, http://www.nytimes.com/2015/09/05/world/middleeast/obama-and-saudi-king-sidestep-dispute-over-iran-nuclear-deal.html.

43. Barbara Crossette, "Albright, in Overture to Iran, Seeks a 'Road Map' to Amity," *New York Times*, June 18, 1998.

44. For transcript of speech, see "Bush State of the Union Address," CNN, January 29, 2002, http://edition.cnn.com/2002/ALLPOLITICS/01/29/bush.speech.txt/.

45. Kenneth Katzman, "Iran: U.S. Concerns and Policy Responses," Congressional Research Service report to U.S. Congress, July 25, 2014, 53, https://www.fas.org/sgp/crs/mideast/RL32048.pdf.

46. Brian Knowlton, "Nuclear-Armed Iran Risks World War III, Bush says," *New York Times*, October 17, 2007, http://www.nytimes.com/2007/10/17/world/americas/17iht-prexy.4.7932027.html?_r=0.

47. White House, "Remarks by the President on a New Beginning," speech in Cairo, Egypt, June 4, 2009, https://obamawhitehouse.archives.gov/blog/2009/06/04/presidentrsquos-speech-cairo-a-new-beginning.

48. White House, "Key Excerpts of the Joint Comprehensive Plan of Action (JCPOA)," July 14, 2015, https://www.whitehouse.gov/the-press-office/2015/07/14/key-excerpts-joint-comprehensive-plan-action-jcpoa.

49. Louis Charbonneau and Parisa Hafezi, "Iran Pursues Ballistic Missile Work, Complicating Nuclear Talks," Reuters, May 16, 2014, http://uk.reuters.com/article/2014/05/16/uk-iran-nuclear-missiles-idUKKBN0DV21X20140516.

50. Patrick Goodenough, "Defiant Iran Says No One Will Stop It from Developing Ballistic Missiles," *cnsnews*, August 24, 2015, http://www.cnsnews.com/news/article/patrick-goodenough/defiant-iran-says-no-one-will-stop-it-developing-ballistic-missiles.

51. See Indyk, speech to the Washington Institute for Near East Policy, May 18, 1993, http://www.washingtoninstitute.org/policy-analysis/view/the-clinton-administrations-approach-to-the-middle-east; see also Indyk et al., "Symposium on Dual Containment."

52. For a full transcript, see "Text of Clinton Statement on Iraq," CNN, transcript, February 17, 1998, http://www.cnn.com/ALLPOLITICS/1998/02/17/transcripts/clinton.iraq/.

53. White House, "President Bush Outlines Iraqi Threat," October 7, 2002. See also "Remarks by President Bush on Iraq in the Rose Garden," September 26, 2002, https://georgewbush-white house.archives.gov/news/releases/2002/09/20020926-7.html.

54. The full text of the State of the Union address is at http://whitehouse.georgewbush.org / news/2003/012803-SOTU.asp.

55. Rao Prashant, "Maliki Tells US' Boehner Iraqi Troops Are Ready," *Agence France Presse*, April 16, 2011; Aaron Davis, "Maliki Seeking Consensus on Troops," *Washington Post*, May 12, 2011.

56. U.S. Department of State, "U.S. Foreign Policy Toward Iraq," testimony by Brett McGurk, House Foreign Affairs Committee, Subcommittee on the Middle East and Africa, November 13, 2013, https://foreignaffairs.house.gov/hearing/subcommittee-hearing-u-s-foreign-policy-toward -iraq/.

57. Missy Ryan, "U.S. Renews Training of Elite Forces in Jordan," Reuters, May 7, 2014. See also Statement by Rear Admiral John Kirby on the Authorization to Deploy Additional Forces to Iraq, Release No. NR- 562–14, November 7, 2014, https://www.defense.gov/News/News-Releases/ News-Release-View/Article/605265/statement-by-pentagon-press-secretary-rear-admiral-john-kirby-on-the-authorizat/.

58. Harold Brown, interview, *Wall Street Journal*, July 1, 1980, 22.

59. See U.S. Senate, *First Concurrent Resolution on the Budget, Fiscal Year 1981* (Washington, DC: Congressional Budget Office, 1981), 384.

60. See U.S. Congress, *Rapid Deployment Forces: Policy and Budgetary Implications* (Washington, DC: Congressional Budget Office, 1983), xiv, 4, 8, 11.

61. For detailed discussion see Yetiv, *America and the Persian Gulf*, 81–84.

62. Kenneth Katzman, "Kuwait: Security, Reform, and U.S. Policy," Congressional Research Service report to U.S. Congress, April 29, 2014, https://www.fas.org/sgp/crs/mideast/RS21513.pdf.

63. Christopher M. Blanchard, "Qatar: Background and U.S. Relations," Congressional Research Service, November 4, 2014, http://www.fas.org/sgp/crs/mideast/RL31718.pdf, 5.

64. Martin Indyk, "US Policy Priorities in the Gulf: Challenges and Choices" (Washington, DC: Brookings Institution, December 2004).

65. The commission concluded that the Saudi government had become "locked in mortal combat with Al Qaeda." National Commission on Terrorist Attacks upon the United States, *The 9/11 Commission Report: Final Report of the National Commission on Terrorist Attacks upon the United States* (New York, 2004), 373.

66. Christopher M. Blanchard, "Saudi Arabia: Background and U.S. Relations," Congressional Research Service, June 14, 2010, http://fpc.state.gov/documents/organization/145596.pdf, 27.

67. Judith Kipper quoted in Patrick E. Tyler, "Stability Itself Is the Enemy," *New York Times*, November 10, 2003.

68. U.S. Department of the Treasury, "Testimony of Daniel L. Glaser, Deputy Assistant Secretary Office of Terrorist Financing and Financial Crimes," November 8, 2005, http://www.treasury .gov/press-center/press-releases/Pages/js3011.aspx.

69. "Country Reports on Terrorism, 2008," April 30, 2009; U.S. State Department Office of the Coordinator for Counterterrorism, Country Reports on Terrorism 2012, May 30, 2013.

70. Testimony of U.S. Department of the Treasury Undersecretary for Terrorism and Financial Intelligence Stuart A. Levey before the Senate Finance Committee, April 1, 2008.

71. U.S. Department of State, "Country Reports on Terrorism 2014," http://www.state.gov/j /ct/rls/crt/2014/239407.htm.

72. "Technical Cooperation Agreement between the United States of America and the Kingdom of Saudi Arabia," U.S. State Department, December 2, 2008. http://www.state.gov/documents /organization/109344.pdf.

73. "Statement of General Lloyd J. Austin III, U.S. Army Commander, Central Command before the House Appropriations Committee for Defense on the Posture of U.S. Central Command," March 5, 2013, http://appropriations.house.gov/uploadedfiles/hhrg-113–ap02–wstate-austing -20130418.pdf.

74. Simon Webb, "Saudi Builds Security Force of 35,000 to Guard Oil," Reuters, November 16, 2007, http://www.reuters.com/article/2007/11/16/us-opec-summit-saudi-security-idUSL1528 115720071116.

75. "Moving in the Right Direction—A Conversation with Ambassador Ford Fraker," Saudi-US Relations Information Service, December 1, 2008, 2014, http://susris.com/2008/12/01/susris -exclusive-moving-in-the-right-direction-a-conversation-with-ambassador-ford-fraker-part-3/.

76. "Bahrain Joins Anti-ISIS Coalition," *Aranews*, February 16, 2015, http://aranews.net/2015 /02/bahrain-joins-anti-isis-coalition/.

77. U.S. State Department, Foreign Military Financing Account Summary, https://2001-2009 .state.gov/t/pm/ppa/sat/c14560.htm .

78. Ibid.

79. White House, "Remarks by the President on the Middle East and North Africa," May 19, 2011, http://www.whitehouse.gov/the-press-office/2011/05/19/remarks-president-middle-east -and-north-africa%20.

80. David Pollock, "Kuwait: Keystone of U.S. Gulf Policy," Washington Institute for Near East Policy, November 2007, 2.

81. "DoD Commemorates Kuwaiti Major Non-Nato Ally Status," U.S. Department of Defense, April 1, 2004.

82. Senate Foreign Relations Committee staff discussions, Kuwait, February 2012, in U.S. Senate, "The Gulf Security Architecture: Partnership with the Gulf Cooperation Council" https://www .foreign.senate.gov/imo/media/doc/746031.pdf.

83. Kenneth Katzman, "The United Arab Emirates (UAE): Issues for U.S. Policy," Congressional Research Service report to U.S. Congress, May 15, 2014, http://www.fas.org/sgp/crs/mideast/ RS21852.pdf, 12.

84. Greg Jaffe, "U.S. Rushes to Upgrade Base for Attack Aircraft," *Wall Street Journal*, March 14, 2003.

85. Philip Finnegan, "Oman Seeks U.S. Base Upgrades," *Defense News*, April 12, 1999.

86. Quoted in Marc J. O'Reilly, *Unexceptional America's Empire in the Persian Gulf: 1941–2017* (Lanham, MD: Lexington Books, 2008), 180.

87. Ibid.

88. Christopher M. Blanchard, "The Gulf Security Dialogue and Related Arms Sale Proposals," Congressional Research Service, October 8, 2008, https://www.fas.org/sgp/crs/weapons/RL34322 .pdf.

89. Ibid.

90. "Persian Gulf," Report to Congressional Requesters, U.S. Government Accountability Office, September 2010, http://www.gao.gov/assets/310/309821.pdf.

91. U.S. Department of State, "Joint Communiqué From the Third Ministerial Meeting for the U.S.-GCC Strategic Cooperation Forum," September 26, 2013, http://www.state.gov/r/pa/prs/ ps/2013/09/214834.htm.

92. "Remarks by Secretary Hagel at the Manama Dialogue from Manama, Bahrain," tran-

script, U.S. Department of Defense, December 7, 2013, http://archive.defense.gov/transcripts/tran script.aspx?transcriptid=5336.

93. U.S. Department of State, "Gulf Cooperation Council and Ballistic Missile Defense," remarks by Frank A. Rose, May 14, 2014, https://www.hsdl.org/?view&did=753250.

94. Ibid.

95. "Saudi Seeks Stronger US-Gulf Military Cooperation," *Defense News*, May 14, 2014, http://www.defensenews.com/article/20140514/DEFREG04/305140029/Saudi-Seeks-Stronger-US-Gulf -Military-Cooperation?odyssey=mod_sectionstories.

96. Ibid.

97. U.S. Department of State, "Gulf Cooperation Council and Ballistic Missile Defense," remarks by Frank A. Rose, May 14, 2014, https://www.hsdl.org/?view&did=753250.

98. "U.S.-Gulf Cooperation Council Camp David Joint Statement," White House, May 14, 2015, https://www.whitehouse.gov/the-press-office/2015/05/14/us-gulf-cooperation-council-camp -david-joint-statement.

99. Kenneth Katzman, "Iraq: Politics, Governance, and Human Rights," Congressional Research Service, April 19, 2012, http://www.fas.org/sgp/crs/mideast/RS21968.pdf, 34.

100. Senate Armed Services Committee, "Senate Armed Services Committee Holds Hearing on Iraq Security Issues," November 15, 2011.

101. Kenneth Katzman, "Iraq: Politics, Security, and U.S. Policy," Congressional Research Service, RS21968 June 22, 2015, https://fas.org/sgp/crs/mideast/RS21968.pdf.

102. "Remarks by Secretary Hagel at the Manama Dialogue from Manama, Bahrain," transcript, U.S. Department of Defense, December 7, 2013, http://archive.defense.gov/transcripts/tran script.aspx?transcriptid=5336.

103. Ibid.

104. "Gulf Cooperation Council and Ballistic Missile Defense," remarks by Frank A. Rose, Deputy Assistant Secretary, Bureau of Arms Controls, U.S. Department of State, May 14, 2014, https://www.hsdl.org/?view&did=753250.

105. Remarks by Secretary Hagel at the Manama Dialogue Manama.

106. "Fact Sheet: United States-Saudi Arabia Bilateral Relationship," White House, March 28, 2014, http://www.whitehouse.gov/the-press-office/2014/03/28/fact-sheet-united-states-saudi -arabia-bilateral-relationship.

107. Helene Cooper and Gardiner Harris, "An Arms Deal Is Aimed at Saudis' Iran Worries," *New York Times*, September 3, 2015, http://www.nytimes.com/2015/09/04/us/politics/iran-deal -will -top-agenda-when-saudi-king-visits-white-house.html.

108. Richard F. Grimmett, "U.S. Arms Sales: Agreement with and Deliveries to Major Clients, 2003–2010," Congressional Research Service, R42121, December 16, 2011, https://fas.org/sgp/crs/ weapons/R42121.pdf.

109. Walter Hickey, "We're Now Selling the Most Advanced Missile System to This Islamic State," June 6, 2012, http://www.businessinsider.com/lockheed-martin-sells-thaad-missile-system -to-uae-2012-6.

110. Blanchard, "Saudi Arabia," CRS Report for Congress, February 12, 2014, http://www.fas .org/sgp/crs/mideast/RL33533.pdf.

111. Ibid., 4.

112. Senate Armed Services Committee, "Senate Armed Services Committee Holds Hearing on Iraq Security Issues," November 15, 2011.

113. John Hudson, "Iraqi Ambassador: Give Us Bigger Guns, and Then We'll Help on Syria," *Foreign Policy*, July 17, 2013.

114. U.S. Department of State, "U.S. Foreign Policy Toward Iraq," testimony, House Foreign Affairs Committee, Subcommittee on the Middle East and North Africa, November 13, 2013, https://foreignaffairs.house.gov/hearing/subcommittee-hearing-u-s-foreign-policy-toward-iraq/.

115. "The Gulf Security Architecture: Partnership with the Gulf Cooperation Council," U.S. Committee on Foreign Relations report, June 19, 2012, https://www.foreign.senate.gov/imo/media/doc/746031.pdf.

116. "Remarks by Secretary Hagel at the Manama Dialogue from Manama, Bahrain," U.S. Department of Defense, December 7, 2013, http://archive.defense.gov/transcripts/transcript.aspx?transcriptid=5336.

Chapter 4

1. John Duke Anthony, "The U.S.-GCC Relationship: Is It a Glass Leaking or a Glass Filling?" National Council on U.S.-Arab Relations, July 1, 2003, http://ncusar.org/publications/Publications/2003-07-01-US-GCC-Relationship.pdf.

2. "Saudi Tops Sovereign Wealth Fund Assets in GCC," albawaba, August 13, 2013, http://www.albawaba.com/business/saudi-arabia-sovereign-wealth-fund-gcc-513325.

3. Stasa Salacanin, "GCC Sovereign Wealth Funds Manage over USD 1.7 Trillion," bqdoha, December 9, 2013, http://www.bqdoha.com/2013/12/gcc-sovereign-wealth-funds-manage-usd-1-7-trillion.

4. "Trade in Goods with Saudi Arabia," U.S. Census Bureau, 2013, http://www.census.gov/foreign-trade/balance/c5170.html#2013.

5. Excluding military arms sales and other governmental services.

6. "U.S. 2013 Export to Arab World Set Record—NUSACC," SUSRIS Saudi-US Relations Information Service, February 8, 2014, http://susris.com/2014/02/08/u-s-exports-to-arab-world-set-record-nusacc/.

7. Glen Carey, "U.S. Companies Seek New Investments in Saudi Arabia amid China Competition," Bloomberg, June 6, 2010, http://www.bloomberg.com/news/2010-06-06/u-s-companies-seek-new-investments-in-saudi-arabia-amid-china-competition.html.

8. "Saudi-US Relations Remain Strong," Arab News, March 12, 2014, http://www.arabnews.com/news/538866.

9. See Carey, "U.S. Companies Seek New Investments in Saudi Arabia Amid China Competition."

10. Ibid.

11. James B. Smith, "US-Saudi Relations: Eighty Years as Partners," Arab News, March 20, 2013, http://www.arabnews.com/news/445436.

12. Mamarinta P. Mbabaya, "The Role of Multinational Companies in the Middle East: The Case of Saudi Arabia" (PhD diss., University of Westminster, 2002), 362.

13. "Opportunities Ahead—Commerce Secretary Pritzker," Saudi-US Relations Information Service, September 24, 2013, http://susris.com/2013/09/24/trade-and-investment-opportunities-ahead-commerce-secretary-pritzker/.

14. John Sfakianakis, "U.S.-Saudi Trade Relations," Saudi-US Relations Information Service, June 10, 2009, http://susris.com/2009/06/10/us-saudi-trade-john-sfakianakis/.

15. Ibid.

16. Office of the U.S. Trade Representative, "Middle East Free Trade Area Initiative (MEFTA)," accessed March 18, 2014, http://www.ustr.gov/trade-agreements/other-initiatives/middle-east-free-trade-area-initiative-mefta.

17. Office of the U.S. Trade Representative, "United Arab Emirates," May 8, 2014, http://www.ustr.gov/countries-regions/europe-middle-east/middle-east/north-africa/united-arab-emirates.

18. Ibid.

19. Maximilian Bossdorf, Christian Engels, and Stefan Weiler, "EU GCC Invest Report 2013," GCC Invest EU, April 2013, http://www.eu-gccinvest.eu/file/EU%20GCC%20Invest%20Report%202013.pdf.

20. "Qatar," Office of the U.S. Trade Representative, May 6, 2014, http://www.ustr.gov/coun tries-regions/europe-middle-east/middle-east/north-africa/qatar. See also "U.S. 2013 Export to Arab World Set Record—NUSACC," Saudi-US Relations Information Service, February 8, 2014, http://susris.com/2014/02/08/u-s-exports-to-arab-world-set-record-nusacc/.

21. "Kuwait," Office of the U.S. Trade Representative, April 29, 2014, http://www.ustr.gov/countries-regions/europe-middle-east/middle-east/north-africa/kuwait.

22. "Saudi Arabia Fact Sheet," Chevron, May 2014, http://www.chevron.com/documents/pdf/saudiarabiafactsheet.pdf.

23. "Saudi Arabia Activities," ExxonMobil, accessed June 10, 2014, http://corporate.exxon mobil.com/en/company/worldwide-operations/locations/saudi-arabia/about/overview.

24. "Aramco in $5bn China deal," *Arabnews*, March 31, 2007, http://www.arabnews.com/node /296629.

25. "Chevron to Establish Sustainable Energy Efficiency Center in Qatar," Chevron, February 17, 2009, http://www.chevron.com/news/press/release/?id=2009-02-17.

26. Joe Carroll, "Exxon to Build $10 Billion U.S. LNG Export Plant with Qatar," Bloomberg, May 9, 2013, http://www.bloomberg.com/news/2013-05-09/exxon-to-build-10-billion-u-s-lng -export-plant-with-qatar-1-.html.

27. "Kuwait," ExxonMobil, accessed March 13, 2014, http://corporate.exxonmobil.com/en/company/worldwide-operations/locations/kuwait.

28. "U.S.-Saudi Arabia Memorandum of Understanding on Nuclear Energy Cooperation," Saudi-US Relations Information Service, May 16, 2008, http://susris.com/2008/05/16/us-saudi -arabia-memorandum-of-understanding-on-nuclear-energy-cooperation/.

29. "Unconventional Gas Program," Saudi Aramco, August 7, 2014, http://www.jobsataramco .eu/unconventional-gas-program.

30. Ali al-Naimi, "Natural Gas: A View from Saudi Arabia" (paper presented at the International Energy Forum held in Mexico, November 12, 2014), https://www.ief.org/_resources/files/events/4th-ief-igu-ministerial-gas-forum/minister-al-naimi-keynote-speech.pdf.

31. "Technically Recoverable Shale Oil and Shale Gas Resources: An Assessment of 137 Shale Formations in 41 Countries Outside the United States," Energy Information Administration, June 10, 2013, http://www.eia.gov/analysis/studies/worldshalegas.

32. "Saudi Aramco 2014 Annual Review," Saudi Aramco, May 11, 2015, 25.

33. Abdelghani Henni, "Saudi Aramco to Supply Shale Gas to Industrial Projects," Society of Petroleum Engineers, May 5, 2015, http://www.spe.org/news/article/saudi-aramco-to-supply-shale -gas-to-industrial-projects.

34. Mike Bird, "Saudi Arabia Is Putting Aside Billions for Its Own Gas-Fracking Revolution," *Business Insider*, January 27, 2015, http://www.businessinsider.com/saudi-arabia-wants-its-own -shale-gas-2015-1.

35. Saudi Aramco 2014 Annual Review," Saudi Aramco, May 11, 2015, 48.

36. Ibid., 46.

37. "Aramco Opens R&D Center in Houston," Aramco Services Company, September 19, 2014, http://www.aramcoservices.com/News-Events/Houston-RC-Inauguration.aspx.

38. Heather Saucier, "Aramco Seeks Innovation at US Research Centers," American Association of Petroleum Geologists, November 2013, http://www.aapg.org/Publications/News/Explorer/Emphasis/ArticleID/130/Aramco-Seeks-Innovation-At-U-S-Research-Centers.

39. James Perkins, "Saudi Aramco Hiring US Shale Workers," *Shale Energy Insider*, March 19, 2015, http://www.shaleenergyinsider.com/2015/03/19/saudi-aramco-hiring-us-shale-workers/.

40. "Joint Statement of the U.S.-Iraq Joint Coordinating Committee on Energy, U.S. Department of State, April 23, 2012, https://2009-2017.state.gov/e/enr/rls/188344.htm.

41. "U.S. Foreign Policy toward Iraq," testimony before the House Foreign Affairs Committee, Subcommittee on the Middle East and North Arica, U.S. Department of State, November 13, 2013, https://foreignaffairs.house.gov/hearing/subcommittee-hearing-u-s-foreign-policy-toward-iraq/.

42. "Iraq," ExxonMobil, accessed May 26, 2014, http://corporate.exxonmobil.com/en/company/worldwide-operations/locations/iraq/about/overview.

43. "Chevron Signs Iraq Kurd Oil Deal," *Al Arabiya*, June 17, 2013, http://english.alarabiya.net/en/business/energy/2013/06/17/Chevron-signs-Iraq-Kurd-oil-deal.html.

44. Tim Arango and Clifford Krauss, "China Is Reaping Biggest Benefits of Iraq Oil Boom," *New York Times*, June 2, 2013, http://www.nytimes.com/2013/06/03/world/middleeast/china-reaps-biggest-benefits-of-iraq-oil-boom.html?_r=0.

45. *Andrew E. Kramer*, "U.S. Companies Get Slice of Iraq's Oil Pie," *New York Times*, June 15, 2011, http://www.nytimes.com/2011/06/15/business/energy-environment/15iht-srerussia15.html?_r=0.

46. Kelly Gilblom, "Saudi Arabia Wooing Fired U.S. Shale Workers to 'Join Our Team,'" Bloomberg, March 16, 2015.

47. James B. Smith, "US-Saudi Relations: Eighty Years as Partners," *Arab News*, March 20, 2013, http://www.arabnews.com/news/445436.

48. "Saudi Sabic in Talks to Enter US Shale Gas Market," *Arab News*, January 22, 2014, http://www.arabianbusiness.com/saudi-s-sabic-in-talks-enter-us-shale-gas-market-535740.html#.U4EMzHJdWWb.

49. Andy Sandbridge, "US Shale Boom to Have Minimal Impact on Gulf," *Arabia Business*, November 23, 2013, http://www.arabianbusiness.com/us-shale-boom-have-minimal-impact-on-gulf-s-p-527451.html#.U4EMAnJdWWY.

50. Ibid.

51. "Saudi Says US Shale Oil Surge Is Good for Market," Reuters, January 19, 2014, http://www.arabianbusiness.com/saudi-says-us-shale-oil-surge-is-good-for-market-535246.html.

52. Clifford Krauss, "Free Fall in Oil Price Underscores Shift Away from OPEC," *New York Times*, November 28, 2014, http://www.nytimes.com/2014/11/29/business/energy-environment/free-fall-in-oil-price-underscores-shift-away-from-opec.html?&hpw&rref=business&action=click&pgtype=Homepage&module=well-region&region=bottom-well&WT.nav=bottom-well.

53. Interestingly, Venezuelan foreign minister Rafael Ramirez said that he accepted the OPEC decision not to cut production because he hoped that lower prices would help drive some of the higher-cost U.S. shale oil production out of the market. Cited by Alex Lawler, David Sheppard, and Rania El Gamal, "Saudis Block OPEC Output Cut, Sending Oil Price Plunging," Reuters, November 28, 2014, http://www.reuters.com/article/2014/11/28/us-opec-meeting-idUSKCN0JA0O320141128.

54. Golnar Motevalli, "Iran Wary of Oil 'Shock Therapy' as OPEC Vies for Market," Bloomberg, December 1, 2014, http://www.bloomberg.com/news/2014-11-30/iran-wary-of-oil-shock-therapy-as-opec-vies-for-market-share.html.

55. Andrew Critchlow, "OPEC: Saudi Prince Says Riyadh Won't Cut Oil Unless Others Follow," *Telegraph*, December 2, 2014, http://www.telegraph.co.uk/finance/newsbysector/energy/oilandgas/11268611/OPEC-Saudi-Prince-says-Riyadh-wont-cut-oil-unless-others-follow.html.

56. Krauss, "Free Fall in Oil Price."

57. See Lawler et al., "Saudis Block OPEC Output Cut, Sending Oil Price Plunging."

58. David M. Herszenhorn, "Fall in Oil Prices Poses a Problem for Russia, Iraq and Others," *New York Times*, October 15, 2014, http://www.nytimes.com/2014/10/16/world/europe/fall-in-oil -prices-poses-a-problem-for-russia-iraq-and-others.html?_r=0.

59. Quoted in "Iran Says Lower Oil Prices a New Tactic to Undermine Its Economy," Reuters, October 21, 2014, http://www.reuters.com/article/2014/10/21/iran-oil-prices-idUSL6N0SG3PS 20141021.

60. Lyuba Lyulko, "Obama Wants Saudi Arabia to Destroy Russian Economy," Pravda.Ru, October 3, 2014, http://english.pravda.ru/world/asia/03-04-2014/127254-saudi_arabia_russia_obama-0/.

Chapter 5

1. On that potential, see Christopher Coker, *The Improbable War: China, the United States, and the Logic of Great Power Conflict* (Oxford: Oxford University Press, 2015). Also see Richard Rosecrance, ed., *The Next Great War?* (Cambridge, MA: MIT Press, 2014).

2. Michael Levi, "Go East, Young Oilman: How Asia Is Shaping the Future of Global Energy," *Foreign Affairs* 94, no. 4 (July–August 2015): 108–117.

3. Louise Levathes, *When China Ruled the Seas: The Treasure Fleet of the Dragon Throne, 1405– 1433* (New York: Simon & Schuster, 1994).

4. Lillian Craig Harris, *China Considers the Middle East* (London: I. B. Tauris, 1993), 28.

5. Steve A. Yetiv and Chunlong Lu, "China, Global Energy, and the Middle East," *Middle East Journal* 61, no. 2 (2007): 200.

6. On China's changing priorities since Mao, see David M. Lampton, *Following the Leader: Ruling China, from Deng Xiaoping to Xi Jinxing* (Berkeley: University of California Press, 2014).

7. See the series "The End of Reform in China," *Foreign Affairs* (May/ June 2015).

8. "China," U.S. Energy Information Administration, accessed June 10, 2014, http://www.eia .gov/countries/analysisbriefs/China/china.pdf.

9. "Keeping It to Themselves," *Economist*, March 31, 2012, http://www.economist.com/ node/21551484.

10. International Energy Agency, *World Energy Outlook 2013*, November 12, 2013.

11. "China's 2014 Oil Demand, Imports to Grow Faster—CNPC Research," Reuters, January 15, 2014, http://www.reuters.com/article/2014/01/15/china-oil-demand-idUSL3N0KP1PR20140115.)

12. "'Don't Rely on Shale Oil' Warns International Energy Agency," *Euronews*, December 11, 2013.

13. See "Brookings Doha Energy Forum 2012: Policy Paper," Brookings Institution, 2012, http://www.brookings.edu//media/research/files/reports/2012/5/23%20energy%20forum%20re port/energy%20forum%20report_english.

14. See Minxuan Cui, ed., "*Zhongguo nengyuan shiwu guihua jianjie* [Brief introduction of China Energy Tenth Five-Year Plan]," in *Zhongguo nengyuan fazhan baogao 2006* [The energy development report of China 2006] (Beijing: Shehui kexue wenxian chubanshe, 2006). Pak K. Lee, "China's Quest for Oil Security: Oil (Wars) in the Pipeline?" *Pacific Review* 18, no. 2 (2005): 265– 301.

15. Zhong Xiang Zhand, "The Overseas Acquisitions and Equity Oil Shares of Chinese National Oil Companies: A Threat to the West But a Boost to China's Energy Security?" *Energy Policy* 48 (September 2012): 698–701.

16. Ibid.

17. Scott Anderson, "A Potential Partnership: Sino-Saudi Relations," *Wilson Journal of International Affairs* 2 (2004): 58–73.

18. "Riyadh and Beijing Spur Global Economic Growth," *Arab News*, October 1, 2013, http://www.arabnews.com/news/466321.).

19. "Saudi King Arrives in China to Discuss Energy," *China Daily*, January 23, 2016, http://www.chinadaily.com.cn/english/doc/2006-01/23/content_514686.htm.)

20. "China, Saudi Arabia Sign Energy Cooperation Deal," Xinhua News Agency, January 24, 2006, http://www.china.org.cn/english/BAT/156149.htm.)

21. "China, Saudi Arabia Extend Energy Ties," *Asia Times*, January 25, 2006, http://www.atimes.com/atimes/China_Business/HA25Cb04.html.

)22. Hassan M. Fattah, "Avoiding Political Talk, Saudis and Chinese Build Trade," *New York Times*, April 23, 2006, http://www.nytimes.com/2006/04/23/world/asia/23saudi.html?_r=1&.).

23. "Riyadh and Beijing Spur Global Economic Growth."

24. "Chinese President Arrives in Riyadh at Start of 'Trip of Friendship, Cooperation,'" *Xinhua*, February 10, 2009, http://news.xinhuanet.com/english/2009-02/10/content_10796711.htm.

25. "Chinese President Arrives in Riyadh."

26. "Premier Wen Jiabao Visits Three Gulf Countries," Office of the Commissioner of the Ministry of Foreign Affairs of the People's Republic of China in the Hong Kong Special Administrative Region, January 20, 2012.

27. "Saudi FM Tells China Violence by Assad Must Be Stopped," *Al Arabiya*, May 18, 2013, http://english.alarabiya.net/en/News/middle-east/2013/05/18/Saudi-FM-tells-China-violence-by-Assad-must-be-stopped-.html.

28. "Saudi Crown Prince to Begin Four-Day Visit to China," *BBC Monitoring Middle East*, March 11, 2014.

29. Bruce Wakefield and Susan L. Levenstein, eds., *China and the Persian Gulf: Implications for the United States* (Washington, DC: Woodrow Wilson International Center, 2011), 38.

30. Bates Gill, *Chinese Arms Transfers: Purposes, Patterns, and Prospects in the New World Order* (Westport, CT: Praeger, 1992), 96–99.

31. Levenstein, *China and the Persian Gulf*, 16.

32. John W. Garver, *China and Iran: Ancient Partners in a Post-Imperial World* (Seattle: University of Washington Press, 2006), 13–17.

33. Scott W. Harols and Alireza Nader, *China and Iran: Economic, Political, and Military Relations* Santa Montica, CA: Rand Corporation, May 2, 2012), 4.

34. Ben Blanchard, "Iran's Ahmadinejad to Visit as China Slams New Sanctions," *Reuters*, May 23, 2013, http://www.reuters.com/article/2012/05/23/us-china-iran-idUSBRE84M05A20120523.

35. Thomas Erdbrink and Chris Buckley, "China and Iran to Conduct Joint Naval Exercises in the Persian Gulf," *New York Times*, September 21, 2014, http://www.nytimes.com/2014/09/22/world/middleeast/china-and-iran-to-conduct-joint-naval-exercises-in-the-persian-gulf.html?_r=0.

36. Ibid.

37. Brian Spegele, "Oil-Thirsty China a Winner in Iran Deal," *Wall Street Journal*, July 14, 2015.

38. Yetiv and Lu, "China, Global Energy, and the Middle East," 202.

39. Suzanne Xiao Yang, *China in the UN Security Council Decision-making on Iraq* (Hoboken, NJ: Taylor and Francis, 2012), 136–50.

40. Qin Jize, "China Welcome to Explore Iraqi Oil Resources: Envoy," *China Daily*, June 19, 2007, http://www.chinadaily.com.cn/cndy/2007-06/19/content_897160.htm.

41. "China to Write Off Iraqi Debts," *China Daily*, May 4, 2007, http://www.china.org.cn/english/international/209907.htm.

42. "China and Iraq," Ministry of Foreign Affairs of the People's Republic of China, August 22, 2011, http://www.fmprc.gov.cn/eng/wjb/zzjg/xybfs/gjlb/2823/.

43. "China, Iraq Pledge Further Reciprocal Cooperation as PM Visits," Xinhua, July 18, 2011, http://news.xinhuanet.com/english2010/china/2011-07/18/c_13993129.htm.

44. "China and Iraq Announce Strategic Partnership," Diplomat, December 23, 2015, http://thediplomat.com/2015/12/china-and-iraq-announce-strategic-partnership/.

45. "Officials Expect 5th China-Arab Cooperation Forum to Lay New Cornestone for Ties," English.news.cn, May 30, 2012.

46. Abdul Hannan Tago, "Sino-Arab Forum Boosts Ties," Arabnews, June 5, 2014, http://www.arabnews.com/node/582066.

47. Geoffrey Kemp, The East Moves West: India, China, and Asia's Growing Presence in the Middle East (Washington, DC: Brookings Institution Press, 2010). 135.

48. "Kuwaiti Prime Minister Nasser Meets with Visiting Chinese Foreign Minister Yang Jie-chi," Embassy of the People's Republic of China in the State of Kuwait, September 5, 2008, http://kw.chineseembassy.org/eng/sbgx/t590943.htm.

49. "Wen Jiabao Meets with Kuwaiti Emir Al-Sabah," Embassy of the People's Republic of China in the State of Kuwait, May 11, 2009, http://kw.chineseembassy.org/eng/sbgx/t562033.htm.

50. "China, Kuwait Issue Communique, Stressing Trade, Energy Resources Co-Op," Xinhua, May 12, 2009, http://news.xinhuanet.com/english/2009-05/12/content_11357753.htm.

51. "Kuwait, China Sign Energy Agreement," China Post, May 11, 2009, http://www.chinapost.com.tw/business/middle-east/2009/05/11/207637/Kuwait-China.htm.

52. "China, Kuwait Vow to Boost Economic Ties," BBC Monitoring Asia Pacific, April 17, 2014.

53. "Kuwait Signs Landmark Crude Oil Supply Deal with China," BBC Monitoring Middle East," August 22, 2014.

54. "Foreign Minister Meets with His Chinese, Thai and S.Korean Counterparts," Bahrain News Agency, June 22, 2004.

55. "PM Hail Bahraini-Chinese Relations," Bahrain News Agency, May 25, 2006.

56. "Trade between Bahrain and China on a Rise," Albawaba, September 21, 2011.

57. "Bahrain King Hails Success of China Visit," TradeArabia, September 26, 2013.

58. "China and the United Arab Emirates," Embassy of the People's Republic of China in United Arab Emirates, 2011.

59. "China Eyes Closer Strategic Partnership with UAE," Xinhua, March 29, 2012.

60. "China, UAE Issue Joint Statement," China.org.cn, January 18, 2012.

61. "China Eyes Closer Strategic Partnership with UAE."

62. "Qatar-China Trade Jumps 45% to $8.45bn Last Year," Construction Week Online, February 27, 2013.

63. Chris Zambelis, "China, Qatar Forge Tricky Partnership," Asia Times, October 25, 2012.

64. "China, Qatar Announce Strategic Partnership," BBC Monitoring Asia Pacific, November 4, 2014.

65. "China, Oman Vow to Enhance Cooperation, Friendship," Xinhua, November 8, 2010.

66. Ibid.

67. Yetiv and Lu, "China, Global Energy, and the Middle East," 200.

68. Roland O'Rourke, "China Naval Modernization: Implications for U.S. Navy Capabilities-Background and Issues for Congress," Congressional Research Service, Report prepared for Member and Committees of Congress September 30, 2013.

69. Thomas J. Christensen, The China Challenge: Shaping the Choices of a Rising Power (New York: Norton, 2015), 99.

70. Brian M. Downing, "New Port Marks China's Growing Presence in the Persian Gulf Region," World Tribune, February 21, 2013.

71. Ibid.

72. Mustafa Salama, "Navy Exercises Bring Iran, China closer," *Al-Monitor*, October 19, 2014.

73. John Calabrese, "China and the Persian Gulf: Energy and Security," *Middle East Journal* 52, no. 3 (1998): 350–366.

74. "The Strait of Hormuz Is the World's Most Important Oil Transit Chokepoint," U.S. Energy Information Administration, January 4, 2012.

75. Nader, *China and Iran*.

76. Calabrese, "China and the Persian Gulf," 365.

77. Evan S. Medeiros and Bates Gill, *Chinese Arms Exports: Policy, Players, and Process* (Carlisle, PA : Strategic Studies Institute, U.S. Army War College: 2000).

78. Richard F. Grimmett, "Conventional Arms Transfers to Developing Nations, 1998–2005," Congressional Research Service, 2006, https://fas.org/sgp/crs/weapons/RL33696.pdf .

79. Richard F. Grimmett and Paul K. Kerr, "Conventional Arms Transfers to Developing Nations, 2004–2011," Congressional Research Service, 2012.

80. Ibid.

81. Garver, *China and Iran,* 156–59.

82. Peter Fritsch, "Chinese Evade U.S. Sanctions on Iran," *Wall Street Journal*, January 4, 2010, http://www.wsj.com/articles/SB126256626983914249.

83. Indira A. R. Lakshmanan, "U.S. Concerned Chinese Companies May Be Aiding Iran Nuclear Weapon Effort," Bloomberg, March 10, 2011.

84. "China Opens Missile Plant in Iran," UPI, April 23, 2010.

85. Nader, *China and Iran*.

86. Grimmett and Kerr, "Conventional Arms Transfers to Developing Nations."

87. Al-Naimi, "Energy for a New Asian Century Conferment Ceremony of Honorary Doctorate from Peking University," Overseas Exchange Centre, Peking University, www.saudiaramco.com, November 13, 2009. Also see "Saudi Arabia to Cooperate with China on Nuclear," *China Business News*, August 21, 2014.

Chapter 6

1. See the series on "The End of Reform in China," *Foreign Affairs* (May/June 2015).

2. Abdel Aziz Aluwaisheg, "The GCC Turns East," *Arab News*, December 16, 2012; "GCC's Trade Surplus to Hit $493 Billion in 2012–13," *Albawaba*, March 28, 2012.

3. "GCC Trade and Investment Flows," *Economist* (Economist Intelligence Unit, 2014), 25–27, http://fichiers.acteurspublics.com/redac/pdf/Décembre/L40CGC.pdf.

4. Robert Bailey, "China and GCC: Growing Ties," *Gulf Business*, April 16, 2013.

5. "GCC Trade and Investment Flows."

6. Tamsin Carlisle, "China Is Right Market at Right Time for Gulf," *National*, August 18, 2009.

7. "China's 2014 Iran Crude Oil Imports up 28 Pct-Customs," Reuters, January 23, 2015, http://in.reuters.com/article/2015/01/23/china-oil-iran-idINL4N0V126B20150123.

8. "China Exceeds US to Become Saudi Arabia's Top Oil Customer," *Global Times*, February 23, 2010.

9. "We Recognized China's Importance Early," *China Daily*, September 26, 2011.

10. Mohammed Turki Al-Sudairi, "Sino-Saudi Relations: An Economic History," GRC Gulf Paper, Gulf Research Center, August 2012.

11. Jad Mouawad, "China's Growth Shifts the Geopolitics of Oil," *New York Times*, March 19, 2010.

12. Ibid.

13. "Saudi Aramco Sees Strong Potential in China Market," *Saudi Gazette*, January 16, 2009.

14. "China and GCC Widen Energy Ties," *Middle East Economic Survey*, January 23, 2012.

15. Quoted in Mouawad, "China's Growth Shifts the Geopolitics of Oil."

16. "Sinopec, Exxon Mobil, Saudi Aramco, and Fujian Petrochemical Sign Agreements to Progress Fujian Manufacturing and Marketing Projects," ExxonMobil Corporation, August 25, 2004.

17. John Calabrese, "China and the Persian Gulf: Energy and Security," *Middle East Journal* 52, no. 3 (1998): 350–366.

18. John Calabrese, "Saudi Arabia and China Extend Ties beyond Oil," Uyghur American Association, September 27, 2005, https://uyghuramerican.org/article/saudi-arabia-and-china-extend -ties-beyond-oil.html.

19. Kevin Jianjun Tu, "The Strategic Considerations of the Sino-Saudi Oil Deal," *China Brief*, March 29, 2006.

20. "China Makes First Announcement on Strategic Oil Reserves," Reuters, November 20, 2014, http://www.reuters.com/article/2014/11/20/china-oil-reserves-idUSL3N0TA1QE20141120.

21. "China Will Build Special Railway for Muslim Pilgrims in Saudi Arabia," *Telegraph*, February 11, 2009.

22. "Plant Planned with CNPC in Yunnan," *Oil and Gas News Online*, September 26, 2011.

23. "Company Board Meets in China," Saudi Aramco, 2010.

24. David D. Kirkpatrick, "Chinese Visit to Saudi Arabia Touches on Oil and Politics," *New York Times*, January 15, 2012.

25. "New Saudi-Sinopec Oil Refinery," Reuters, January 15, 2015.

26. Chris Buckley, "China's Wen Presses Saudi Arabia for Oil Access," Reuters, January 14, 2012.

27. Habib Shaikh, "Saudi Arabia Looks East as It Expands Industries," *Business Times Singapore*, October 2, 2006.

28. "SABIC Mulls New Plants to Boost Output," Reuters, December 6, 2009.

29. "GCC Trade and Investment Flows," *Economist* (Economist Intelligence Unit, 2014).

30. "Premier Wen Jiabao Visits Three Gulf Countries," Ministry of Foreign Affairs of the People's Republic of China, January 20, 2012, http://www.fmprc.gov.cn/mfa_eng/wjb_663304/zzjg _663340/xybfs_663590/xwlb_663592/t898613.shtml.

31. "Saudi Arabia, Russia Sign Nuclear Power Cooperation Deal," Reuters, June 19, 2015, http://www.reuters.com/article/2015/06/19/saudi-russia-nuclear-idUSL5N0Z516320150619.

32. Naser M. Al-Tamimi, *China-Saudi Arabia Relations, 1990–2012: Marriage of Convenience or Strategic Alliance?* (Hoboken, NJ: Taylor and Francis, 2013).

33. Naser Al-Tamimi, "China-Saudi Relations: Booming Trade," *Al Arabiya News*, February 22, 2013, http://www.alarabiya.net/views/2013/02/22/267670.html.

34. "China Global Investment Tracker" (Washington, DC: American Enterprise Institute and Heritage Foundation, 2013).

35. "Looking East: The Saudis Are Hedging Their Bets," *Economist*, December 9, 2010.

36. "World Energy Outlook 2012: Executive Summary," International Energy Agency, 2012.

37. Roy D. Kamphausen, "The Iraq Energy Factor in Sino-Japanese Relations," Uyghur American Association Policy Brief 7, no. 6, March 21, 2007, https://uyghuramerican.org/article/iraq-energy -factor-sino-japanese-relations.html.

38. "Kingdom to Ship Same Oil Volumes to China in 2014," *Arab News*, January 15, 2014.

39. Katherine Zoepf, "Iraq Signs $3.5 Billion Deal for China to Develop Oil Field," *New York Times*, November 11, 2008.

40. "Iraq Considers Lessons from First Bid Round," *Petroluem Intelligence Weekly*, July 13, 2009.

41. Catherine Hunter, "Halfaya Contact Signed Off in Iraq as Ministry Works to End-January Deadline," *Global Insight*, January 28, 2010.

42. Samuel Ciszuk, "CNOOC, TPAO Sign Development Contract for Iraq's Maysan Oilfields," *Global Insight*, May 18, 2010.

43. "China, Indonesia to Join Exxon at Giant Iraqi Oilfield," Reuters, August 22, 2013.

44. "PetroChina Buys 7.7% More of West Qurna-1 for $442 Million," plsx.com, May 16, 2014, https://www.plsx.com/news/article/petrochina-buys-77-more-of-west-qurna-1-for-442-million.

45. Du Juan, "PetroChina Poised to Dominate Iraqi Oil," *China Daily*, August 13, 2013.

46. Ibid.

47. "Iraq Approves $526 mln Drilling Deal for West Qurna Oilfield," Reuters, May 19, 2015, http://www.reuters.com/article/2015/05/19/iraq-energy-west-qurna-idUSL5N0YA4RN20150519.

48. "China's Antonoil $140m Oilfield Deal in Iraq," *TradeArabia*, July 21, 2015.

49. Tim Arango and Clifford Krauss, "China Is Reaping Biggest Benefits of Iraq Oil Boom," *New York Times*, June 2, 2013, http://www.nytimes.com/2013/06/03/world/middleeast/china-reaps-biggest-benefits-of-iraq-oil-boom.html?_r=0.

50. Erica S. Downs, "China-Gulf Energy Relations" (Washington, DC: Brookings Institution, August 1, 2011).

51. For instance, in 2008, CNPC recovered its 1997 contract to develop the al-Ahdab field, but it had to accept a less profitable and riskier contract. "China's CNPC Signs First 20-Year Iraqi Service Contract," International Petroleum Finance, September 8, 2008.

52. Hunter, "Halfaya Contract Signed Off in Iraq."

53. Aseel Kami, "China's Shanghai Works on $1 bln Power Deal in Iraq," Reuters, May 29, 2010.

54. "Iraqi Sewage Plant Project Worth 156 Million US Dollars Is Won by CCCC," China Communications Construction Company, December 11, 2013, http://en.ccccltd.cn/newscentre/companynews/201312/t20131220_28549.html.

55. UN Commodity Trade Statistics Database (New York: United Nations, various dates).

56. "GCC Trade and Investment Flows," *Economist*, 2014.

57. Chen Qian, "China's Natural Gas Imports: On a Rising Path," Shipping Intelligence Network, May 24, 2013.

58. Julie Jiang and Jonathan Sinton, "Overseas Investments by Chinese National Oil Companies: Assessing the Drivers and Impacts," International Energy Agency, February 2011.

59. "China-Qatar Cooperation Benefits Both Countries," Xinhua, June 23, 2012, http://lr.china-embassy.org/eng/majorevents/t468200.htm.

60. Joey Aguilar, "China-Qatar 2013 Trade Volume Projected to Reach $10bn," *Gulf Times*, December 30, 2013.

61. "China," U.S. Energy Information Administration, February 4, 2014.

62. "World's LNG Liquefaction Plans and Regasification Terminals," Global LNG Info, July 2015.

63. "China's Liquified Natural Gas Import Deals," Reuters, November 11, 2013.

64. UN Commodity Trade Statistics Database (New York: United Nations, accessed January 15, 2015.

65. "Oman," U.S. Energy Information Administration, October 10, 2013.

66. Al-Tamimi, *China-Saudi Arabia Relations, 1990–2012*, 146.

67. "China's Iranian Crude Imports Drop 2.2 pct in 2013," Reuters, January 21, 2014.

68. "China," U.S. Energy Information Administration, May 14, 2015.

69. "Oman Oil & Gas Report: Includes 10–Year Forecasts to 2022," *Oman Oil and Gas Report*, no. 4 (2013).

70. Bijan Khajehpour, "Iran's Pivot to the East," *Al-Monitor*, July 19, 2013.

71. Scott W. Harold and Alireza Nader, *China and Iran: Economic, Political, and Military Relations* (Santa Monica, CA: Rand Corporation, May 2, 2012).

72. "China," U.S. Energy Information Administration, May 14, 2015.

73. "CNPC Gains Upstream Foothold," *Middle East Economic Digest*, September 3, 2014.

74. Jiang and Sinton, "Overseas Investments by Chinese National Oil Companiess," 21–23.

75. "CNPC to Develop Azadegan Oilfield," *China Daily*, January 16, 2009.

76. "Iran, China Signs $1.7bln Oil Contract," Fars News Agency, January 15, 2009.

77. "Research and Markets: Iran Petrochemicals Report Q2 2011," Reuters, March 09, 2011.

78. "Defiant Iran Forges Ahead with Dams Plan," *UPI*, April 6, 2011.

79. Kenneth Katzman, "Iran Sanctions," Congressional Research Service, January 31, 2014.

80. Ibid.

81. John Daly, "Iran Tears Up Azadegan Contract with China," Oilprice.com, May 4, 2014, http://oilprice.com/Energy/Energy-General/Iran-Tears-Up-Azadegan-Contact-With-China .html.

82. See Erica S. Downs, "China–Middle East Energy Relations," testimony before the U.S.-China Economic and Security Review Commission, Brookings Institution, June 6, 2013.

83. Chen Aizhu, "China State Firms to Start Pumping New Oil in Iran," Reuters, July 31, 2015, http://www.reuters.com/article/2015/07/31/china-iran-oil-idUSL3N10B29620150731. See also Chen Aizhu, "China's Iran oil imports to hit record on new production: sources," *Reuters*, January 5, 2017, http://uk.reuters.com/article/us-china-iran-oil-idUSKBN14P15W.

84. Abdel Aziz Aluwaisheg, "China-GCC Strategic Dialogue Resumes," *Arab News*, January 19, 2014.

85. Zhong Xiang Zhand, "The Overseas Acquisitions and Equity Oil Shares of Chinese National Oil Companies: A Threat to the West But a Boost to China's Energy Security?" *Energy Policy* 48 (September 2012): 698–701.

86. *Degang Sun, "China's Soft Military Presence in the Middle East,"* Middle East Studies Institute, March 11, 2015, http://www.mei.edu/content/map/china%E2%80%99s-soft-military-pres ence-middle-east.

87. Joseph P. Giljum, "The Future of China's Energy Security," *Journal of International Policy Solutions* 11 (Spring 2009): 12–24.

88. Jiang and Sinton, "Overseas Investments by Chinese National Oil Companies."

89. "China: State Firms Face Scrutiny for Overseas Losses," Oxford Analytica, October 20, 2011. Another issue is related to wide concerns about huge losses incurred when investing abroad. A study by China University of Petroleum suggests that China's "big three" oil corporations (CNPC, Sinopec, CNOOC) had invested in some 144 overseas projects totaling $70 billion by the end of 2010, but two-thirds of such overseas investments suffered losses.

90. Mikkal Herberg, "China's Global Quest for Resources and Implications for the United States," testimony before the US–China Economic and Security Review Commission, January 26, 2012.

91. Jiang and Sinton, "Overseas Investments by Chinese National Oil Companies," 22–23.

92. On how China has sought to secure energy assets worldwide from the Middle East to Africa, see Elizabeth C. Economy and Michael Levi, *By All Means Necessary: How China's Resource Quest Is Changing the World* (New York: Oxford University Press, 2014).

93. Statement of Mikkal E. Herberg before the U.S.-China Economic and Security Review Commission June 14, 2007.

94. "China Buying Oil from Iran with Yuan," *BBC News*, May 8, 2012.

Chapter 7

1. On Russian views of this matter, see Ministry of Foreign Affairs of the Russian Federation, "Russsian Foreign Minister Sergey Lavrov Interview to Interfax News Agency," December 26, 2011.

2. "Crisis Prevented Russia from Doubling GDP as Promised—Putin," RIANovosti.ru, June 1, 2011.

3. "Vladimir Putin: Sejchas dlja Rossii vazhen ne kolichestvennyj, a kachestvennyj rost ekonomiki" [Vladimir Putin: Qualitative not quantitative growth is important for Russia]," *Rossiyskaya Gazeta* [Russian gazette], June 1, 2011.

4. "Russia's Medvedev Sees No Alternative to Modernization," RIAnovosti.ru, September 10, 2010.

5. "Putin: Cherez 10 let RF vojdet v pjaterku krupnejshih ekonomik mira [Putin: After 10 years, Russia will become the fifth largest economy in the world]," Golos Rossii [Voice of Russia], May 26, 2011.

6. Alexander Kilyakov, "Russia's President Promises a New Model for Economic Growth," *Russia beyond the Headlines*, October 8, 2012.

7. Ivan Krylov, "Vladimir Putin: V ekonomike Rossija stavit pered soboj ambicioznye celi [Vladimir Putin: Russia's economy has set itself ambitious goals]," *russkiymir.ru* [Russian world], May 26, 2011.

8. Ibid.

9. Neil Buckley, "Economy: Oil Dependency Remains a Fundamental Weakness," *Financial Times*, June 20, 2012.

10. "Zasedanie komissii po modernizacii i tehnologicheskomu razvitiju ekonomiki Rossii [Meeting of the Commission for Modernization and Technological Development of Russian Economy], Prezident Rossii [president of Russia]," kremlin.ru, September 26, 2011.

11. "Rossija, vperjod! Stat'ja Dmitrija Medvedeva, [Forward, Russia! Article by Dmitry Medvedev], Prezident Rossii [president of Russia]," kremlin.ru, September 10, 2009.

12. "Dmitrij Medvedev: Rossija cherez 10 let dolzhna stat' sil'nym gosudarstvom [Dmitry Medvedev: Russia in 10 years to become a strong state]," *Rossiyskaya Gazeta*, [Russian gazette], June 20, 2011.

13. Quoted in Jon Meacham, *Franklin and Winston* (New York: Random house 2003), 339.

14. *Washington Post*, October 2, 1980, A1.

15. Thus, great U.S. attention, reflected in the Iran-Contra fiasco in 1986–1987, focused on severing Moscow's relations with Iran, for fear that these two states could undermine U.S. regional interests. For instance, see the declassified memo, Graham Fuller to the director of the CIA, "Towards a Policy on Iran," May 17, 1985.

16. See, for instance, the statement by former Under Secretary of State for Security Assistance Matthew Nimitz, "U.S. Security Framework," *Current Policy* 221 (September 1980): 1–4.

17. Richard K. Herrmann and Michael P. Fischerkeller, "Beyond the Enemy Image and Spiral Model," *International Organization* 49, no. 3 (1995): 449–450.

18. Cyrus R. Vance, *Hard Choices: Critical Years in America's Foreign Policy* (New York: Simon and Schuster, 1983), 391.

19. See Richard F. Grimmett, *Conventional Arms Transfers to Developing Nations, 1992–1999* (Washington, DC: CRS, August 18, 2000), 44, 53.

20. "Land of Crisis and Upheaval," *Jane's Defence Weekly*, July 30, 1994, 29.

21. Anoushiravan Ehteshami, "Iran's National Strategy: Striving for Regional Parity or Supremacy?" *International Defence Review* 27, no. 4 (April 1994), 35.

22. *Kommersant*, December 1, 1993 in Foreign Broadcast Information Service: Soviet Union/

Central Eurasia (SOV), December 2, 1993, 11. Also see James Bruce, "France Bolsters GCC with Abu Dhabi Accord," *Jane's Defence Weekly*, January 28, 1995, 5.

23. "Russia, Saudi Arabia Set to Finalize Arms Deal," *Agence France-Presse*, August 29, 2009.

24. "Russia, Saudi Arabia in Talks on Major Arms Deal," RIA Novosti, February 15, 2010.

25. "Russia-Saudi Arabia Talks on Large Arms Deals Drag on," *Interfax: AVN Military*, March 7, 2011.

26. Ibid.

27. "Corridors of Power, Russia, Saudi Arabia Have So Far Signed One Defense Contract," *Interfax: Russia and CIS Defense Industry Weekly*, March 11, 2011.

28. Marat Terterov, *New Partnerships and Realignments in the Evolving International System: An Introduction to Contemporary Relations between Russia, the CIS and the Gulf*," in Marat Terterov, ed., *Russian and CIS Relations with the Gulf Region: Current Trends in Political and Economic Dynamics* (Dubai: Gulf Research Center, 2009).

29. Andrej Kreutz, *Russia in the Middle East: Friend or Foe?* (Westport, CT: Greenwood Press, 2007).

30. Mark A. Smith, "Russia and the Persian Gulf: The Deepening of Moscow's Middle East Policy," Conflict Studies Research Centre, August 2007.

31. "Medvedev: RF-Saudi Relations Developing Dynamically," ITAR-TASS, July 14, 2008.

32. "Russian Foreign Minister Starts Visit to Saudi Arabia," ITAR-TASS, May 21, 2006.

33. "Putin Starts 'Historic' Riyadh Visit Today," *Gulf News*, February 11, 2007.

34. Marat Terterov, "Russian Relations to the Gulf Region in a Changing Geopolitical Environment," *Central European Journal of International and Security Studies* 3, no. 1 (2008): 157.

35. "Medvedev: RF-Saudi Relations Developing Dynamically," ITAR-TASS.

36. "Saudi Arabian Minister Conveys King's Message to Russian President," Interfax: Russia and CIS Military Newswire, March 28, 2011.

37. "Saudi U.N. Envoy Slams Russia's Request on Yemen," *Al Arabya*, April 5, 2015.

38. "Putin Lifts Ban on Russian Missile Sales to Iran," *New York Times*, April 13, 2015.

39. "Saudi Arabia and Russia Vie for Global Oil Market Foothold," *Al Arabiya*, June 28, 2015.

40. Abbas Al Lawati, "Putin's Visit to the UAE Marks Special Relationship," Gulfnews.com, September 10, 2007.

41. "Russia/United Arab Emirates/Syria: Putin, UAE Crown Prince to Discuss Situation in Syria," *Asia News Monitor*, September 13, 2013.

42. "Russia/United Arab Emirates: Sanctions vs Russia Not to Hurt Relations with UAE," *Asia News Monitor*, June 9, 2014.

43. "Russian FM Is in Bahrain to Discuss Bilateral Ties and Persian Gulf," ITAR-TASS, February 19, 2009.

44. "Bahrain Politics: Bahrain Strengthens Ties with Russia," *EIU ViewsWire*, May 6, 2014.

45. Embassy of the Russian Federation in Canada, "Summary of Remarks by Russian Foreign Minister Sergey Lavrov at the First Ministerial Meeting of the Strategic Dialogue between Russia and the Cooperation Council for the Arab States of the Gulf," press release, November 7, 2011.

46. "Russia CIS Diplomatic Panorama," *Interfax*, December 8, 2004.

47. Government of the Russian Federation, "Prime Minister Vladimir Putin Met the Prime Minister of Iraq, Nouri al-Maliki," April 10, 2009.

48. Ministry of Foreign Affairs of the Russian Federation, "O vizite Ministra inostrannykh del Rossii S.V.Lavrova v Irak [The visit of Russian Foreign Minister Sergey Lavrov in Iraq]," May 10, 2011.

49. "Iraqi PM Arrives on Russia Visit Despite Warning of 'Some Forces,'" TASS.ru, May 21, 2015.

50. Amanda Macias, "Russia Is Making Moves in Iraq," Reuters, May 21, 2015.

51. See the text of Foreign Minister Qatbzadeh's message to Andrei Gromyko in Tehran Domestic Service, in Foreign Broadcast Information Service, South Asia, August 15, 1980, I-5–6.

52. Interview with Iran's ambassador to the U.S.S.R., *Tehran Keyhan*, in Foreign Broadcast Information Service, South Asia, April 15, 1987, 13.

53. Commentary in *Pravda*, in *Current Digest of the Post-Soviet Press*, April 3, 1985, 9.

54. Reported in *Pravda*, in *Current Digest of the Post-Soviet Press*, February 22, 1989.

55. Excerpt of the agreements, cited in Moscow International Service, in Foreign Broadcast Information Service: USSR, August 3, 1989, 11.

56. For Moscow's justification to Arab states of this sale, see Kuwait Al-Qabas, in Foreign Broadcast Information Service: Near East and South Asia (NESA), July 28, 1989, 18.

57. For example, see *Pravda*, in Foreign Broadcast Information Service: USSR, July 20, 1989, 30. Also see *Tass*, August 20, 1989, in Foreign Broadcast Information Service: USSR, August 21, 1989, 25.

Chapter 8

1. Official Web Portal of President of Russia, "The Foreign Policy Concept of the Russian Federation," July 12, 2008.

2. "Investments Is Promising Sphere in Ties with Persian Gulf States," ITAR-TASS, November 10, 2008.

3. "Sergey Lavrov Attends First Meeting of Russia-Gulf Cooperation Council Dialogue," Rossiyaksya Gazeta Online, November 3, 2011.

4. Alex Rodriguez, "Iran Gets Nuclear Fuel from Russia: But Tehran Says Deal Won't Stop Enrichment" *Tribune Business News*, December 18, 2007.

5. Nabi Abdullaev, "Putin Talks Arms, Nuclear Power in Gulf Visit," *DefenseNews*, February 19, 2007.

6. *Mezhdunarodnye otnosehniya na Blizhnem I Srednem Vostoke in Politika Rossii* [International relations in the Near and Middle East in politics of Russia] (Moscow: Russian National Fund, 1995), quoted in Andrej Kreutz, *Russia in the Middle East: Friend or Foe?* (Westport, CT: Greenwood Press, 2007), 90.

7. *AP Worldstream*, November 26, 2001, quoted in Kreutz, "Russia and Iraq," 94.

8. John Sfakianakis, "Saudi-Russian Trade Relations Deepen," *Arab News*, November 21, 2007.

9. Natalia Rybakova, "Russian-Arab Business Council to Attract Investments to Russia," Tatar-Inform Information Agency, June 10, 2009.

10. "Saudi Arabia to Host Business Forum, Russia's Exhibition in October 2009," ITAR-TASS, June 3, 2009.

11. Courtney Trenwith, "Saudi Arabia, Russia Sign $10bn Investment Deal," *Arabian Business*, June 21, 2015.

12. D. O. Biryukov, "Arabskie investitsii v rossiiskuyu ekonomiku [Arab investments in Russian economy]," Institut Blizhnego Vostoka [Institute for Middle East], May 27, 2011.

13. "Russia, Saudi Arabia to Cooperate, Not to Compete—Ambassador," ITAR-TASS, April 7, 2009.

14. "Qatar, Russia Working on 12 Major Projects," *Gulf Times*, February 11, 2011.

15. Ministry of Foreign Affairs of the Russian Federation, "Rossiisko-Katarskie Otnosheniya [Russian-Qatari relations]," October 10, 2011.

16. Ibid.

17. Peninsula Qatar.com, "Gazprombank Announce Closing of Russia Fund," January 3, 2011.

18. Ibid.

19. "Russia's Putin, "Emir of Qatar Willing to Discuss 'Sensitive' Cooperation," Interfax, November 2, 2010.

20. Ibid.

21. "Qatar's SWF Commits $2bn Investment to Russia," Arabianbusiness.com, May 24, 2014.

22. Ministerstvo Inostrannykh del Rossiiskoi Federatsii [Ministry of Foreign Affairs of the Russian Federation], "Rossiisko-Emiratskie Otnosheniya [Russian-emirate relations]," October 10, 2011, http://www.mid.ru/en/maps/ae/?currentpage=main-country.

23. Ibid.

24. "Russia, UAE to Settle USSR Debt Issue, and to Sign Space Cooperation Agreement," ITAR-TASS, September 9, 2007.

25. "Abu Dhabi Fund Invests in Russia," *Wall Street Journal*, November 30, 2010.

26. "Rosneft Joins UAE Gas Project as Russia Seeks Mideast Partners," *Oil Daily*, June 8, 2010.

27. "UAE's Gulftainer Eyes Growth in Russia, Asia," Arabianbusiness.com, April 2, 2012.

28. Ministerstvo Inostrannykh del Rossiiskoi Federatsii, "Rossiisko-Emiratskie Otnosheniya [Russian-emirate relations]."

29. Ibid.

30. "Russia/United Arab Emirates: Sanctions vs Russia Not to Hurt Relations with UAE," *Asia News Monitor*, June 9, 2014.

31. Ministerstvo Inostrannykh del Rossiiskoi Federatsii [Ministry of Foreign Affairs of the Russian Federation], "Rossisko-Kuveitskie Otnosheniya," [Russian-Kuwaiti relations]," October 10, 2011.

32. Ibid.

33. "First Meeting of the Sub-Commission on Trade, Economic, Technical, Financial and Investment Cooperation Was Held in El-Kuwait," Ensat.ru, September 12, 2011.

34. Ministerstvo Inostrannykh del Rossiiskoi Federatsii [Ministry of Foreign Affairs of the Russian Federation] "Rossiisko-Bakhreinskie Otnosheniya [Russian-Bahraini relations]," October 10, 2011.

35. Ibid.

36. "Bahrain Reinforces Ties with Russia," *Gulf News*, January 28, 2015, http://gulfnews.com/news/gulf/bahrain/bahrain-reinforces-ties-with-russia-1.1447458.

37. "Bahrain, Russia Sign New Trade Agreements," *Trade Arabia*, April 29, 2014.

38. Ministerstvo Inostrannykh del Rossiiskoi Federatsii [Ministry of Foreign Affairs of the Russian Federation] "Rossisko-Omanskie Otnosheniya" [Russian-Omani relations], October 10, 2011.

39. World Bank, "World Development Indicators: Contribution of Natural Resources to Gross Domestic Product, accessed June 16, 2016."

40. Energy Information Administration, "Russia," http://www.eia.gov/beta/international/analysis.cfm?iso=RUS.

41. Dave Cohen, "Has Russia's Oil Production Peaked?" *Energy Bulletin*, April 23, 2008.

42. Ministry of Energy of the Russian Federation, "Energy Strategy of Russia: For the Period up to 2030," 2010.

43. Leonard Coburn, "Russian Oil-A Long Term View," International Association for Energy Economics (Fall 2010).

44. "Gazprom Neft Pursues Iran and Cuba Oil Projects to expand resource base," Gulfnews.com, June 30, 2010.

45. "LUKoil Set to Expand Oil and Gas Cooperation with Iran," RIA Novosti, December 13, 2007.

46. "Interview with Boris Silbermints, Deputy CEO for Exploration and Production of Gazprom Neft," Interfax, January 28, 2010.

47. "Russia, Iran to Boost Energy Cooperation," ITAR-TASS, October 15, 2008.

48. "Russia's Lukoil Says Iran Project Dropped over Sanctions," RIA Novosti, March 24, 2010.

49. "Gazprom Neft Forced Out of Iranian Project," *Moscow Times*, October 11, 2011.

50. "Lukoil Executive: Iran Tension to Effect Long Term on Oil Market," RT.com, February 3, 2012.

51. "Iran Again Invites Russia to Join Its Oil and Gas Projects," RT.com, February 12, 2013.

52. "Russia's Gazprom Neft Signs Contract to Develop Iraqi Oil Field," RIA Novosti, January 28, 2010.

53. "Energy Is One of Most Promising Russia-Iraq Cooperation Spheres—Shmatko," ITAR-TASS, September 11, 2009.

54. Ibid.

55. Going Global East Meets West (blog), "Iraq and Russia—Lukoil Starts Drilling at Iraq's West Qurna-2 Field," April 25, 2012, http://musingsoniraq.blogspot.com/2012/04/russias-lukoil -begins-drilling-at-iraqs.html.

56. "Lavrov to Discuss Russia-Iraq Energy, Military-Technological Cooperation in Baghdad," Interfax-AVN Online, May 10, 2011.

57. "Gazprom Enters New Project in Iraq's Kurdish Autonomous Region with 80% Share," *Trend*, February 26, 2013.

58. "Baghdad to Apply Sanctions against Gazprom in Case of Its Cooperation with Kurdish Autonomy," *Journal of Turkish Weekly*, August 6, 2012.

59. Rebin Yar Ahmad, "Gazprom Prepares to Drill for Oil in Halabja," rudaw.net, May 3, 2015, http://rudaw.net/english/kurdistan/030520152.

60. "Russia, Saudi Arabia Should Strengthen Cooperation amid Crisis—Sechin," ITAR-TASS, December 16, 2008.

61. Kreutz, "Russia and the Arabian Peninsula," 131.

62. "Lukoil Overseas Holding Ltg: Corporate Report," Lukoil-overseas.com, 2009.

63. "Lukoil JV Gives Up on Rub Al-Khali," *Oil and Gas News*, September 21, 2010.

64. "Russian-Saudi Relations," Ministry of Foreign Affairs of the Russian Federation, October 10, 2011.

65. "Saudi Arabia, Russia in Talks over Nuclear Agreement," *Saudi Economic Survey*, November 8, 2010.

66. "Saudi Arabia, Russia Sign Nuclear Power Cooperation Deal," Reuters, June 19, 2015, http://uk.reuters.com/article/2015/06/19/uk-saudi-russia-nuclear-idUKKBN0OZ10R20150619.

67. "Saudi Arabia, China Sign Nuclear Cooperation Pact," *Wall Street Journal*, January 16, 2012, http://online.wsj.com/article/SB10001424052970204468004577164742025285500.html.

68. "Russia, Saudi Arabia Energy Partners, Not Rivals—Putin," RIA Novosti, February 12, 2007, http://en.rian.ru/russia/20070212/60580105.html.

69. Brian Spegele, "Russia, China Warm Up over Oil, Squeezing OPEC," *Wall Street Journal*, January 24, 2015.

70. "Gas Vital to Middle East Economies," *Gulf News*, July 1, 2011, http://gulfnews.com/busi ness/oil-gas/gas-vital-to-middle-east-economies-1.830847.

71. "Crescent Petroleum Discusses Major Projects with Rosneft, Rosteknhnologii," RIA Novosti, August 21, 2010, http://en.rian.ru/world/20100821/160291179.html. See also LeAnne Graves, "Rosfnet considers exiting JV with Crescent in Sharjah," *National*, May 26, 2015, http://www.the national.ae/business/energy/rosneft-considers-exiting-jv-with-crescent-in-sharjah.

72. Miles Johnson, "Rosneft Ventures into Middle East," *Financial Times*, May 20, 2010.

73. Ministerstvo Inostrannykh del Rossiiskoi Federatsii [Ministry of Foreign Affairs of the

Russian Federation] "Rossiisko-Kuveitskie Otnosheniy [Russian-Kuwaiti relations]," October, 10, 2011.

74. "Rossiisko-Bakhreinskie Otnosheniya [Russian-Bahraini relations]," October 10, 2011.

75. Ministerstvo Inostrannykh del Rossiiskoi Federatsii [Ministry of Foreign Affairs of the Russian Federation] "Rossisko-Omanskie Otnosheniya [Russian-Omani relations]," October 10, 2011.

76. "Constituent Session of the Russian-Omani Business Council," Ensat.ru, June 16, 2011.

77. "Russia, Qatar Sign Memorandum on Civilian Nuclear Cooperation," *Interfax: Russia and CIS Business and Investment Weekly*, November 8, 2010.

78. "Qatar Buys into Shell," RT.com, May 11, 2012, http://rt.com/business/news/qatar-shell -stake-buy-003/.

79. Sam Barden, "The Gas Gang," *Sputniknews*, December 8, 2010, https://sputniknews.com/ analysis/20101208161683342/.

80. Yulia Latynina, "The Main International Confrontation of the XXI Century Is between Hydrocarbon Despotism and Pipeline Democracies," *Novaya gazeta*, March 29, 2011, http://en .novayagazeta.ru/politics/8713.html.

81. "Gazprom Maintained Market Share in Most of Europe in 2010—IEA," Interfax: Russia *and* CIS Business and Financial Newswire, Mar 15, 2011.

82. "Gazprom Talking with Qatar about Working in Europe, Pacific Rim Countries," Interfax: Russia *and* CIS Business *and* Investment Weekly, November 8, 2010. Also see "World's LNG Lique-faction Plants and Regasification Terminals," Globallnginfo.com, April 2012, http://www.globallng-info.com/World%20LNG%20Plants%20&%20Terminals.pdf.

83. "Worrying Times for Energy Investors," *Petroleum Economist*, October 28, 2010, http:// www.petroleum-economist.com/Article/2730869/A-worrying-time-for-LNG-investors.html.

84. "Russia Courts Qatar as LNG Partner," *Energy Intelligence Group*: NEFTE Compass, July 22, 2010.

85. Jeannie Stell, "South Stream Project On Again . . . for Now," *Offshore Engineer*, May 11, 2015.

86. "Energy Production and Imports," accessed June 20, 2013, Eurostat, http://ec.europa.eu/ eurostat/statistics-explained/index.php/Energy_production_and_imports

87. "Poland Signs $550 Million Gas Deal with Qatargas," *LNGPedia*, July 1, 2010. See also Jo Harper, "Świnoujście gas terminal: all systems go," *Financial Observer*, November 11, 2015, http:// www.financialobserver.eu/poland/swinoujscie-gas-terminal-all-systems-go/.

88. Leslie Palti-Guzman, "Qatar-Russia: Friends or Enemies?" *Energy Intelligence Group: Energy Compass, April 9, 2010.*

89. "Gazprom Sets Up Shop in Qatar," UPI, February 12, 2013, http://www.upi.com/Business_ News/Energy-Resources/2013/02/12/Gazprom-sets-up-shop-in-Qatar/UPI-73201360666276/.

90. "Qatar Says Not a Gas 'Alternative' to Russia," *Agence France-Presse*, September 23, 2014, http://news.yahoo.com/qatar-says-not-gas-alternative-russia-100516188.html.

91. "Nabucco Needs Gas from Iran to be a Game Changer—Bartuska," ICIS.news, July 24, 2009, http://www.icis.com/Articles/2009/07/24/9235044/nabucco-needs-gas-from-iran-to-be-a -game-changer-bartuska.html.

92. "Iran," U.S. Energy Information Administration, June 19, 2015.

93. "Iran to Resume Abandoned LNG Projects," Press TV, June 25, 2015, http://www.presstv.ir /Detail/2015/06/25/417492/iran-gas-lng-exports-sanctions-kameli.

94. Dmitry Zhdannikov, "Russia Faces Oil Price Battle as Iraqi Output Grows," Reuters, July 29, 2011.

95. Ibid.

96. "Summary of Russian Press for Tuesday 13 February 2007," Defense News—BBC Monitoring Former Soviet Union, February 13, 2007.

97. See Carol R. Saivetz, "Moscow's Iranian Policies: Opportunities and Dangers," Middle East Brief, Brandeis University, January 2007.

98. "Medvedev Bans Sale of S-3 00 Missiles, Other Weapons to Iran (Update 1)", RIA Novosti, September 22, 2010, http://en.rian.ru/mlitary_news/20100922/160688354.html.

99. "Russia Is Upgrading S-300 Defense Missiles Intended For Iran," Radio Free Europe Radio Liberty, August 1, 2015, http://www.rferl.org/content/russia-upgrading-s300-defense-missiles-intended-for-iran/27162140.html.

100. See Mark N. Katz, "Russian-Iranian Relations in the Obama Era," Middle East Policy 17 (Summer 2010): 62–69.

101. Judy Dempsey, "If Gas Talks Fail, Europe Has a Backup Plan," New York Times, January 9, 2012, http://www.nytimes.com/2012/01/10/world/europe/10iht-letter10.html.

102. "Strakhi titana [Giant's fear]," RBCDaily, January 21, 2010, http://www.rbcdaily.ru/2010/01/21/tek/453620.

103. Anna Shiryaevskaya, "Putin's Global Gas Plan Falters as Gazprom Dithers on LNG," Bloomberg, August 3, 2010, http://www.bloomberg.com/news/2010-08-04/putin-s-global-plan-for-gas-domination-falters-as-gazprom-dithers-on-lng.html.

104. Garibov Konstantin, "Russia Defends Its Stance at the Gas Exporting Countries Forum," Voice of Russia, November 16, 2011, http://english.ruvr.ru/2011/11/16/60483996.html.

105. Ibid.

Chapter 9

1. Richard F. Grimmett and Paul K. Kerr, "Conventional Arms Transfers to Developing Nations, 2004–2011" (Washington, DC: Congressional Research Service, 2012).

2. Wael Mahdi, "Iran Needs Higher Oil Prices for 2013 Budget, Apicorp Says," Bloomberg, July 26, 2013, http://www.bloomberg.com/news/2013-07-26/iran-needs-higher-oil-price-for-2013-budget-apicorp-says.html.

3. See World Population Review, "Iran Population 2014," accessed May 23, 2015, http://worldpopulationreview.com/countries/iran-population/.

4. For example, see a histogram comparing the capabilities of Saudi Arabia, Iran, Iraq, Israel, Egypt and Syria: James W. Moore, "An Assessment of the Iranian Rearmament Program," Comparative Strategy 13: 381.

5. "The Most Powerful Militaries in the Middle East," Business Insider, accessed November 10, 2015, http://www.businessinsider.com/most-powerful-militaries-in-the-middle-east-2014-8#no-3-saudi-arabia-14.

6. Global FirePower, "Countries Ranked by Military Strength," 2015, accessed March 10, 2016, https://knoema.com/GFP2016/global-firepower-2015.

7. "Iran Able to Block Strait of Hormuz, General Dempsey Says on CBS," Bloomberg, January 8, 2012, https://www.bloomberg.com/news/articles/2012-01-08/iran-able-to-block-strait-of-hormuz-general-dempsey-tells-cbs.

8. For an extensive analysis of this literature and of Iran's capabilities, see Caitlin Talmadge, "Closing Time: Assessing the Iranian Threat to the Strait of Hormuz," International Security 33 (Summer 2008): 82–117.

Chapter 10

1. See Gal Luft and Anne Korin, eds., *Energy Security Challenges for the 21st Century* (Santa Barbara, CA: Praeger Security International, 2009).

2. See Barry Buzan, *Theory of World Security* (Cambridge: Cambridge University Press, 2007); Paris Roland, "Human Security: Paradigm Shift or Hot Air?" *International Security* 26, no. 2 (Fall 2001): 87–102; Thomas Homer-Dixon, "Straw Man in the Wind," *National Interest*, January 2, 2008; Richard Wyn Jones, *Security, Strategy, and Critical Theory* (Boulder, CO: Lynne Rienner, 1999); Jessica Tuchman Mathews, "Redefining Security," *Foreign Affairs* 68, no. 2 (Spring 1989): 162–177.

3. Charles L. Glaser, "How Oil Influences U.S. National Security," *International Security* 38, no. 2 (Fall 2013): 112–146. Also see Meghan L. O'Sullivan, "The Entanglement of Energy, Grand Strategy, and International Security," in Andreas Goldthau, ed., *The Handbook of Global Energy Policy* (Hoboken, NJ: Wiley-Blackwell, 2013), 30–47.

4. See Robert Looney, "Oil Prices and the Iraq War: Market Interpretations of Military Developments," *Strategic Insights* 2, no. 4 (April 2003), http://calhoun.nps.edu/bitstream/handle /10945/25431/Oil_Prices_and_the_Iraq_War_Market_Interpretations_of_Military_Developments .pdf?sequence=1&isAllowed=y.

5. For an overview of causes of the 2008 oil price shock, see, for instance, James D. Hamilton, "Causes and Consequences of the Oil Shock of 2007–08," Brookings Institution, 2009.

6. "World Oil Transit Chokepoints," U.S. Energy Information Administration, updated August 22, 2012, http://www.marsecreview.com/wp-content/uploads/2012/08/World-Oil-Transit-Choke points.pdf.

7. See "World Oil Transit Chokepoints," U.S. Energy Information Administration, November 10, 2014.

8. "Iran Threatens to Block Strait of Hormuz Oil Route," BBC, December 28, 2011, http:// www.bbc.com/news/world-middle-east-16344102.

9. "Iran Able to Block Strait of Hormuz, General Dempsey Says on CBS," *Businessweek*, January 11, 2012, http://www.businessweek.com/news/2012-01-11/iran-able-to-block-strait-of-hormuz -general-dempsey-says-on-cbs.html.

10. On insurance rates, Steve Yetiv's discussion with Steve Carmel, vice president of Maersk Line Limited, Norfolk, Virginia, August 3, 2014.

11. See, for instance, "West Africa Piracy Endangering Commodities Shipping," *Insurance Journal*, July 18, 2013, and "Pirate Attacks Increase in the Gulf of Guinea," *Oilprice*, July 18, 2013.

12. "Iran Able to Block Strait of Hormuz, General Dempsey Says on CBS." Also, see "U.S. Adds Forces in Persian Gulf," *New York Times*, July 3, 2012.

13. "Naval Co-operation in the Gulf War," in David Fouquet, ed., *Jane's NATO Handbook, 1988–1989* (London: Jane's, 1988), 198.

14. Bates Gill and Evan S. Medeiros, "Foreign and Domestic Influences on China's Arms Control and Nonproliferation Policies," *China Quarterly* 161 (March 2000): 75.

15. Paul Mann, "No Breakthrough on Chinese Proliferation," *Aviation Week and Space Technology*, March 11, 2002, 57.

16. See Edward D. Mansfield and Jack Snyder, *Electing to Fight: Why Emerging Democracies Go to War* (Cambridge, MA: MIT Press, 2005).

17. Public Opinion in Iran and America on Key International on Key International Issues, Questionnaire: (PIPA), WorldPublicOpinion.org, 2006.

18. For a concise case of the threats of Iran's nuclear aspirations, see Matthew Kroenig, "Time to Attack Iran," *Foreign Affairs* 91, no. 2 (January/February 2012): 76–86.

19. *National Military Strategy to Combat Weapons of Mass Destruction* (Washington, DC: Chairman, Joint Chiefs of Staff, February 13, 2006).

20. See "Iranian Officials Publicly Cite Impact of Sanctions," *Washington Post*, July 3, 2012.

21. For instance, see "Foreign Ministry Spokesman Kong Quan's Regular Press Conference on 17 January 2006," Ministry of Foreign Affairs of the People's Republic of China, accessed March 27, 2012, at http://www.fmprc.gov.cn/eng/xwfw/s2510/2511/t231665.htm.

22. *Cooperative Defense Initiative Against Weapons of Mass Destruction in Southwest Asia* (Washington, DC: Department of Defense, United States Central Command, 2002). The members of the GCC, which was formed in May 1981, are Saudi Arabia, Kuwait, Oman, Qatar, the United Arab Emirates, and Bahrain.

23. Ibid.

24. See Joseph A. Kechichian, "Can Conservative Arab Gulf Monarchies Endure a Fourth War in the Persian Gulf?" *Middle East Journal* 61 (Spring 2007): 297–299.

25. On GCC threat perceptions, see Thomas R. Mattair, "Mutual Threat Perceptions in the Arab/Persian Gulf: GCC Perceptions," *Middle East Policy* 14 (Summer 2007): 133–140.

26. See Joshua R. Itzkowitz Shifrinson and Miranda Priebe. "A Crude Threat: The Limits of an Iranian Missile Campaign against Saudi Arabian Oil," *International Security* 36 (2011): 167–201.

27. Brynjar Lia and Ashild Kjok, "Energy Supply as Terrorist Targets?" in Daniel Heradstveit and Helge Hveem, eds., *Oil in the Gulf* (London: Ashgate, 2004).

28. See "Sea Terrorists Threaten Oil," *Oil and Gas Journal*, June 18, 2007, 30.

29. Neal Adams, *Terrorism and Oil* (Tulsa, OK: PennWell Corporation, 2003), 102.

30. Lia and Kjok, "Energy Supply as Terrorist Targets?" 111.

31. "Big Oil Ready for Possible Terror Strike," *Oil Daily*, February 18, 2003.

32. See Daniel Byman, *Deadly Connections: States That Sponsor Terrorism* (Cambridge: Cambridge University Press, 2005), 235–38.

33. See Kenneth Katzman, "The Persian Gulf States: Issues for U.S. Policy, 2006," Congressional Research Service, August 21, 2006.

34. Andrew England, "Saudis Set Up Force to Guard Oil Plants," *Financial Times*, August 26, 2007, http://www.freerepublic.com/focus/f-news/1886993/posts.

35. For post-9/11 views of this threat, see John E. Peterson, *Saudi Arabia and the Illusion of Security* (London: Oxford University Press for the International Institute for Strategic Studies, 2002). See also Sherifa Zuhur, *Saudi Arabia: Islamic Threat, Political Reform, and the Global War on Terror* (Carlisle Barracks, PA: Strategic Studies Institute, March 2005), http://ssi.armywarcollege.edu/pdf files/pub598.pdf.

36. On the Nixon, Carter, and Reagan doctrines, see Michael A. Palmer, *Guardians of the Gulf* (New York: Free Press, 1992), chaps. 5, 6, esp. 118.

37. "U.S. Fears Prospect of Saudi Coup, Weighs Invasion Plans," *Worldtribune*, November 1, 2015, http://www.worldtribune.com/worldtribune/WTARC/2005/ss_saudi_11_01.html.

38. F. Gregory Gause III, *Oil Monarchies: Domestic and Security Challenges in the Arab Gulf States* (New York: Council on Foreign Relations Press, 1994), 122.

39. See Jahangir Amuzegar, *Managing the Oil Wealth: OPEC's Windfalls and Pitfalls* (London: I. B. Tauris, 1999), 41–43.

40. See ibid.

41. See Lawrence Freedman and Efraim Karsh, *The Gulf Conflict, 1990–1991: Diplomacy and War in the New World Order* (Princeton, NJ: Princeton University Press, 1993), 56–57.

42. Quoted in "Coping with High Oil Prices: A Summary of Options," CRS Issue Brief RL30459, April 19, 2000.

43. Quoted in "The US Role with OPEC," *Oil and Gas Journal*, April 24, 2000, 19.

44. Congressional Research Service, *Coping with High Oil Prices*, April 19, 2000.

45. "Iran Slams U.S. Pressure on OPEC to Raise Output," Xinhua News Agency, March 20, 2000.

46. Quoted in "Iran Accuses U.S. of Pressuring OPEC," *United Press International*, July 18, 2000.

47. "OPEC on Top," *Middle East Economic Digest*, July 21, 2000.

48. See, for instance, "OPEC Resists Calls for Increased Oil Output," *Oil and Gas Journal*, October 16, 2000, 40. See also A. F. Alhajji, "OPEC Cannot Manage World Oil Markets with a Price Band," *World Oil* (October 2000): 131.

49. "Iran Cautions OPEC Members against Oversupply of Crude," Xinhua News Agency, September 11, 2000.

50. "Saudi Prince Vows Stable Oil Market," *New York Times*, January 14, 2001.

51. See Kechichian, "Can Conservative Arab Gulf Monarchies Endure a Fourth War in the Persian Gulf?" 297–99.

52. See Zhong Xiang Zhand, "The Overseas Acquisitions and Equity Oil Shares of Chinese National Oil Companies: A Threat to the West But a Boost to China's Energy Security?" *Energy Policy* 48 (September 2012): 698–701. See also Julie Jiang and Jonathan Sinton, "Overseas Investments by Chinese National Oil Companies: Assessing the Drivers and Impacts," Information Paper, International Energy Agency, February 2011, http://www.iea.org/publications/freepublications / publication/overseas_china.pdf.

53. Erica S. Downs, "The Chinese Energy Security Debate," *China Quarterly* 177 (March 2004): 21–41.

54. "Financial and Economic Data Relating to NATO Defence," NATO Press Release 28, February 24, 2014.

55. See John Gordon, Stuart Johnson, F. Stephen Larrabee, and Peter A. Wilson, "NATO and the Challenge of Austerity," *Survival* 54, no. 4 (August/September 2012): 121–142.

56. Ivo Daalder and James Stavridis, "NATO's Victory in Libya," *Foreign Affairs* 91, no. 2 (2012): 2–7.

57. Anders Fogh Rasmussen, "The Atlantic Alliance in Austere Times," *Foreign Affairs* 90, no. 4, (July / August 2011): 2–6.

58. "World Energy Outlook 2012," International Energy Agency, November 12, 2012, 81.

59. Leonard Coburn, "Russian Oil—A Long Term View," International Association for Energy Economics, second quarter of 2011, accessed June 25, 2014, http://www.energystrategy.ru/projects /docs/ES-2030_(Eng).pdf, 12–13.

60. Nayla Razzouk and Anthony Dipaola, "Iraq Oil Production Beating Iran Ends Saddam Legacy," Bloomberg, May 11, 2012.

61. Tim Arango and Clifford Krauss, "China Is Reaping Biggest Benefits of Iraq Oil Boom," *New York Times*, June 2, 2013, http://www.nytimes.com/2013/06/03/world/middleeast/china-reaps -biggest-benefits-of-iraq-oil-boom.html.

62. "China's CNPC Signs First 20-Year Iraqi Service Contract," International Petroleum Service, May 18, 2010, https://www.highbeam.com/doc/1G1-185405923.html. For a difference between PSC and SC, see http://www.academia.edu/3300791/Production_Sharing_Contracts_vs_Service_ Contracts_from_the_View_Point_of_an_IOC.

63. Catherine Hunter, "Halfaya Contract Signed Off in Iraq as Ministry Works to End-January Deadline," Global Insight, January 28, 2010.

64. Arango and Krauss, "China Is Reaping Biggest Benefits of Iraq Oil Boom."

65. Zarchary Keck,, "China Doubles Down on Iraqi Oil," *Diplomat*, October 18, 2013, http:// thediplomat.com/2013/10/china-doubles-down-on-iraqi-oil-gamble/.

Chapter 11

1. "Lost Civilizations: The Roman Empire," NBC, July 23, 1995).

2. For a good brief description of these views in the 1990s, see William C. Wohlforth, "The Stability of a Unipolar World," *International Security* 24 (Summer 1999): 5–9. On balancing, see Kenneth N. Waltz, *Theory of International Politics* (Reading, MA: Addison-Wesley, 1979). On this literature, also see Christopher Layne, *The Peace of Illusions: American Grand Strategy from 1940 to the Present* (Ithaca, NY: Cornell University Press, 2006), 12–16. Although unipolarity and hegemony differ, these articles are instructive: Nuno P. Monteiro, "Unrest Assured: Why Unipolarity Is Not Peaceful," *International Security* 36 (Winter 2011/12): 9–40, and Randall L. Schweller and Xiaoyu Pu, "After Unipolarity: China's Visions of International Order in an Era of U.S. Decline," *International Security* 36 (Summer 2011): 41–72.

3. See Robert A. Pape, "Soft Balancing against the United States," *International Security* 30 (Summer 2005): 7–45. Also see T. V. Paul, "Soft Balancing in the Age of U.S. Primacy," *International Security* 30 (Summer 2005): esp. 58–59.

4. For a seminal view of this kind, see Robert O. Keohane, *After Hegemony: Cooperation and Discord in the World Political Economy* (Princeton: Princeton University Press, 1984). Also see Helen Milner and Andrew Moravcsik, eds., *Power, Interdependence and Non-State Actors in World Politics* (Princeton: Princeton University Press, 2009).

5. Alexander Wendt, *Social Theory of International Politics* (Cambridge: Cambridge University Press, 1999).

6. Notwithstanding the differences between hegemony and unipolarity, see Wohlforth, "The Stability of a Unipolar World," and William C. Wohlforth, "Unipolarity, Status Competition, and Great Power War," *World Politics* 61 (January 2009): 28–57. For her part, Carla Norloff argues that the United States still possesses three critical features that give it "positional advantages" over all other states—the largest domestic economy, the key world currency, and the strongest military—and that its hegemonic burdens are outweighed by the benefits of provisioning public goods. Carla Norloff, *America's Global Advantage: US Hegemony and International Cooperation* (Cambridge: Cambridge University Press, 2010). Like Norloff, Robert Lieber focuses more on how America is not in decline. Robert J. Lieber, *Power and Willpower in the American Future: Why the US Is Not Destined to Decline* (Cambridge: Cambridge University Press, 2012).

7. See G. John Ikenberry, ed., *America Unrivaled: The Future of the Balance of Power* (Ithaca, NY: Cornell University Press, 2002).

8. See John M. Owen IV, "Transnational Liberalism and U.S. Primacy," *International Security* 26 (2002): 117–52.

9. For example, Michael Greenstone and Adam Looney, "Paying Too Much for Energy? The True Costs of Our Energy Choices" *Daedalus* 141, no. 2 (Spring 2012): 10; John S. Duffield, Over a Barrel: The Costs of U.S. Foreign Oil Dependence (Stanford: Stanford University Press, 2008); James A. Griffin, A Smart Energy Policy: An Economist's Rx for Balancing Cheap, Clean, and Secure Energy (New Haven, CT: Yale University Press, 2009); Roger J. Stern, "United States Cost of Military Force Projection in the Persian Gulf, 1976–2007," Energy Policy 38, no. 6 (June 2010): 2816–2825.

10. Stern, "United States Cost of Military Force Projection in the Persian Gulf."

11. For a sweeping analysis of this literature, see Mark A. Delucchi and James Murphy, "U.S. Military Expenditures to Protect the Use of Persian-Gulf Oil for Motor Vehicles," Institute of Transportation Studies, University of California, Davis, October 2006, esp. Tables 15–16.

12. Steve A. Yetiv, *Explaining Foreign Policy: U.S. Decision-Making and the Persian Gulf Wars*, 2nd ed. (Baltimore, MD: Johns Hopkins University Press, 2011).

13. George Bush and Brent Scowcroft, *A World Transformed* (New York: Knopf, 1998), 358.

14. On the causes of terrorism, see Daniel L. Byman, "Al-Qaeda as an Adversary: Do We Understand Our Enemy?" *World Politics* 56, no. 1 (October 2003): 143–148; Lisa Anderson, "Shock and Awe: Interpretations of the Events of September 11," *World Politics* 56, no. 2 (January 2004): 303–325.

15. On perceived and real occupation as a source of terrorism, see Robert A. Pape, *Dying to Win: The Strategic Logic of Suicide Terrorism* (New York: Random House, 2005).

16. bin Laden video (CNN, October 21, 2001), transcript at: http://edition.cnn.com/2002/WORLD/asiapcf/south/02/05/binladen.transcript/.

17. On his view of the Gulf, see Yossef Bodansky, *Bin Laden: The Man Who Declared War on America* (New York: Prima, 1999), esp. chap. 12. Also see John L. Esposito, *Unholy War: Terror in the Name of Islam* (New York: Oxford University Press, 2002), esp. 20–23.

18. Baghdad INA, in Foreign Broadcast Information Service, October 10, 1990, 27.

19. See islamic-news.co.uk. The transcript also appears in Barry Rubin and Judith Colp Rubin, eds., *Anti-American Terrorism and the Middle East* (New York: Oxford University Press, 2002), 137–142.

20. On foreign occupation as the primary cause of terrorism, see Robert A. Pape, *Dying to Win: The Strategic Logic of Suicide Terrorism* (New York: Random House, 2005).

21. Interview with Osama bin Laden, "Hunting the Enemy," *Frontline* (May 1998), http://www.pbs.org/wgbh/pages/frontline/shows/binladen/who/family.html.

22. Roland Jacquard, *In the Name of Osama Bin Laden* (Durham, NC: Duke University Press, 2002), 110–111. Yoram Schweitzer and Shaul Shay, *The Globalization of Terror* (New Brunswick, NJ: Transaction Publishers, 2009), 29.

23. Jacquard, *In the Name of Osama Bin Laden*, 96.

24. See Fawaz A. Gerges, *The Rise and Fall of Al-Qaeda* (New York: Oxford University Press, 2014).

25. Joseph E. Stiglitz and Linda J. Bilmes, *The Three Trillion Dollar War: The True Cost of the Iraq Conflict* (New York: Norton, 2008).

26. See Abdel Bari Atwan, *The Secret History of Al-Qaeda* (Berkeley: University of California Press, 2006).

27. On such forces, see Shadi Hamid, *Temptations of Power: Islamists and Illiberal Democracy in a New Middle East* (New York: Oxford University Press, 2014).

28. Waltz, *Theory of International Politics*; Christopher Layne, "The Unipolar Illusion Revisited: The Coming End of the United States' Unipolar Moment," *International Security* 31 (Fall 2006): 12–16.

29. See Pape, "Soft Balancing against the United States," and Paul, "Soft Balancing in the Age of U.S. Primacy," esp. pp. 58–59. Also see Christopher Layne, "America's Middle East Grand Strategy after Iraq: The Moment for Offshore Balancing Has Arrived," *Review of International Studies* 35, no. 1 (January, 2009): 5–25.

30. On Iran's rising power, see this set of 2013 Council on Foreign Relations articles: http://www.cfr.org/issue/proliferation/ri31. Also, for the roots of this development, see Val Nasr, *The Shia Revival: How Conflicts within Islam Will Shape the Future* (New York: Norton, 2007).

31. William A. Callahan and Elena Barabantseva, eds., *China Orders the World* (Baltimore: Johns Hopkins University Press, 2011).

32. Laurie Pearcey, "Xi Jinping's New Silk Road: Chinese Foreign Policy, Energy Security and Ideology," *Conversation*, September 16, 2013, http://theconversation.com/xi-jinpings-new-silk-road-chinese-foreign-policy-energy-security-and-ideology-17994.

33. Christopher Williams, "Russia's Closer Ties with China: The Geo-Politics of Energy and the Implications for the European Union," *European Studies: A Journal Of European Culture, History and Politics* 27, no. 1 (2009): 151–166.

34. On Russia's pipelines, see "The Commercial and Political Logic for the Altai Pipeline," Oxford Institute for Energy Studies, December 1, 2014, https://www.oxfordenergy.org/wpcms/wp -content/uploads/2014/12/The-Commercial-and-Political-Logic-for-the-Altai-Pipeline-GPC-4.pdf.

35. Ibid.

36. Ben Hubbard, "Cables Released by WikiLeaks Reveal Saudis' Checkbook Diplomacy," *New York Times*, June 21, 2015, 10.

37. Ikenberry, *America Unrivaled*.

38. Stephen M. Walt, *Taming American Power: The Global Response to U.S. Primacy* (New York: Norton, 2005), 124, 187–191.

39. On how China is a free rider in the field of energy security, see Andrew Kennedy, "China and the Free Rider Problem: Exploring the Case of Energy Security," *Political Science Quarterly* 130 (Spring 2015): 27–50. Also see Bingbing Wu, "Strategy and Politics in the Gulf as Seen from China," in Bryce Wakefield and Susan L. Levenstein, eds., *China and the Persian Gulf: Implications for the United States* (Washington, DC: Woodrow Wilson International Center for Scholars, 2011), 10–26.

40. Andrew Kennedy, "China and the Free Rider Problem: Exploring the Case of Energy Security," *Political Science Quarterly* 130 (Spring 2015): 36–38.

41. Thomas L. Friedman, "Foreign Policy by Whisper and Nudge," *New York Times*, August 24, 2013.

42. Gal Luft, "What Does America's Shale Gasoline Revolutions Mean for China?" *Journal of Energy Security* (July 2013), http://www.ensec.org/index.php?option=com_content &view=article&id=452:what-does-americas-shale-gas-revolution-mean-for-china&catid=137 :issue-content&Itemid=422.

43. John Calabrese, "Dragon by the Tail: China's Energy Quandary," *Middle East Institute Perspective*, March 23, 2004.

44. For the literature on and nature of hedging, see Mohammad Salman and Gustaaf Geeraerts, "Strategic Hedging and China's Economic Policy in the Middle East," *China Report* 51, no. 2 (2015): 102–120.

45. See Carol R. Saivetz, "Moscow's Iranian Policies: Opportunities and Dangers," Middle East Brie, Brandeis University, January 2007.

46. "Medvedev Bans Sale of S-300 Missiles, Other Weapons to IRAN (Update 1)," RIA Novosti, September 22, 2010, http://en.rian.ru/mlitary_news/20100922/160688354.html.

47. "MID Rossii obyavil novye sanktsii protiv Irana oshibkoi [Russian Foreign Ministry announced new sanctions against Iran are a mistake]," *RT*, January 24, 2012, http://inotv.rt.com /2012-01-24/MID-Rossii-obyavil-novie-sankcii.

48. Alexei Anishchuk, "Russia Hopes Iran Nuclear Talks Will Resume Soon," January 23, 2012, http://www.reuters.com/article/2012/01/23/us-iran-russia-idUSTRE80M0Y720120123.

49. David M. Herszenhorn and Steven Lee, "Putin Flexes Diplomatic Muscle on Iran," *New York Times*, July 15, 2015.

50. For instance, see "Foreign Ministry Spokesman Kong Quan's Regular Press Conference on 17 January 2006," Ministry of Foreign Affairs of the People's Republic of China, accessed March 16, 2012, at http://www.fmprc.gov.cn/eng/xwfw/.

51. "Foreign Ministry Spokesman Qin Gang's Regular Press Conference on 28 March 2006," Ministry of Foreign Affairs of the People's Republic of China accessed at http://www.fmprc.gov.cn/ eng/xwfw/s2510/2511/t2430]8.htm.

52. Chen Aizhu, "China Extends Iran Oil Import Cut as Sanctions Mount," Reuters, January 5, 2012, http://www.reuters.com/article/2012/01/05/iran-oil-china-idUSL3E8C5EFP20120105.

53. Under U.S. law enacted in December 2011, financial institutions in countries that do not qualify for exemptions by significantly lowering their purchases of Iranian oil would risk being cut off from the U.S. financial system if they attempted to settle oil trades with Iran's central bank. See, for example, "US Exempts China, Singapore from its Iran Oil Sanctions," Bloomberg, June 28, 2012, http://www.bloomberg.com/news/2012-06-28/u-s-exempts-china-singapore-from-its-iran-oil-sanctions.html.

54. For example, in 2011, Chinese investments in the United States totaled around $16 billion and U.S. imports from China reached around $330 billion. In contrast, Sino-Iranian overall trade and investment totaled $39 billion and $1 billion, respectively. UN Comtrade statistical database.

55. See Mark N. Katz, "Russian-Iranian Relations in the Ahmadinejad Era," *Middle East Journal* 62, no. 2 (Spring 2008): 202–216.

56. For a good, brief analysis of differences in relations, see Mark N. Katz, "Russian-Iranian Relations in the Obama Era," *Middle East Policy* 17 (Summer 2010): 62–69.

57. See Ivan Arreguin-Toft, *How the Weak Win Wars: A Theory of Asymmetric Warfare* (Cambridge: Cambridge University Press, 2005).

58. See Joseph S. Nye Jr., *The Future of Power* (New York, NY: Public Affairs, 2011. Zeev Maoz, for instance, has argued that bringing greater capabilities to a power attempt can sometimes backfire by causing a counterreaction by inferior actors. Zeev Maoz, "Power, Capabilities, and Paradoxical Conflict Outcomes," *World Politics* 41 (January 1989): 239–266. Also see David Baldwin, "Power Analysis and World Politics: New Trends Versus Old Tendencies," *World Politics* 31 (January 1979): 19–38.

59. Joseph S. Nye Jr., *Is the American Century Over?* (Cambridge, MA: Polity Press, 2015). Ian Bremmer, *Superpower: Three Choices for America's Role in the World* (New York, NY: Portfolio Penguin, 2015).

60. Charles Tripp, *A History of Iraq*, 2nd ed. (Cambridge; Cambridge University Press, 2002), chap. 1.

61. Yitzhak Nakash, *The Shi'is of Iraq*, 2nd ed. (Princeton, NJ: Princeton University Press, 2003).

62. For a discussion of these views, see various analyses in Carnegie Endowment for International Peace, *Is Saudi Arabia Stable?* (Washington, DC: Carnegie Endowment for International Peace, August 15, 2013). Also, for earlier analyses, see Rachel Bronson, *Thicker Than Oil: America's Uneasy Partnership with Saudi Arabia* (New York: Oxford University Press, 2007); John E. Peterson, *Saudi Arabia and the Illusion of Security* (London: Oxford University Press for the International Institute for Strategic Studies, 2002); Robert Baer, *Sleeping with the Devil* (New York: Crown, 2003); Michael T. Klare, *Blood and Oil: The Dangers and Consequences of America's Growing Petroleum Dependency* (New York: Metropolitan Books, 2004), 84–90.

63. See Paul Stevens and Matthew Hulbert, "Oil Prices: Energy Investment, Political Stability in the Exporting Countries and OPEC's Dilemma," Chatham House, October 2012.

64. Michael L. Ross, "Will Oil Drown the Arab Spring?" *Foreign Affairs* 90, no. 5 (September/October 2011): 2–7.

65. For example, Riyadh sent troops to help Bahrain control its predominantly Shia population, which may otherwise have influenced their Shia brethren in Saudi Arabia's oil-rich Eastern Province. This province had been the locus of several massive demonstrations against the regime, particularly in 1979 in the wake of the Iranian Revolution.

66. Christopher M. Blanchard, "Saudi Arabia: Background and U.S. Relations," Congressional Research Service, RL33533, April 29, 2015, 9.

Chapter 12

1. See Barry Buzan and George Lawson, *The Global Transformation* (Cambridge: Cambridge University Press, 2015).

2. Michael Beckley, "China's Century: Why America's Edge Will Endure," *International Security* 36, no. 3 (Winter 2011/2012): 41–78. Joseph S. Nye Jr., "The Twenty-First Century Will Not Be a 'Post-American' World," International Studies Quarterly 56, no. 1 (2012): 215–217.

3. Albert Hirschman, *National Power and the Structure of Foreign Trade* (Berkeley: University of California Press, 1945).

4. See Henry A. Kissinger, *On China* (New York: Penguin Books, 2012), 498–503.

5. For example, John Ikenberry, "The Rise of China and the Future of the West: Can the Liberal System Survive?" *Foreign Affairs* 87, no. 1 (2008): 23–37; and Henry A. Kissinger, "Future of US-Chinese Relations: Conflict Is a Choice, Not a Necessity," *Foreign Affairs* 91 (2012): 44.

6. See Richard Rosecrance, ed., *The Next Great War?* (Cambridge, MA: MIT Press, 2014). John J. Mearsheimer, "Can China Rise Peacefully?" *National Interest*, October 25, 2014, http://nationalinterest.org/commentary/can-china-rise-peacefully-10204, and Robert Kaplan, "The South China Sea Is the Future of Conflict," *Foreign Policy* 188 (2011): 76–85.

7. See Richard Rosecrance, ed., *The Next Great War?* (Cambridge, MA: MIT Press, 2014), and Christopher Coker, *The Improbable War: China, the United States, and the Logic of Great Power Conflict* (Oxford: Oxford University Press, 2015).

8. For a balanced view that sees a war with China as unlikely though not impossible, see Thomas J. Christensen, *The China Challenge: Shaping the Choices of a Rising Power* (New York: Norton, 2015).

9. See Brock Tessman and Wojtek Wolfe, "Great Powers and Strategic Hedging: The Case of Chinese Energy Security Strategy," *International Studies Review* 13 (2011): 214–240.

10. Gilbert Rozman, *The Sino-Russian Challenge to the World Order: National Identities, Bilateral Relations, and East versus West in the 2010s.* (Stanford: Stanford University Press, 2014).

11. Nayla Razzouk and Anthony Dipaola, "Iraq Oil Production Beating Iran Ends Saddam Legacy," Bloomberg, May 11, 2012.

12. Fernand Braudel, *The Mediterranean and the Mediterranean World in the Age of Philip II* (New York: Harper, 1972).

13. Paul Kennedy, *The Rise and Fall of the Great Powers: Economic Change and Military Conflict from 1500 to 2000* (New York: Random House, 1987); Charles S. Maier, *Among Empires: American Ascendancy and Its Predecessors* (Cambridge, MA: Harvard University Press, 2006); Bernard Porter, *Empire and Superempire: Britain, America and the World* (New Haven, CT: Yale University Press, 2006).

14. Paul K. MacDonald, "Those Who Forget Historiography Are Doomed to Republish It: Empire, Imperialism and Contemporary Debates about American Power," *Review of International Studies* 35 (2009): 45–67.

15. Marc O'Reilly, *Unexceptional: America's Empire in the Persian Gulf, 1941–2007* (Lanham, MD: Lexington Books, 2008). Christopher Layne, *The Peace of Illusions: American Grand Strategy from 1940 to the Present* (Ithaca, NY: Cornell University Press, 2006).

16. MacDonald, "Those Who Forget Historiography," 65.

17. Joseph S. Nye Jr., *Bound to Lead: The Changing Nature of American Power* (New York: Basic Books, 1990).

18. On British control, see Bruce R. Kuniholm, "Great Power Rivalry and the Persian Gulf," in Robert F. Helms II and Robert H. Dorff, eds., *The Persian Gulf Crisis: Power in the Post–Cold War World* (Westport, CT: Praeger, 1993), 44–51.

19. Jane Burbank and Frederick Cooper, *Empires in World History: Power and the Politics of Difference* (Princeton: Princeton University Press, 2010).

20. For an example of such exploration, see Charles L. Glaser and Rosemary A. Kelanic, eds., *Crude Strategy: Rethinking the US Military Commitment to Defend Persian Gulf Oil* (Washington, DC: Georgetown University Press, 2016).

21. Robert Looney, "Oil Prices and the Iraq War: Market Interpretations of Military Developments," *Strategic Insights* 2, no. 4 (April 2003), http://calhoun.nps.edu/handle/10945/25431.

22. On the rise of American capability, see Steve A. Yetiv, *Crude Awakenings: Global Oil Security and American Foreign Policy* (Ithaca, NY: Cornell University Press, 2004), chap. 4.

23. Ibid.

24. Michael A. Palmer, *Guardians of The Gulf: A History of America's Expanding Role in the Persian Gulf, 1833–1992* (New York: Free Press, 1992).

25. On how China is a free rider in the field of energy security, see Andrew Kennedy, "China and the Free Rider Problem: Exploring the Case of Energy Security," *Political Science Quarterly* 130 (Spring 2015): 27–50. Also see Bingbing Wu, "Strategy and Politics in the Gulf as Seen from Chin,'" in Bryce Wakefield and Susan L. Levenstein, eds., *China and the Persian Gulf: Implications for the United States* (Washington, DC: Woodrow Wilson international Center for Scholars, 2011), 10–26.

26. Kennedy, "China and the Free Rider Problem," 36–38.

27. On how China is a free rider in the field of energy security, see ibid. Also see Bingbing Wu, "Strategy and Politics in the Gulf," 10–26.

28. Robert O. Keohane, *After Hegemony: Cooperation and Discord in the World Political Economy* (Princeton: Princeton University Press, 1984), as well as thinkers in the institutionalist school that he founded following his book's publication.

29. Mamoun Fandy, *Saudi Arabia and the Politics of Dissent* (New York: St. Martin's Press, 1999).

30. On this history and for an argument on how America will be needed for many years to come, see Jeffrey R. Macris, *The Politics and Security of the Gulf: Anglo-American Hegemony and the Shaping of a Region* (London: Routledge, 2009).

31. Karl E. Meyer and Shareen Blair Brysac, *Tournament of Shadows* (Washington, DC: Counterpoint, 1991), 117.

32. Joseph S. Nye Jr., *Soft Power: The Means to Success in World Politics* (New York: Public Affairs, 2004).

33. On soft power, see ibid.; Matthew Kroenig, Melissa McAdam, and Steven Weber, "Taking Soft Power Seriously," *Comparative Strategy* 29, no. 5 (2010): 412–431; Jan Melissen, ed., *The New Public Diplomacy: Soft Power in International Relations* (New York: Palgrave Macmillan, 2007); Inderjeet Parmar and Michael Cox, eds., *Soft Power and US Foreign Policy* (New York: Routledge, 2010); Jonathan McClory, *The New Persuaders III: A 2012 Global Ranking of Soft Power* (Charlotte, NC: Institute of Government, 2013).

34. Joseph S. Nye Jr., *The Future of Power* (New York: Public Affairs, 2011). Nye, *Soft Power*.

35. Nye, *The Future of Power*, 83.

36. On definitions of power, see ibid.

37. On this strain in American thoughts, see Hilde Eliassen Restad, "Old Paradigms in History Die Hard in Political Science: US Foreign Policy and American Exceptionalism," *American Political Thought* 1 (May 2012): 53–76.

38. Amaney Jamal, *Of Empires and Citizens: Pro-American Democracy or No Democracy at All* (Princeton: Princeton University Press, 2012).

39. Sabri Ciftci and Güneş Murat Tezcür, "Soft Power, Religion, and Anti-Americanism in the Middle East," *Foreign Policy Analysis*, May 19, 2016.

40. See, for instance, David Shambaugh, "China's Soft-Power Push," *Foreign Affairs* 94, no. 4 (July/August 2015): 1–15. Joshua Kurlantzick, *Charm Offensive: How China's Soft Power Is Transforming the World* (New Haven, CT: Yale University Press, 2007).

41. Quoted in Mareike Ohlberg and Bertram Lang, "How to Counter China's Global Propaganda Offensive," *New York Times*, September 21, 2016.

42. See, for instance, "Middle Eastern Students Abroad: In Numbers," Top Universities.com, April 10, 2015, http://www.topuniversities.com/blog/middle-eastern-students-abroad-numbers.

43. Jonathan McClory, *The New Persuaders III: A 2012 Global Ranking of Soft Power* (London: Institute of Government, 2013).

44. See Anthony Fensom, "Asia's Soft Power Deficit," July 22, 2015, http://thediplomat.com /2015/07/asias-soft-power-deficit/.

Index